THREAD PAINTING AND SILK SHADING EMBROIDERY

Techniques and projects

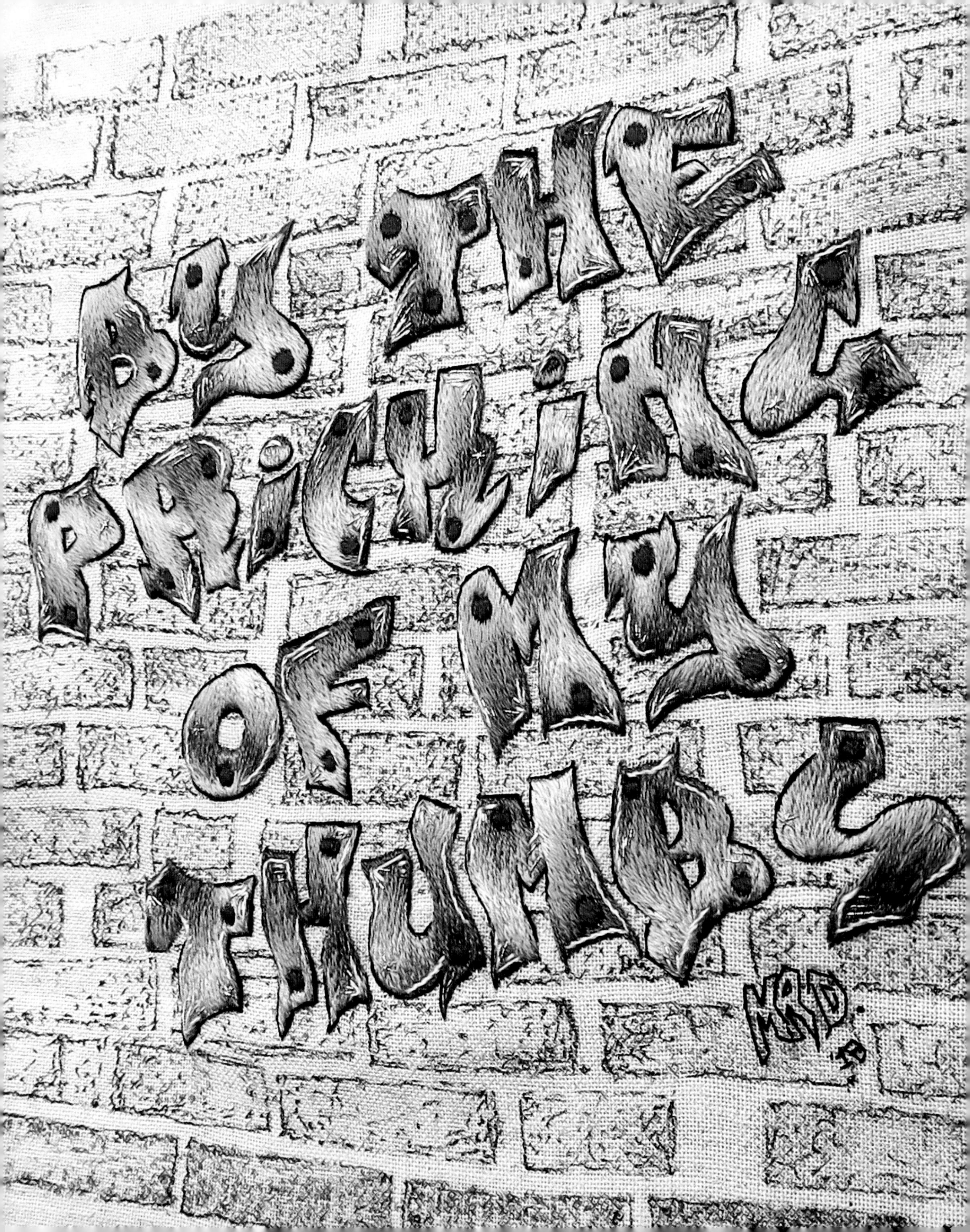
BY THE PRICKING OF MY THUMBS

THREAD PAINTING AND SILK SHADING EMBROIDERY

Techniques and projects

MARGARET DIER

THE CROWOOD PRESS

First published in 2018 by
The Crowood Press Ltd
Ramsbury, Marlborough
Wiltshire SN8 2HR

enquiries@crowood.com

www.crowood.com

This impression 2024

British Library Cataloguing-in-Publication Data
A catalogue record for this book is available from the British Library.

ISBN 978 1 78500 477 3

Typeset by Servis Filmsetting Ltd, Stockport, Cheshire
Printed and bound in India by Thomson Press India Ltd

Contents

Introduction

I am an acupictor. I didn't know this until I started researching for this book. It is a Latin term for embroiderer. But when translated literally, it means 'painter with a needle', which I most certainly am.

Thread painting, needle painting, long and short stitch, silk shading – so many names for essentially one embroidery technique. So why this one? Apart from being my favourite it also has an air of mystery about it. 'Is it painted?', 'Is it done by machine?' are just a couple of the comments that frequently arise when people see thread painting for the first time. They just can't quite believe it is embroidery.

I started embroidery as a child, little canvas kits of birds and my grandma trying to teach me feather stitch with a needle so sharp I didn't want to hold it. I moved on to working my own designs, teaching myself satin and chain stitch from old books. I then found an article about The Royal School of Needlework. Could I do my hobby as a career? Embroidery *all* day, every day? It sounded too good to be true, but it wasn't. I was accepted on to their three-year apprenticeship and yes, did embroidery all day every day. It opened a door to types of embroidery I didn't know existed. Thread painting being one of them.

This wild rose is the first piece of thread painting I attempted. The design is a mixture of an antique painting for the rose to which I added leaves from my parents' garden. There is so much about it I would now change; the turnovers on the flowers were padded, that is something I would not do now; I would use more colours in the rose and make the shading more sophisticated; you can also see that the edges of some of the petals are quite uneven and messy. However, I love it as it started me on my journey of discovery of thread painting. Every piece of thread painting has taught me something new and it is important to continually improve and learn from each piece you do.

I love thread painting; yes, I found the idea of it daunting, but I found it the most wonderful technique to learn and subsequently use for so much of my embroidery. I love that you do not need lots of specialist or expensive equipment and can just use needle and thread to create

OPPOSITE: A naturally shaded wild rose worked in stranded cottons. The centre is padded satin stitch and there are shaded French knots for stamens.

such works of art. You can create a picture with huge amounts of detail, with amazing shading, with texture and depth. I promise you it is achievable. I have taught so many students over the years to love thread painting and it is such a sense of achievement to stitch an embroidery of a favourite pet or a beautiful scene from a holiday.

I also love the freedom that comes from thread painting; although there are rules which you learn at the start, as you develop your thread painting you will break the rules to create your own style.

Thread painting is an embroidery subject that many people feel is too difficult or just a bit scary. It has no obvious way of working like many other techniques do. How do you choose the colours? How do you make it look like the stitches are curving? How do you know which direction to stitch? For the most part it is just one stitch that you have to learn. That's it.

Thread painting is just long and short stitch. It either goes straight down the fabric without changing direction, known as tapestry shading, or it changes angle known as natural shading. Both these techniques give the effect of painting with the needle; tapestry shading is perhaps more suited to buildings and scenery. Natural shading as suggested by its name suits flowers and animals.

Silk shading is another term for thread painting, referring to the traditional way of stitching with silk thread. These days, however, we have so many different types of threads available that it is a misnomer to refer to this technique just as silk shading.

The key to long and short stitch is practice. There are lots of little tips that will help you achieve beautiful embroideries, and there will be some unpicking. Or backward stitching as it is also known! However, you learn every time you take a stitch out. It is worth it, I promise you.

Using this Book

I hope that this book is a practical workbook to help you get started on your thread painting journey and then continue to inspire you to work on your own designs.

There are practice exercises to try before you start on any of the projects.

This beautiful church embroidery shows tapestry shading on the face and veil. Additional stitches have been worked over the top of the long and short to add facial details and to catch down the longer stitches on the veil. (Royal School of Needlework, RSN2217)

If you have never attempted this type of embroidery before I recommend you do practise these exercises as they will help you understand the projects. It is presumed in all the projects that you can embroider long and short stitch and blend colours. If you have tried long and short stitch before then please read the practice exercises chapter in case you have tried a different way of working.

Most of the projects have a design template at the back of the book, which you can use to trace and then transfer to your fabric. These templates are actual size.

All the projects have the threads and fabric used in the sample picture listed just before the instructions. You may wish to use different threads in your projects, which is fine, but you may need to make the projects larger or smaller accordingly. For example, the poppy project is stitched in one strand of stranded cotton; this project would also work well in wools but you should enlarge the design in order to be able to stitch the detail in the small spaces. In the same way the Jacobean crewel work leaf has been stitched in very thick wools, so if you decided to work it in a fine thread you should make the design much smaller.

Try and stitch your first project with the same type of thread as listed, so you can see how the projects work before you start altering the thread types.

The projects have a guide on how many and what sort of colours to use. This is just a guide. You may have more or less colours in your sample. Use the photographs of the finished projects to match the colours. If you do not have the same number of colours then it does not matter, you will still get a good result. Remember this type of embroidery is quite a free style and therefore it is perfectly acceptable to put your own slant on it. If you wish to add more colours, then that is acceptable too. I have kept the colours to a working minimum to hopefully keep the projects manageable for beginners – if you are more experienced then add more colours as you wish.

You can adapt the instructions to stitch your own designs. For example, the bullfinch project is in a classic bird pose. You can use the instructions to embroider a bird in a similar pose. The instructions for the order of working may differ slightly but they will teach you how to embroider different areas of a bird. Just start at the back of the bird and work your way forward.

This book should lead you onto hopefully creating your own designs too, which is incredibly satisfying. There are helpful tips on what to look for when creating your own designs, how to choose your fabrics and colours and how to mount your work when you have finished.

So pick up a needle, thread it up and start your love of thread painting.

CHAPTER 1

Inspiration and Designing

Embroidering your own designs is so satisfying. Kits are great for starting out but if you want to do thread painting, your options are limited so designing your own pieces is necessary. Creating your own designs can seem daunting and perhaps have you running away with bad memories of school art lessons. However, with a few guidelines and some inspiration ideas, almost anything can be thread painted.

What to Embroider and How to Find Your Design?

Start with images that you like and are inspired by; flowers, landscapes, family, magazine and book covers, animals, advertising, films, still life, stamps, a favourite photograph you have taken, an abstract idea, a child's drawing – anything you enjoy looking at.

Embroidering an image that you like will be much more enjoyable than one you feel indifferent about. You will be looking at it for a long time, so it helps if you have a connection to it.

Sketchbook For Ideas

Think of a sketchbook as a pin board in book form. Bits and pieces that you have collected and put into a book for easy reference and transport. It does not have to be a book filled with sketches, unless that is what you want. You may wish to use a pin board as a starting point for a project and transfer that information to a book, then start another board.

A sketchbook is useful for collecting ideas you may have; photographs, magazine cuttings, seed packets, postcards and greeting cards. Do not try and make a sketchbook neat, tidy and pristine; it is a tool. It is there to spark an idea and collect thoughts. It is personal and for you only. Write all over it; poems, quotes and ideas that come to you in the middle of the night. Or have no words at all and make it a visual reference book to dip into when creative block strikes.

Sketchbooks come in all sizes; a mini one for popping in your bag when out and about and travelling means you will never be without a way of recording an idea.

Larger sizes are useful for planning projects at home and sticking in all the bits and pieces that you need to create an embroidery project. Remember threads and scraps of material can be attached to your scrapbooks. You can also use them to record the projects you have done, what threads you have used, what went well, what you didn't like about the project or what you would change. It is also good to list where you got the fabric you have used in case you want to repeat the project in the future – you could add a little scrap of it too.

OPPOSITE: A selection of pansy jewellery embroidered in stranded cottons on silk fabric.

This is a page of an embroiderer's sketchbook; it has photos, sketch ideas, bits of fabric and some watercolour sketches. There is no theme or order; it is just a page of ideas as they happen.

Although in focus, this image of a honeysuckle flower may be a confusing subject for a thread painting; it has shadows cast on it from other areas of the plant which may not make sense if you take it out of its context. Its stem and leaves are also cut off, so you would have to make up these parts if you wanted to add them to your embroidery design.

This would be a much better option for a thread painting. The shadows that are cast on it are from its own petals and leaves so would make sense when embroidered. The background colours in this photograph could also be helpful in choosing your fabric backing. A beautiful sky blue would show this embroidery off perfectly as we can see the sky does in this photograph.

Photography

Although there is unlimited photography on the internet and in magazines, it is much more satisfying to take your own photographs for your embroidery designs.

Camera phones are fine for a starting point for photography. Obviously, you may be limited in details for close and distance focus but they often have good editing tools that can be useful. A stand-alone camera will have more options for focus. Get used to snapping things that you think could be embroidered. Think about how much detail you would like in your embroidery.

For example, if you wanted to embroider a flower, do you want to zoom in on the petals and the centre of the flower and perhaps make the design more abstract? Or do you want to have a couple of flowers and perhaps a bud or leaf for a more traditional design style? Think about the background. Take the flower photo from a different direction. It may then give you an idea for a colour backing you want to use. Or you may want to include other images in the embroidery such as an insect or piece of wall the flower may be against. Notice the shadows that are being cast on your subject; do they make it hard to see the colours? Are you yourself casting a shadow on the subject? Do you need an extra light source to make a better photograph?

Get used to seeing images when you are out and about as ideas for a thread painting; a window display, a meal, a scene on holiday, an interesting building. Use your camera to capture these little snap shots of your life. Very often you can look back on a photo you have taken and see a thread painting design in it.

With today's digital age many photographs are just left on computers, phones or storage devices and very often you forget how inspired you were about a subject you have seen. Try and print out or at least put in a dedicated folder images that you thought would make good thread paintings. Creative block does strike and if you have somewhere your inspiring photographs are all collected, then you can use them to spark new ideas.

Copyright

Going on the internet or photocopying out of a book is a very convenient way of getting a design, but really that is someone else's design, someone else's hard work; even if it is a photograph, it does not belong to you. Use these sources as inspiration and a starting point but *do not* copy. The satisfaction of embroidering your own piece that you have designed is immense. It does not take much to change an image to create something that is truly yours.

Drawing

Sitting and drawing your own design is daunting if you have never done it before. Practice does make perfect so it is worth trying a few drawing and sketching exercises to see where it may lead.

Perhaps start by tracing an image with a pencil to get a feel for it and the shapes it contains; this could be a photograph you have taken as a starting point. Trace as much or as little as you like. It is just an exercise in looking at your image in detail. Then copy this tracing on to white paper by drawing freehand with a pencil. Do not worry if some of the shapes are different, it is just for you so it does not matter how it turns out. If you are not happy with this design then repeat the exercise. Really look at the shapes you are drawing; is it true to life or are you just drawing what you think is there? Very often we have an idea in our mind of what something looks like but in reality, it is totally different.

Museums

Museums are hugely inspiring for getting ideas. Obviously, textile collections are relevant and can spark ideas of ways of using your embroidery. Historical collections are a reminder of how embroidery has been used for centuries and seeing historical methods can spark a whole new approach to a project.

Historical portraiture is also an amazing resource. Many old master painters, such as Holbein and Marcus Gheeraerts II, would replicate in detail the embroidery and textiles of their sitters. There are many portraits of Queen Elizabeth I where her embroidered gowns are covered in thread painted flowers and beasts.

Many fashion designers reference historical styles in their collections, often as thread painting. Fashions always evolve, but many times they look back to do so.

Other Embroidery and Textile Artists

Seeing how other artists approach their subject is invaluable. Inspiration from other embroiderers is very important and it should push you to create your own style and body of work. Exhibitions, textile magazines and social media are a good way to experience embroidery artists. It does not need to be thread painting particularly but it can help you get out of a creative rut or spark an idea. Use other artists' work as a starting block to develop your *own* ideas, not as a way of copying the method or style they have used. A favourite embroidery artist may have embroidered stylized pop stars for example – could you use this as an idea to create famous landmarks or animals in your own style?

This little silk-shaded rabbit from an embroidered casket is a perfect motif for a springtime embroidery design. The hillock could be stitched in tapestry shading with greener shades perhaps and the oversized leaves could be replaced with little sprigs of flowers. The bunny is perfect as he is! (Private collection)

How to Refine your Design For Embroidery

Once you have chosen your design you will need to refine it for a thread painting embroidery project. You will need to do this regardless of how you transfer your design to the fabric. It needs to be simplified so that the image on your fabric is not confusing and is easy to stitch. If you have a design on your fabric with lots of lines it can be hard to see which part of your design is which.

Equipment needed: design source at the size you are doing your embroidery, tracing paper, HB pencil, eraser, sticky tape, plain white paper.

Secure your design to your work surface with tape and place your tracing paper over the top. Make your tracing paper size larger than your finished design size; tape this just at the top edge and a little down the sides. Start tracing just the outside lines of your design. Move then to tracing any important internal lines that you think you will need. If there are lines that are very close together then perhaps just simplify these to one line. Make sure that you trace any important markings or strong shadow lines on to your tracing paper. If they are important to your design, then you need them on the tracing.

Place a piece of white paper under your tracing. This is a good way to check what the design will look like on your fabric. If there is anything that looks odd, lift your tracing paper to see what has happened. Perhaps the design source has darker areas that make it harder to see lines. You may have to draw these on freehand. Keep checking the design with the white paper to make sure it is complete.

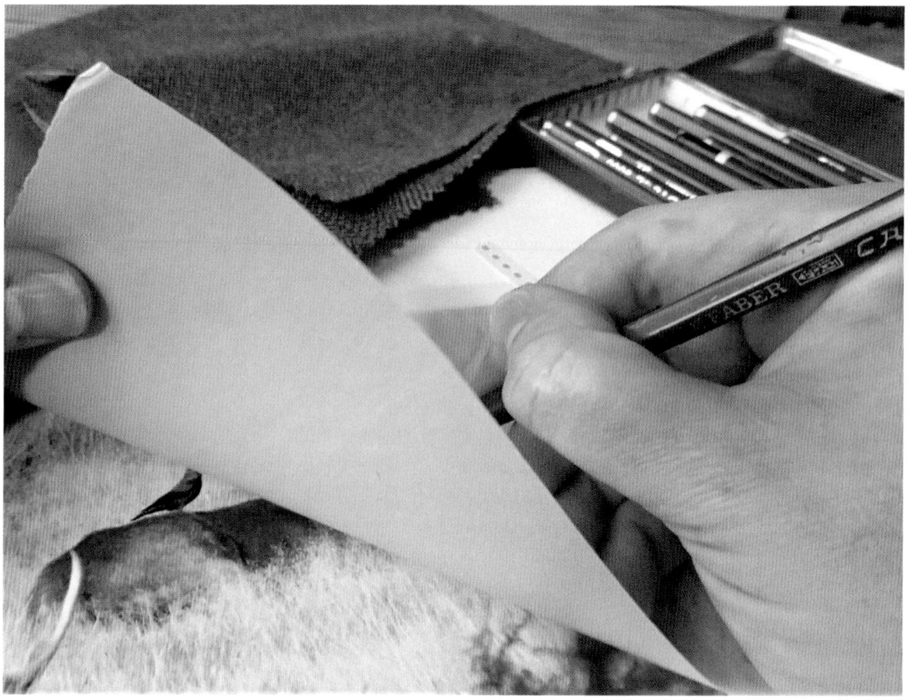

This shows the photograph and the tracing taped down but with the sides and bottom of the tracing unattached, so it is easily lift-able to check details on the photograph.

Refer to your original design and imagine you were stitching it. Would you be able to work out which part is which?

Try not to copy every line. Just the ones that will enable you to stitch. This is especially important if you are using the prick and pounce method of transferring. Too many lines or ones that are very close together will allow too much of the pounce powder onto your fabric making it hard to mark your design on.

When you have finished your design transfer to the tracing paper, it is useful to copy this so you have reference to write notes on, plan stitch directions and so on. Photocopying or scanning your design to white paper is a good way of doing this.

The pencil tracing is now ready to be pricked for the prick and pounce method or retraced for the tracing method. *Do not* use the pencil version of your design for tracing, the pencil can transfer to your fabric. Even though the tracing will be underneath the fabric, pencil, if transferred, can mark your embroidery threads. If you are retracing the design, then use a permanent black ink pen on tracing paper. This is to allow maximum light through when tracing using a light box or window. (*See* Chapter 4 for more on these transfer methods.)

Colour and Shading In Your Design

Once you have your design in linear format you need to create a shaded and coloured version. If you are working from a photograph that you have taken, you could just use that and get stitching but as a starting exercise it is a good idea to look at the colours you are going to use and how the shading works in your design. It will help you when choosing your colours if you have already studied the colour ranges in your source picture.

Start with the greyscale shaded drawing; make a copy of your design on to white paper, so it is just the lines you are going to use for your transfer. Using a graphite pencil start shading in the darkest parts of the designs, this will be the shadows and heavy markings. Press hard on the pencil so that it is obvious where the darkest parts are going to be. Then with less pressure on the pencil, shade in the medium tones. Do the same with the lightest tones. Now look and see if there are any other tones, something between medium and dark. Adjust your shading to show this. The more detail you put in the more you are really looking at the light and dark in your design.

This photo shows how a little watercolour sketch can become an embroidery design. The design has been refined to take off the top of the twig and extra highlights have been added to the acorn, as it is very dark otherwise. It has also been made slightly larger and longer than the original – as a designer you can change whatever you want to make the design more pleasing to you.

You may find converting your original coloured image to greyscale on a photocopier or printer can help you in this process.

The next step is to create your own coloured version of your design. Yes, you may be working with a photograph, but perhaps the original is a pink flower and you want to make it a bit purple, or bring in other colours. This stage will also help you with choosing threads; you will have looked closely at the colours and noticed little details and odd patches of colour that will help to make your embroidery more natural.

How you colour in your design is up to you. Colouring pencils are good for beginners as they can be rubbed out easily and you can layer up the colours. Computer graphics can be used or perhaps watercolours. Whatever you are confident in. This is not supposed to be an amazing coloured artwork for a gallery, it is a tool to help you in your embroidery. It is for your benefit.

What Doesn't/Does Work in Thread Painting

If you want to stitch it… try it. Some things will be easier than others to stitch, but you can edit the design to suit your embroidery and your vision.

Once you have embroidered a few projects you will understand the easy and hard parts of long and short stitch, so this will help you in your choice of design.

Lots of tiny details and small spaces on a design will be harder to stitch. If you are embroidering traditional long and short stitch, you want to try and get a flow to the stitches so think about that when choosing your design. Making your design bigger can help with little details. You will have more room to turn your angles, more space for your shading and therefore perhaps more colours.

This little forget-me-not necklace has been inspired directly from plants in the garden. It is exciting to take directly from nature when embroidering. Nature has been the most inspiring subject for artists; you will never fail to be inspired when you look to nature.

Your imagination is the only thing stopping you. There are rules to traditional long and short but once you have learnt them, break them! It is your embroidery, so create the effect you want. Thread painting is an art form, it is a way to create beautiful art in a technique going back thousands of years, and over the years those techniques have changed many times. They need to continue to do so.

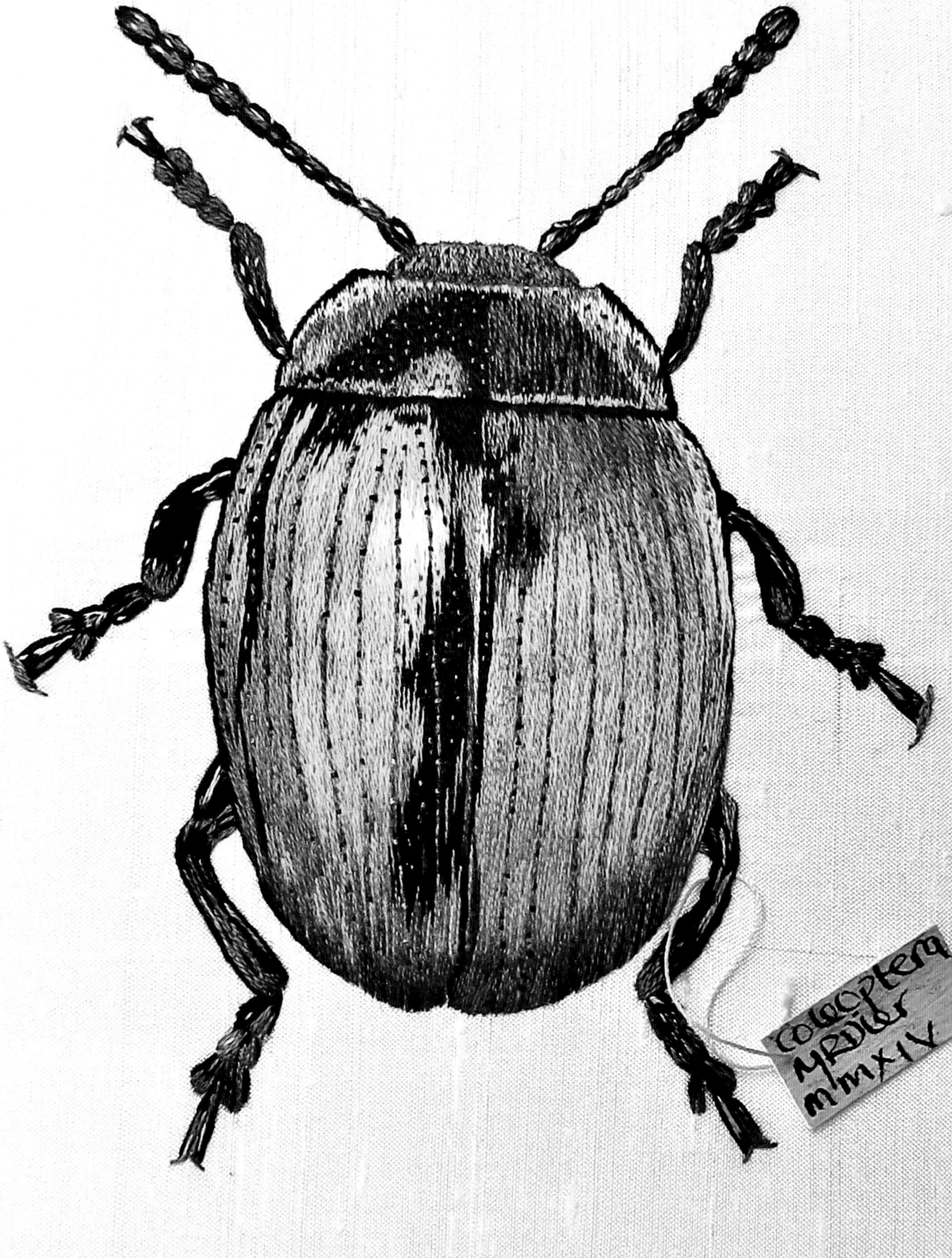
Coleoptera
MMXIV

CHAPTER 2

COLOUR THEORY AND ITS USE IN THREAD PAINTING

We use colour theory to a certain extent every day without realizing it. What scarf to wear with a coat? What colour to paint the walls to go with the new sofa? These are all questions that you may use colour theory to answer. You know that a certain scarf looks better with one coat than another. In fact, this is colour theory – you do use it, just without knowing it.

You may feel that colour theory is something that can be overlooked in thread painting; it is too scientific, too complex. Surely you just choose a picture to stitch, look at the thread availability and choose your colours? Not quite, very often the background colour you choose to stitch on can make a huge difference to the outcome of your embroidery. The wrong colour backing can make your embroidery disappear into the background, the right colour can make the embroidery pop out and enliven your work. Then there is the problem of the thread range not having the right colours. Can you still embroider the picture successfully?

OPPOSITE: A blue beetle embroidered in natural shading with stranded cottons. The identification tag was based on one of Charles Darwin's own labels.

The guidelines below will help you understand a little about colour theory for thread painting. We can obviously not mix colours as such, like a watercolour painter, but there are ways we can blend our threads or stitch one shade next to another to give the impression of another colour.

Scientists estimate that we can possibly see up to 10 million different colours. The thread ranges we use have a limited amount of choice; sometimes a good thing, other times not. It is sometimes very tempting to decide to embroider a flower that is perhaps yellow and pick every yellow that the manufacturer makes. This will just confuse things hugely and you will be using some colours that are almost identical. Another option is just to choose a run of colours that belong to the same range, for example five colours that go from light to dark very smoothly. Sometimes this will make your embroidery look very stylized and perhaps flat, which is fine if that is the effect you want, but to make it look natural you will need other colours.

So, it is understanding that although the flower is yellow, to make it look natural you may have to add grey, white, and perhaps colours like lilac. Really looking closely at what we see around us is fascinating, seeing what colours make up our surroundings rather than what we *think* they are is a constant surprise.

THE COLOUR WHEEL

Sir Isaac Newton was one of the first scientists to explore, develop and understand colour theory. His circular diagram of looking at colours and therefore the relationship one colour has with another is still used today.

We can use the theories in the traditional artist's colour wheel to make good choices in picking our backgrounds and our thread colours.

Primary colours: Primary colours are those that cannot be formed from any other colours. They are red, yellow, and blue. All other colours are a result of mixing these colours together.

Secondary colours: Secondary colours are colours that are formed from a

Hints and tips

You can make your own version of a colour wheel with embroidery, coloured paper, watercolour or by buying a colour wheel tool from an arts shop.

This is a version of the traditional colour wheel made up from machine spools. It is an invaluable resource for an embroiderer when choosing background colours for your work. It can also help with choosing card mounts or coloured picture fames when you have finished your embroidery.

combination of two primary colours. They are green from blue and yellow, orange from red and yellow, and purple from blue and red.

Tertiary colours: Tertiary colours are colours that are formed from a combination of mixing a primary colour with a secondary colour, usually from next to it on the colour wheel. Yellow-orange, red-orange, red-purple, blue-green, and yellow-green.

Left to right; primary, secondary and tertiary colours.

Colour Harmony

Colour harmony is a way of using the colour wheel to pick colours that work together in a pleasing way. These combinations of colours will be more balanced and natural. There are many formulas for picking colours from the wheel but the examples here are a few simple ways to help you use the colour wheel in your thread painting projects.

Complementary Colours

These are colours that are opposite each other on the colour wheel, for example orange and blue. The contrast of complementary colours will create a lively, vibrant effect. They create a high contrast. Use this idea when you want something to stand out.

This is useful when choosing a background colour so that your embroidery does not fade into the background.

These four blues all stand out on the orange silk; an embroidery worked in these threads will glow and be enhanced by the background.

These same blues on a turquoise background will just fade away. The turquoise colour sucks the vibrancy out of the thread.

Triadic Colours

These are usually three colours that are evenly spaced around the colour wheel. Imagine an equilateral triangle placed on the wheel, the points of the triangle being the chosen colours. This is useful when you want to create a harmonious design using more than one colour. Sometimes it is useful to make one of these colours dominant and use the other colours a lesser amount. They then become the accent colours that make the dominant colour 'pop'.

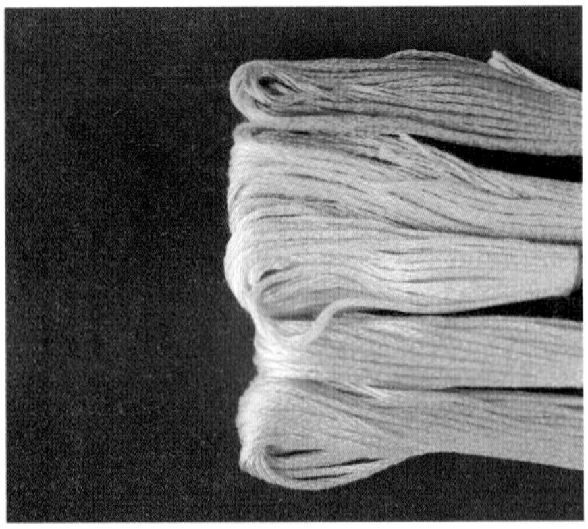

This photo has a red-purple background, with blue-green and yellow-orange threads. The main part of embroidery could be worked in yellow-orange with small touches of blue-green to make the embroidery come 'alive'.

Analogous Colours

These are colours that are next to each other on the colour wheel. These colours can create a balanced and harmonious effect on your design, are often found in nature and can blend well.

This is useful when you do not have the exact colour you require when stitching. For example, you may have an orange-yellow colour in your design but you do not have the correct colour in your thread range. Blending orange and yellow together in the needle or stitching these colours next to each other can give the impression of the correct colour needed.

A close-up of an embroidery showing that rather than just using a range of blues, extra colours have been added from a blue-green and green range to enhance the main blue shell of the beetle and create new colours. The blue-green and green shades are stitched next to the blue colours to create a turquoise effect. In the darker areas of the head a grey-purple colour has been stitched next to the darker blue colours to create shade without it going too dark a blue.

Split Complementary Colours

These are formed by taking one colour and using it with the two colours either side of its direct opposite on the colour wheel. This scheme is again vibrant and contrasting but less so than the simple complementary colours. Sometimes you may have a brilliant colour fabric that you want to use as a background and are unsure what colours to embroider on it. Using this colour rule would help you pick the best thread colours.

A vibrant blue silk fabric with orange-red and orange-yellow threads. All these colours will work together to produce a vibrant design.

Colour Temperature

The temperature of colours is referred to as cool and warm. The colour wheel can be split in two to show this. Generally, we think of red, orange and yellow as warm, and blue, green and purple as cool. However, all these colours can also be both warm and cool. A colour wheel can be used to find a cooler version of a colour. If it goes towards red, it is warmer and towards blue it is cooler.

Warmer colours are vivid and can come out of the design towards you.

Cooler colours are sometimes thought of as calming and generally recede from you.

This rule can be useful if you feel the colour of threads you are working with needs a lift and you want the embroidery to stand out more. You may be using quite a cool range of colours with a warmer background fabric; try adding a cooler

This blue feather on an orange background looks fine and stands out well, but it is quite plain.

The same feather with reds and pinks added is totally transformed. In this sample lots of red has been introduced to show in the photograph, but even just a little touch of red or pink that may not be immediately obvious would have transformed it. Try adding unusual colours to your embroidery in a very subtle way to give it an artistic slant.

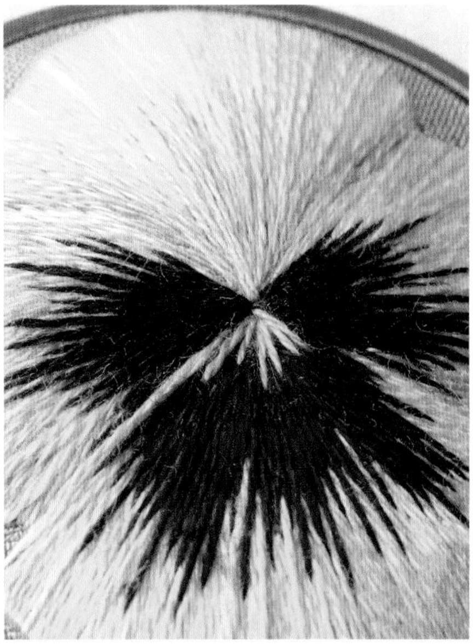

The centre of this pansy could have been very easily stitched in black, but a much more interesting colour combination is a dark purple and dark berry colours to stop the centre of this flower from looking flat.

colour to your stitching and seeing how much of a difference it makes.

Exceptions to the Rule

All the rules above are useful aids for helping with colour choice. However, we all see colour differently. We all have our favourite colours and there are colours we would never wear or have in our homes. So, it is perfectly acceptable to just pick the colours you like because that is what feels right and pleases you. They may clash, or blend, but if they work for you, then use them. You do not have to always refer to a colour wheel; nature has its own palette and can provide endless colour combinations so look around you if you are stuck. You may also have a favourite scarf or cushion whose colour combinations you love – use those items to help you choose colours.

How to Choose Colours for a Project

You have your design, your background fabric, you've picked a few colours from your stash. Can you get going? Yes, but how do you know if the colours are right? Do you have enough? Do you have too many?

Thread Colours

Take the colour photograph or version of your design to your stash of threads, colour chart or local shop and match as many colours as you think you can see in the picture. It is better to have too many colours at this stage than not enough. If two colours seem identical then put one of them back. You can of course add more colours once you have started stitching, but if you have to order them or wait then it can be very frustrating.

Look closely at the shadows; have you just chosen a darker version of your main colour, if your subject is yellow do you need some purples or greys to help with the shadows? Do not be tempted to rely on black – it can be very harsh, as there could be a lack of colours to blend with it to stop it jumping out.

Look at the highlights; is the highlight white or is it perhaps a light pink or blue?

Background Colours

Once your threads are chosen, you can then select your background fabric. The

This tomato could be looked at as just having a few reds and a light pink highlight, as the colours to the left of it suggest. These colours used as they are would create a somewhat 'flat' piece of work. To create a more realistic embroidery, look at the colours on the right. Dark rust shades have been chosen for the shadows to give a sense of depth. An orange has been added to the medium tones to give the tomato some vibrancy and in this case the highlight is white, so this has been added instead of a baby pink.

background colour can make or break an embroidery. A very quick and easy way to see if your threads will work with a background colour is to place the threads flat on the fabric and see if they pop out at you. This is where the colour theory talked about earlier in this chapter will help you to create the best combination of colour.

If you have lots of fabrics to choose from then placing your threads on each of them in turn to see which combination is best is vital. Do not just go with your favourite colour, or think that because you are working a flower, your background fabric must be green.

You can also hold your threads like a bunch of flowers and wrap the fabric around the outside to see if it is a pleasing 'bouquet'. Doing this may also show a thread colour that doesn't fit with everything else; if so, remove it. When they are all held together like this it will give you an idea of the overall feel of your embroidery – the colours should all work together.

Colour Samples

A useful way to get to grips with your colours is to make a stitched colour sample on a piece of fabric. If you are working on a large frame, then it is useful to do your colour sample alongside your project. It is then always there for you to refer to. Write the numbers down next to the stitched sample so you know exactly which colour is which.

The sample is invaluable to see if your colours blend smoothly; if you notice a big jump between shades then you can immediately see it and add another colour to make a smoother graduation. You may also find that the skeins of thread look very different to each other in your hand but when they are stitched next to each other, they look almost identical. There is no point having threads that look the same, which could get confusing. Leave one of them out. The background colour you have chosen may also affect how a colour looks, so try and work your samples on the same colour background that you are using for your design.

Start by stitching one single colour in a block, either the darkest or lightest in a range. Then stitch a combination of this colour and the next one in the range. Then a block of single colour, then a mix. Continue until you have worked through all the colours. Remember that two or three different colour ranges can be stitched together too. So, try a few blocks with mixed colours such as pink, orange and peach. See if they blend – see if they are stripy. Do you need extra colours from these ranges to stop the striped

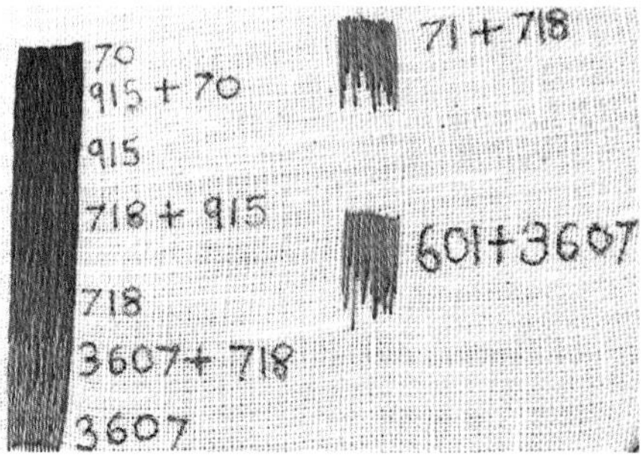

This pink colour range has been stitched from light to dark to see if the colours run through smoothly, and then a couple of extra colour combinations have been stitched on the side to check they are not too stripy together. The bottom sample seems a little stripy, but the top combination seems to blend together well. The colour combinations on the side will help you when you are shading to make a smoother-looking embroidery, it is best to try them out first rather than experimenting on your actual piece and having to unpick.

effect? Do not undo the colour combinations that haven't worked. They are useful to remind you what doesn't work with your threads.

Once you have chosen all your colours for a project, it can help to work a stitched sample with all of them in one long row. This will give you an exact idea of the whole feel of the project by mixing all your colours together before you start. This way you will know exactly which colours to pick when you start stitching.

These samples of threads can also be useful after you have finished a project. Keep them in a notebook with your design and any notes. If you want to re-do an embroidery for any reason, you then have all the colours recorded rather than trying to match to the embroidery, which is difficult when using many colours. You may also stitch a project with similar colours, so you can see what has worked and what hasn't.

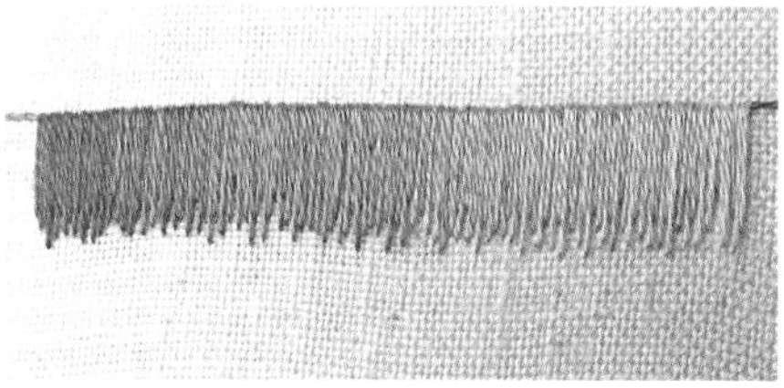

This colour sample shows a range of peaches and oranges. It shows all the combinations of the light colours mixed together and then the medium and dark colours. In this sample the bright orange in the medium range does jump out more than the other colours perhaps, but it will be a useful colour to add a bit of life to an area if it is looking too bland and flat. There also seems to be a bit of a jump between the light and the medium colours, so more blending between them is necessary to create a smooth effect. It is useful to know this before starting on a project, so you are aware of any possible problems.

Looking carefully at your design will help to make the right choice in choosing colours. It is not what you think is there; you need to look and see what is actually there.

This little acorn brooch uses some of the background colour within the embroidered design. This is sometimes a useful way of tying your embroidery and backing together to produce a more pleasing piece. The orange in this leaf is a slightly more subtle shade than the backing to prevent the orange from taking over the embroidery.

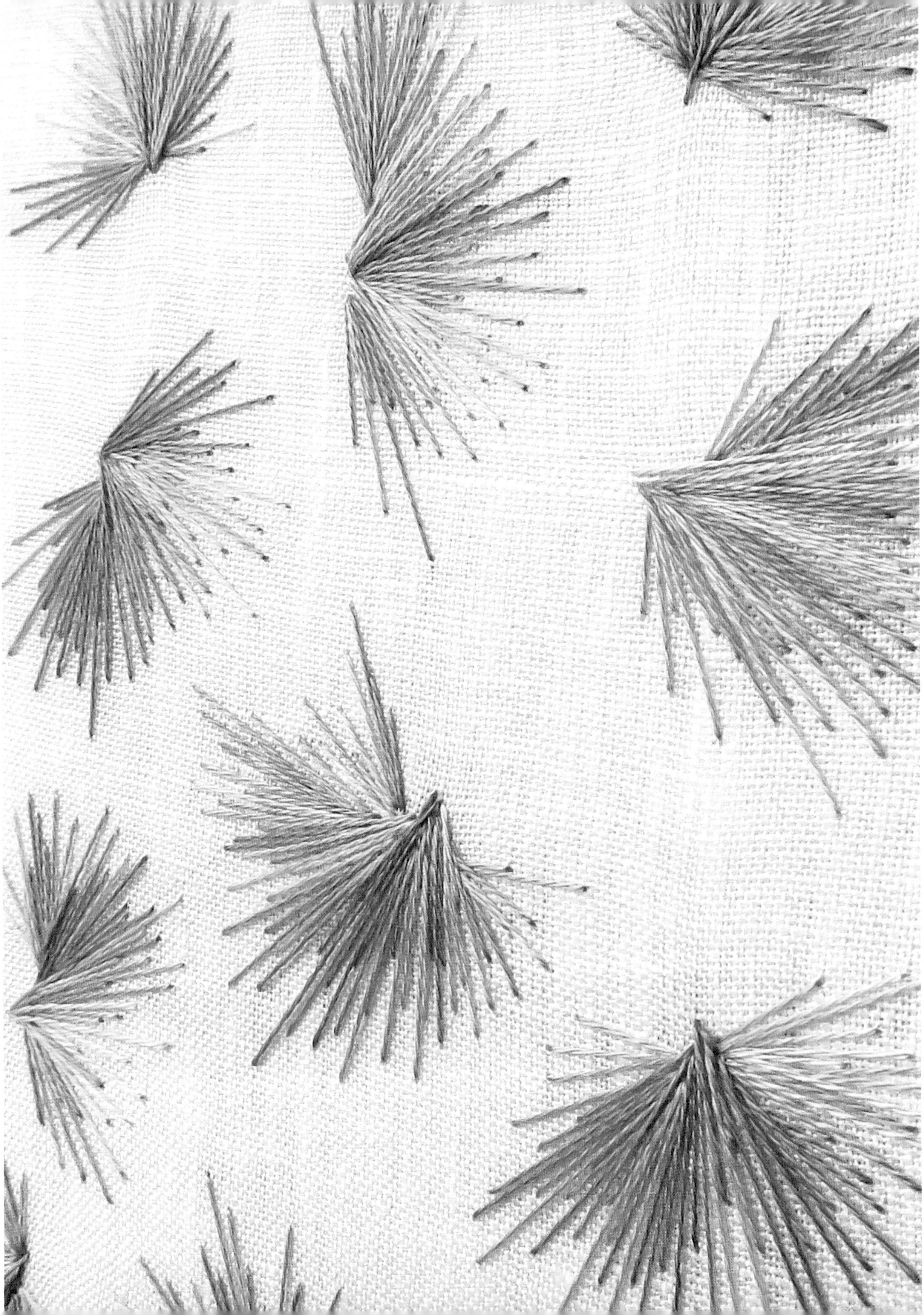

CHAPTER 3

MATERIALS AND EQUIPMENT

Thread painting is a relatively easy technique to get materials for and get started on. At its most simple a small ring frame, a piece of cotton fabric and some thread, needles and scissors are all that you need. As you progress and want to make larger pieces, use different threads and advance your skills, there are lots of equipment and materials to make the process easier and more enjoyable.

Start with basics and then progress to more advanced frames and materials. This chapter will explain the different types of equipment you will need from beginner to advanced ability. You may find that one sort of frame suits you more than another; you may also prefer using wool to cotton for example. There are so many different options out there it is important to find what is best for you.

FRAMES

Working any type of embroidery just in your hand can make the embroidery dirty, cause threads to get tangled and distort the fabric. A frame will make it much easier to stitch your embroidery.

OPPOSITE: A freestyle embroidery stitched in space-dyed threads on a white linen.

RING FRAMES

If you are working on a small project, then a ring frame is more than adequate. It is easy to put the fabric into and you can get started right away. They are also easy to transport, cheap and come in many different sizes. Ring frames can just be held in your hand but ideally they should be supported if possible. Seat and table attachments are available on frames that come with a dowel attached. This allows you to use both hands while embroidering, an important consideration for speed and tension.

Hints and tips

Use a shower cap to cover your work when you have finished stitching on a small ring frame.

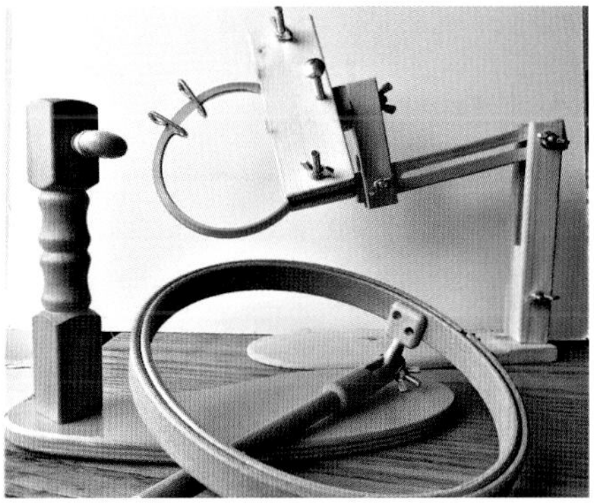

The frame in the foreground has a dowel and works with the seat frame on the left. You can sit on the flat wooden attachment and adjust the height of your frame with the screw. The ring frame also has a hinge and screw setting so you can adjust the fabric tension and angle of the frame as needed. The frame in the background is a plastic clip frame; this would only be suitable for small, simple projects as you cannot adjust the fabric tension. This seat frame has many adjustable parts so is more adaptable for positioning your frame.

SLATE FRAMES

As you progress to larger embroideries or ones that you are going to spend a long time on, you can then start using a slate frame. These require more preparation but

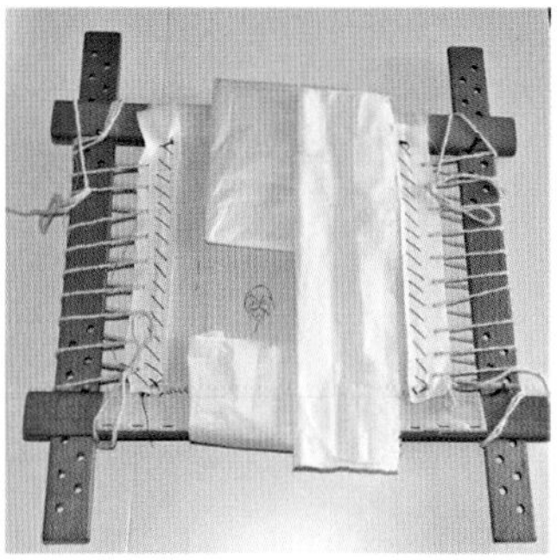

This slate frame is fully 'dressed' and with an embroidery ready to start. Notice that only the part of the fabric that is going to be stitched is uncovered, the excess fabric is all protected with tissue paper.

keep the fabric tighter than you can get in a ring frame, without needing to loosen off. They also allow you to have the fabric pulled evenly in all directions, which helps if you are using two fabrics together. These frames do need to be supported; a pair of trestles is the usual way to work with slate frames but they can be clamped to a table too. They also allow you to stitch with one hand above your embroidery and one hand below. This will enable faster stitching and a more even tension to your stitch, important for all types of embroidery. A slate frame is an investment so make sure you buy one that will accommodate the size of embroidery you wish to do. You should be able to buy extra arms and rollers of different sizes so that they are interchangeable to allow for various sizes of work. If looked after properly, they should last a lifetime.

Other Frames

There are also lots of other frames out there, some for canvas work, others for quilting or appliqué – to a certain extent you could use them for needle painting but it is important to make sure your tension is tight and pulled evenly all the way around the fabric.

Trestles and Floor Stands

To enable you to stitch with both hands it is important that you are not holding the frame with your hand and when you are using a slate frame, you need something to rest it on.

Trestles are used to hold slate frames, they can be moved to the correct height and width and may allow you to adjust the angle. An alternative, although not as comfortable, is to clamp your frame to a table. G-clamps are useful for this and can also be used to clamp a ring frame.

Lighter weight slate frames and ring frames can also be attached to adjustable floor stands. These have the advantage of many hinges so can be very comfortable for working on in terms of the height and angle of your frame, and can fold up easily for storage.

Fabrics

There is such a huge choice of fabrics it can be quite daunting to know where to start. Thread painting is easiest to stitch on a closely woven fabric. Cottons, linen and silk are all suitable. As thread painting is quite an intensive kind of embroidery, sometimes a backing fabric is used. This gives strength to thin fabrics such as silk.

Backing Fabric

A cotton such as calico can be used for backing thinner fabrics. It is best to use a thinner weight as heavier fabric could wear out the thread you are using; also check that it is not too stretchy. The backing fabric supports the thinner fabrics and helps take the strain of the frame. If you are using a thin or translucent top fabric make sure your backing does not have marks, as these can show through on your embroidery surface.

Fabrics to Embroider On

Silk, linen and cottons are all great fabrics to embroider on to. They are all natural fabrics, which make them enjoyable to stitch through. If you are embroidering in silk or fine cotton thread you may want to choose a silk fabric as it will complement your embroidery – silk has a natural shine, therefore embroidery and backing will work well together.

Similarly, if you are embroidering in wool you may want to choose a linen fabric; wool comes in thicker options so a stronger fabric may be suitable and both have a more matt finish.

Silk

Silk comes in many different weights and finishes. Ideally it needs to be closely woven and without slubs. You can check to see if it is closely woven by holding it up to the light, perhaps at a window. If you can see lots of daylight and gaps through the fabric weave, then it is probably too loose to stitch on successfully. Dress weight silk is ideal. This will sometimes require a backing fabric as above. Try to keep silk rolled rather than folded after purchase. Fold lines can be difficult to remove and may stay on the fabric even after being ironed or stretched in a frame. It is best to not use steam when ironing your silk as it can cause water marks.

Shot silks are also an option; these are fabrics which have two colours woven into them, one each way. Depending how the light hits them they can look like very different colours. Do be careful that the effect of the background does not distract from the embroidery and that all the colours complement the colours in your stitching.

These three silks are all perfect for thread painting and are very closely woven; the purple silk has a slight ribbed finish but not enough to distract from the embroidery, the turquoise silk has a very flat smooth finish and although the blue has a small amount of texture, it would not interfere with the stitching at all.

These two silks are not suitable for stitching on; the turquoise silk has a lot of tufts and raised slubs and is very loosely woven, so would get damaged if you stitched on it and would probably wrinkle very easily. The raw peach silk has a very loose weave, so it would be very difficult to get a neat edge when stitching and it would not hold up to the intense stitching needed in thread painting.

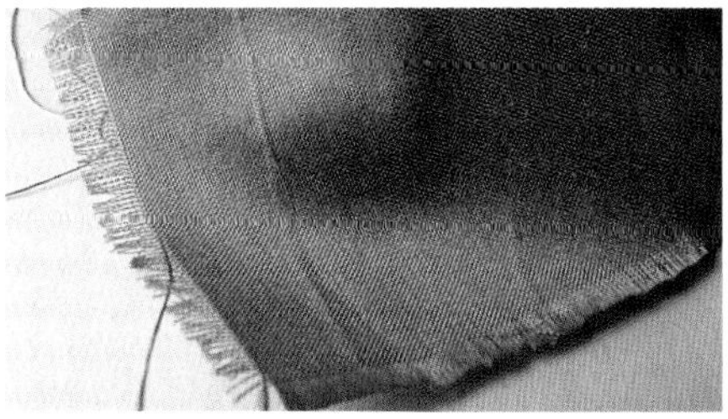

This silk has been woven with both a turquoise and pink thread. So, it can look blue, pink or purple, depending on how the light hits it.

Slubs and textured fabrics

For thread painting a smooth surface is essential to stitch on, especially for beginners as it makes it much easier to embroider. Slubs are often found in the natural process of weaving, especially with natural fibres. They are thicker parts of thread that occur randomly in the fabric causing lumps if you embroider over them. If your chosen fabric, such as a silk dupion, has slubs try and position your design so that you are not embroidering over them. If you try and remove the slubs you will cause a hole and weaken the fabric, so this is not recommended.

Linen

Dress and upholstery linen are both suitable for thread painting. Again it comes in many weights. Usually you will not need a backing fabric if you are embroidering on linen as it is strong and usually closely woven. Traditionally linen twill was used for wool thread painting for items such as curtains and bed hangings.

Even weave linen that is used for counted thread techniques such as cross stitch and black work is not suitable as it is not of a close enough weave. The holes in this linen make it difficult to create a smooth edge.

Other fabrics

Cottons are good to embroider on as long as you follow the rules above. Synthetic fabrics can also be used but be careful of fabrics that are stretchy (especially in one direction and not the other) or have additional threads in their weave such as metals, as it can cause problems when embroidering.

When starting out it is probably best to use a plain coloured fabric rather than one with a pattern. Patterns can get distorted around the embroidery if you have a large amount of dense stitching. This is especially distracting on striped or checked fabric. When you get more confident and your stitch tension improves then it can be fun to experiment with patterned fabrics and even other alternative materials, such as metal and plastics.

Threads

Traditionally silk and wool were used for needle painting. Today we have a huge array of thread for embroidery and thread painting especially. As a beginner it is easy to use stranded cotton and wool as they are cheap and easily available. Silk thread is available by mail or web order unless you are lucky enough to have a shop supplier. It is more expensive but gives the most beautiful results in thread painting embroidery. This is often referred to as silk shading.

Choose the thread that suits you and your budget. Great results can be achieved with only a few colours. You do not need to go out and purchase the whole range of colours when you are starting out.

Stranded Cottons

Stranded cottons are probably the most widely available threads used for thread painting. Usually they come in a skein. As you pull a thread from the skein you can see that the main thread is made up of separate strands, usually six. In this book we will be using either one or two of these separate strands. Stranded cotton is strong and comes in a huge range of colours, which is a big advantage if you are trying to embroider something and colour match it to a specific design.

Find the end of the cotton that pulls out more easily than the other from the skein and pull out a length for working with (no longer than thumb to elbow); now pull out just one strand of thread from this length – do not attempt to pull more than one or it will tangle.

Cut just this one strand off.

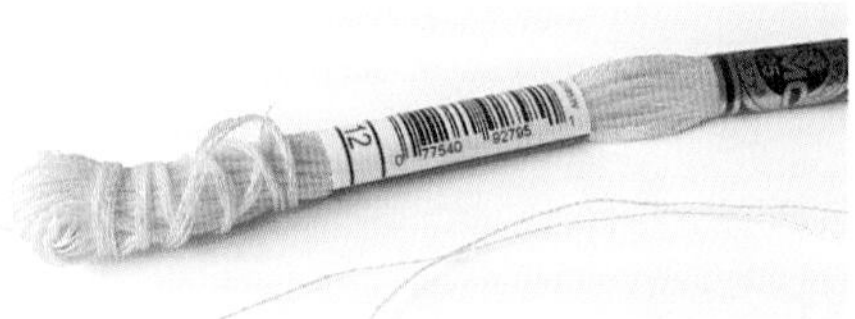

Wrap the other five threads around the end of the skein so that they do not get tangled up. Cutting and wrapping your threads in this way means all the excess threads do not get separated from the skein and mixed up with other colours, which is vital if you are using similar colours in a project. If you cut all six strands off the skein, it can be very easy to mix up all the little bits of threads with one another and potentially damage them.

Wool

Wool comes in many weights and there are specialist wools for embroidery. These are recommended rather than using knitting wools. Very fine crewel wool can give beautiful results and naturally dyed wool is also lovely to use. Wool for embroidery is twisted but you do not separate the strands. You can of course use more than one strand of wool in the needle for a thicker effect.

From left to right: aqua and lilac very fine wool, a skein and reel as used in the toadstool project, pink crewel wool skein as used in the topiary tree project and thick olive wool skein as used in the Jacobean leaf project.

Silk

Silk, although more expensive and perhaps harder to get hold of, has the most amazing allure for the embroiderer. It comes in many types, from ones that are in skeins like stranded cotton and used the same way, to floss that is as thin as human hair and shines magically when stitched.

It is lovely to stitch with silk so if you are able to use it then do. The floss silk can take some getting used to as it can catch on your skin and shred infuriatingly as you embroider but the results are worth it.

Use caution when purchasing old or antique silk thread. Silk does have a tendency to become weak over time. Antique threads will look very enticing in beautiful colours and wooden reels but more often than not will break as you stitch with them, unless you are very lucky. Also, there is a limited supply, which will be a problem if you run out of a colour halfway through a project. Always use a specialist supplier of antique threads rather than threads you pick up in an antique shop, to be sure of their quality.

From left to right: a spool of fine twisted silk as used in the Leek embroidery project, a spool of Japanese silk, this one sold in a one-gram spool as used in the Japanese blossom project (you can see the thread is made up of many individual thinner stands of silk), a fine silk spool as used in the Opus Anglicanum project, and a reel of antique silk that is unsuitable for stitching use. You can see how hairy and fluffy the strands are.

Machine Thread

Machine thread is used to apply your top fabric if you have a double layer, and to secure the two layers together throughout the design with stab stitch. Polyester thread is ideal for this as it is fine and strong and comes in many colours, which is useful for colour matching to your fabric.

Buttonhole and Thick Linen Thread

If you are using a slate frame, then you will need a thick thread to stitch your fabric to the frame. Buttonhole or carpet thread is ideal for this as it is very strong.

When mounting your own work to a board for framing then strong thread is vital, as you need to pull tightly to prevent wrinkles. To check the thread is strong enough hold a piece of thread in each hand and pull tightly in opposite directions; if the thread snaps easily then it is not suitable for mounting. You could use two strands of thread, but they can become tangled and make the process a little trickier. Thick linen thread can also be used.

These threads are all suitable for mounting; the threads are slightly twisted and almost have a tacky feel to them. Some antique threads are suitable for use and you may find old pre-waxed threads like this, which are also suitable for mounting and framing up.

Variegated and Space/ Overdyed Threads

These are individual thread skeins or reels that have been dyed in different colours or one colour in various shades. Therefore, you have no control over the colour shading as you stitch. These are useful if you want a random shaded effect to your work. Hand dyed threads can give an amazing look and very often combine many different colours, either clashing or harmonizing in one skein.

The thread in the foreground is a stranded cotton which is dyed in very harmonizing greens and blues as used in the hydrangea project, the silk spool in the middle is dyed in various shades of pink from dark to light and the thread at the back is dyed in a mixture of colours lemon, pink and orange.

Other Threads

There are so many threads available that once you have mastered the basics of thread painting, there are a whole world of different thread types to explore. Cotton perlé, linen, mixed fibres and variegated or space-dyed threads are all there to play with and create new effects. The only limit is your imagination!

Needles

It is very important when you embroider that you use the correct type and size of needle for the thread you are using. Using the wrong size or type can result in problems with your thread causing it to shred or break. You may also get holes in your embroidery if your needle is too big and your stitching may be less accurate. Needles have a numbering system for the differing sizes available; you will find the size and type of the needle on the packets.

Tapestry needles – which are blunt and used for counted thread work – are not usually used for thread painting.

Antique needles are most definitely to be used if you can get hold of them and they are in good condition and not rusted. Antique needles are a joy to use and have an elegance and strength that is missing in some of the more modern brands.

Embroidery/Crewel Needles

Embroidery/crewel needles have a sharp point and a long, thin eye. They are suitable for stranded cottons and some silks. The higher the number, the thinner the needle. Number 12 is the thinnest embroidery needle readily available. Number 12s do have a tiny eye, so they can be tricky to thread. If they are too hard to thread, then use a larger needle such as a size 10.

Chenille Needles

Chenille needles have a sharp point and a large, wide eye. They are easier to thread and also more suitable for wools and some silk flosses. This is because they make a larger hole as they go through your fabric compared to an embroidery/crewel needle, therefore the thread is not dragged through so much. This can help with some wools which will just shred if the needle is too small. The thinner the chenille needle, the higher the number. Number 24 chenille needles are suitable for fine crewel wools and silk floss; number 18 is suitable for thicker crewel wool or more strands of threads in the needle.

Betweens or Sharps

These needles have a short, small eye and are very often smaller in length. If you can thread them then they are fine to use. They have the same numbering system as the embroidery/crewel needles.

Curved

These needles are not the easiest to get used to using but are vital if you are mounting your own work to a board. They come in a huge variety of sizes and very often come in a mixed size pack.

Darners or Straw

These are usually much longer and generally the same or similar width throughout the needle; they are useful for French knots as they have more needle to hold onto and do not have a bulging eye, which can make an uneven size knot. They are also useful if you are stitching through a lot of padding as they do not get 'lost'.

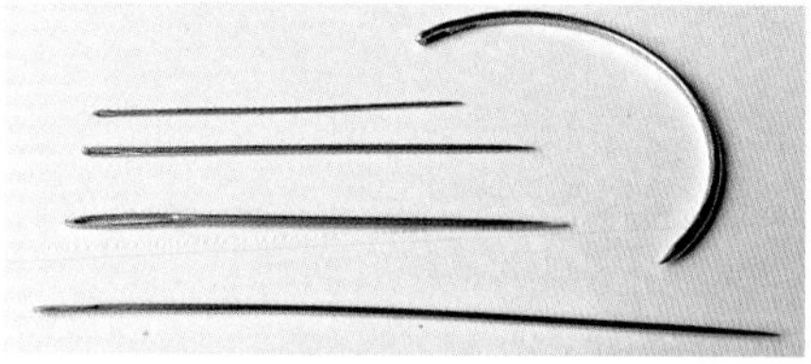

From top to bottom: a number 11 sharp (small eye, short length); number 10 crewel/embroidery (long eye); number 24 chenille (notice the larger rounded eye); a darning needle on the bottom (notice how much longer it is than the other needles); a curved needle on the right.

Hints and tips

Make a needle case from felt and label each page with the different size needles that you use. It is so frustrating going through a tin or pincushion that has hundreds of different needles, none the size or type you want.

Stitching Equipment

Scissors

Small, sharp scissors are vital; specialist embroidery scissors are preferable to craft or paper scissors. There are scissors that have curved ends and angled blades as well as the traditional straight blades. If you can cut your threads easily and they are sharp, then what type you use does not matter.

Dressmaking shears are also useful for cutting your fabrics. They are larger and more heavyweight than embroidery scissors. Some fabrics such as cotton can be ripped on the grain successfully, but many fabrics will need to be cut; it helps if you have larger scissors for this to keep a straight line.

Hints and tips

Do not use your fabric shears or embroidery scissors to cut paper or other materials – this will blunt them!!

Thimbles

Thimbles are a personal choice; if you are using number 12 needles you will find that a thimble is essential, or you will end up with holes in your fingers. It is sometimes the case though that only one hand needs a thimble. Thimbles come in various sizes and you need one that does not fly off if you are stitching. It needs to fit snugly. Leather or silicone thimbles are an alternative if you have a metal allergy.

Pins

Dressmaking pins are useful for securing a top fabric, preparing a slate frame and mounting your work once finished. Make sure they are sturdy and do not bend easily.

From the left: small dressmaking pins are useful for pinning fabrics together; pronged pins can be used for applying a top fabric to a base fabric on a frame but are not vital; large, strong glass-headed dressmaking pins are useful for mounting your work to a board.

Protecting Your Work

As mentioned previously, a shower cap is useful for a small ring frame but larger or square frames need an alternative. White tissue paper is useful for protecting your embroidery and leaning your hand on when stitching. It is also useful for wrapping your work in once it is finished. Make sure it is acid-free for storage.

A white sheet, pillowcase or white table linen is useful for covering larger frames when you are not working on them. They keep the dust off and offer another layer of protection to your work for storage or travel.

Design and Transfer Materials

Design Equipment

This can be as simple as a pencil and a sketch book. A selection of graphite pencils is a great tool to enable you to do tonal drawings of your design. There are tins of about twelve pencils from 5B to 5H that will be more than adequate.

If you are not confident in designing, then tracing paper is a great friend. The thicker tracing paper is preferable as you can use it additionally for making a pricking for transferring your design later. Thinner tracing paper is too weak and will distort and tear rapidly when worked on.

Coloured pencils are useful for making a colour version of your design before you start stitching. However, any colouring medium that you like using, such as watercolours or pastels, will give a great effect.

Transfer Equipment

There are many ways of getting a design on to the fabric for embroidery. As time goes on it seems manufacturers are inventing many products for us to use for marking fabrics; just remember that as they are new, we do not know the future outcome of using these items. If you are unsure, then do not use them or do some trials first.

Prick and pounce method

This method is centuries old and used by old master painters as well as embroiderers. Thick tracing paper is required along with a pricking tool – a pricker. The design is pricked with the tool on to the tracing paper and then a fine powder called pounce is rubbed over the design, the powder drops through the holes onto the fabric. This outline is then painted.

Pounce is made up of either charcoal for light-coloured fabric or cuttlefish bones or chalk for dark fabrics. It is simple to make your own pounce by grinding the substances in a pestle and mortar. To paint the design onto your fabric you will need a very fine paintbrush and watercolour in tubes of the required colour.

Light box

Tracing directly on to your fabric with a light box is a quick and easy method of transfer. Obviously, this is only suitable for lighter coloured fabrics that you can see through. A light box is made up of a translucent material with a light source underneath. The design then the fabric is placed onto the light box surface and traced through. A sharp, hard pencil, such as 2H, or a very fine ink pen is used for the tracing. Best for smaller designs as the fabric can move around if not secured properly.

A window with sunlight shining through is an alternative. If you can guarantee the sunlight!

Transfer paper

Transfer paper works in the same way as carbon paper. It is suitable for all coloured fabrics as the paper comes in many colour options. This method is probably best for small designs as the paper can move around. There are specialist fabric transfer papers available; do not use the type for paper or you will have ink all over your fabric.

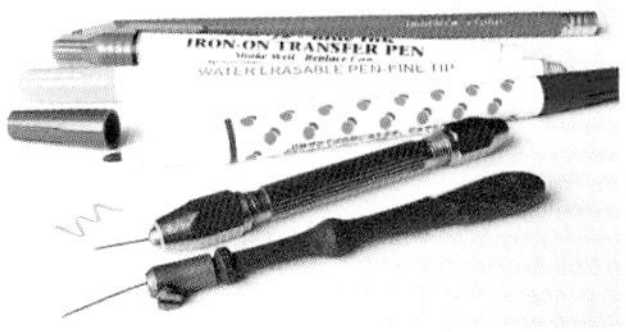

From front to back: a wooden tambour hook used as a pricker; a metal pin vice used as a pricker (from hardware stores); an air-disappearing pen; a water disappearing pen and a selection of transfer pens and pencils.

Transfer pens and pencils

These pens and pencils are used by tracing the design in reverse on to paper and then ironing it on to your fabric. These should always be tested first to make sure they work on your fabric and to see how much pressure and heat is needed from the iron.

Ink pens

If you are confident enough or just want to experiment, then drawing straight on to the fabric is fine. Use a waterproof ink pen for lighter coloured fabrics. Darker fabrics can be marked with a fine metallic gel pen.

If you are not confident in drawing straight on to the fabric, you could use pens that have ink that evaporates after a few days. Then go over the marks you have made with permanent ink. Test the evaporating pen first on a corner to make sure it does indeed disappear.

Lighting

Lighting is so important for all types of embroidery, but especially so for thread painting. You need to be able to identify your colours easily, especially if you have a lot of subtle shades. Bright sunlight is not necessarily the best light for working in. The brightness of sunlight can bleach out what you are looking at and not show up the gentle changes of colours or perhaps spaces between stitches and so on. A bright window with no sunlight directly shining on your work is better.

There are also now a lot of daylight bulbs available, which are invaluable for colour matching and being able to work into the evenings or on a dull day. Although you cannot usually try before you buy, it is worth researching and getting recommendations. Some bulbs can give off huge amounts of heat, which is uncomfortable when you are working so close to them. You also want to place the lamp so that you are not casting a shadow with your hand while working. There are some bulbs especially for artists' purposes rather than general daylight effect. They are more expensive but generally are closer to true daylight and are worth the extra financial outlay.

Magnifiers

Using a magnifier is purely a personal choice. Obviously if you have trouble seeing with or without spectacles, then a magnifier will help. Be aware when using a magnifier there is some distortion and what might look messy in a magnifier may not be as bad as it seems when you take the magnification away.

Hints and tips

Always cover your magnifier when it is not in use with its own cover or make a little drawstring bag to go over it, especially if you work in a window. There have been many instances of an embroidery magnifier setting light to fabric due to sunlight shining through it. Even if you are leaving it for a short time, cover it up.

POISON

CHAPTER 4

How to Use Your Equipment

Starting a new project is exciting and there is a temptation to jump right in. However, preparation is key to a successful project that you may spend many hours on. There is nothing worse than having a project that disappoints you at the end with problems that could have been avoided with just a little time at the start. Refer to the previous chapter for information on the equipment and materials to use.

Fabrics

Use a scrap of fabric and just get started! Yes, you could; however a few checks on your fabric before you start will avoid wrinkles and problems whilst stitching.

Try and cut your chosen fabric straight on the grain. This means a straight line as it has been woven. Some fabric will tear on the grain, you snip it at the edge and rip it apart. It should tear evenly. Many cottons and silks will do this. The very edge may be distorted after ripping so cut that off. If you have a piece already cut then pull a thread from one edge; if it continues all the way to the opposite edge in one piece, then it is cut on the grain. You can also use this method to make a fabric straight, if you are not confident in using scissors.

Make sure you cut your fabric large enough. If you wish to frame your piece or make it into an item later then it is better to have a large piece than add extensions. If you only have a small piece of precious fabric then you can add a backing; this will also allow you to fit a small piece of fabric into a bigger frame.

> **Hints and tips**
>
> Make sure your fabric scissors are sharp by regularly using a scissor sharpener.

Check the fabric for marks, stains and slubs. Antique fabrics and many silks may have marks where they have been folded, or little brown foxing marks. Linens and cottons can mostly be washed successfully, silks can't. You can place your design strategically to cover any problems but be aware of them before you start stitching. Marks on fabrics that are not washed could turn into small holes later.

Iron your fabric – most fabric will have wrinkles or folds due to storage. Using steam will work to remove folds in cotton or linen, but beware of using steam or a water spray on some silks as it can cause water marks. You can also wet the whole piece of fabric under the tap and iron it until dry for stubborn folds. This is not suitable for silks as you will lose the sheen. It is best to test a small piece first just in case. Your fabric will be pulled tight on the frame, so to check pull it tight in your hand and if the folds disappear then it will be fine.

Threads being pulled from the cut edge of a piece of silk, to make sure it is cut on the grain.

OPPOSITE: A hydrangea bouquet worked in stranded cottons over wired edges.

Framing Up

Choose your frame to work on. Stitching your embroidery just in your hand without any frame will cause problems, so use a frame every time. Depending on your transfer method you may need to put the design on the fabric before you frame up.

Ring Frames

It is possible to get your fabric tight in a ring frame. You will have to tighten as you work as the fabric will slacken off. The larger the frame the harder it is to get an even, tight tension all the way round. Be aware of this if you plan to use a large, round quilting frame for example. Heavier weight fabrics and backing fabrics go straight into the ring fame. Binding the top ring with cotton is useful to protect your material and help the ring frame to grip the fabric. Tiny ring frames do not need to do this. Make sure that the fabric that you are using in your ring frame is bigger than the ring frame itself to enable you to be able to pull it from all sides. Wooden ring frames will stain light-coloured fabrics, so bind them to prevent this too.

Place your chosen fabric or backing fabric over the bottom ring, place a layer of acid-free tissue paper over this, then place the top ring over the top. The tissue paper is there to help prevent marks and keep the fabric clean. Tighten the screw gently with a screwdriver while pulling the fabric evenly all the way round. Try not to distort the fabric and try and make the grain as straight as possible (tear away a little bit of tissue if you need to check the grain). Once the fabric is as tight as you can possibly get it, tear the tissue away from the fabric to reveal the area you are going to embroider or add your top fabric to.

If you are working in a ring frame where your applied top fabric (for example an applied silk) is larger than the hoop, you need to apply it before it goes in the ring frame.

If you have a delicate fabric in your ring frame then it is a good idea to loosen it off when you have finished stitching for the day, to try and prevent damaging it.

Binding a ring frame

Cut a very long piece of white or pale cotton about 3cms wide (it is better to have one long piece) that continues all the way around the frame so that you do not have to join in the middle of binding. Wrap the material around the top part of the ring frame overlapping the layers very tightly, starting from the screw fastening and finishing at the other side of the fastening. When you have done a few wraps secure the start with a few stitches using a strong thread. Continue wrapping until you have covered the whole ring frame. Secure the end in the same way, cutting off any excess material.

Binding a ring frame.

Slate Frames

Slate frames are the best way to keep your fabric tight and straight for working longer-term projects. They are made up of two rollers that you stitch your fabric to and two arms that have holes and pegs. The fabric is continually at tension while you work. They also allow you to stitch with one hand above the frame and one hand below. This will allow faster stitching and a more even tension to your work. There is a lot more preparation when framing up a slate frame, but it is worth the extra effort. Slate frame sizes are usually referred to as the size of the webbing tape on the roller.

Equipment:

- Slate frame with pegs
- Tape measure
- Pencil or pen
- Pins
- Fabric
- Scissors
- Chenille needle
- Buttonhole or strong linen thread
- Cotton webbing tape
- Large-eyed needle for the string
- Strong white household string on the ball

1. Firstly, you need to find the middle point between the holes on the rollers. It is important to measure from the *holes* in the rollers and not the rollers themselves or the actual webbing tape. This is because you cannot be sure that the webbing tape has been put on centrally or the holes drilled evenly. Place a tape measure on the inside part of one hole to the inside part of the other. Work out the centre point and mark this on the roller. Check the measurement to be sure. Repeat with the other roller.

2. Now mark the webbing tape at the same point the roller is marked.

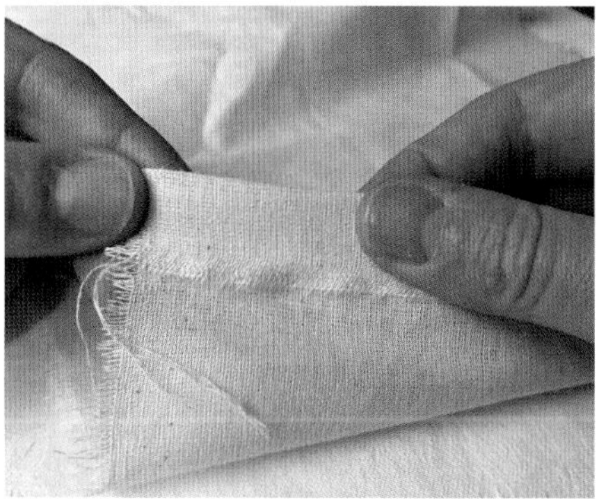

3. Iron the fabric that is going into your frame. Make sure it is straight. The fabric needs to be smaller (preferable) or the same width as the measurement of the webbing on your roller, this is important to enable you to frame up correctly. It can be longer in the other direction, for example longer than the arms of your frame. In fact, this is preferable. Fold the edge that is to be sewn to the roller carefully down with your fingers to make a solid seam that is on the grain; 2cms should be plenty. Repeat with the opposite side.

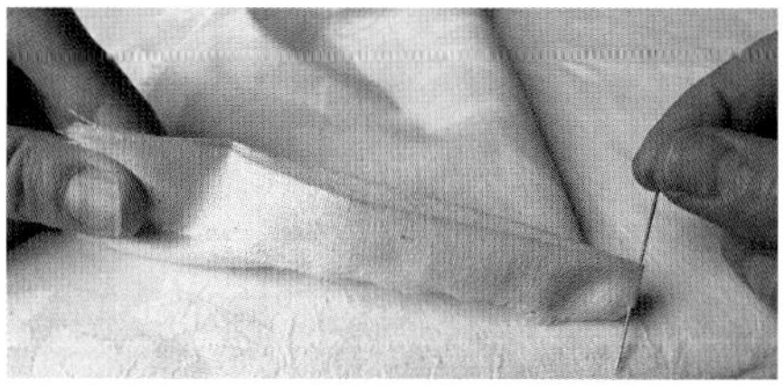

4. Fold the side of fabric that has the seam in half and mark the centre point with a pin. Repeat with the opposite side.

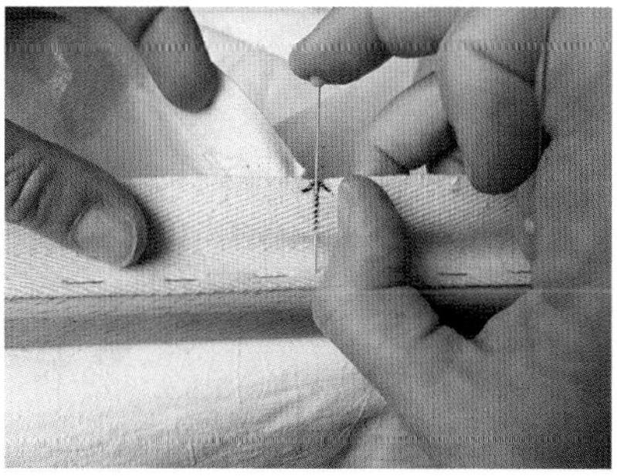

5. Match the pin that marks the centre with your mark on the frame and pin the webbing and fabric together.

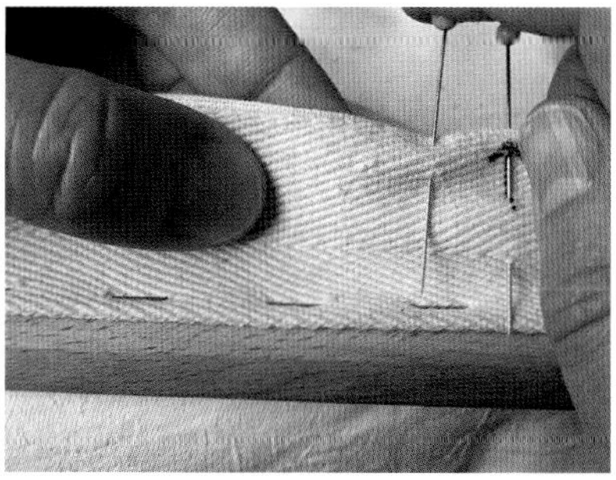

6. Pin all the way along to each end. Notice how the pins are vertical; this is important to keep the measurements accurate. Horizontal pinning can cause the fabric to 'walk'. Repeat with the opposite roller.

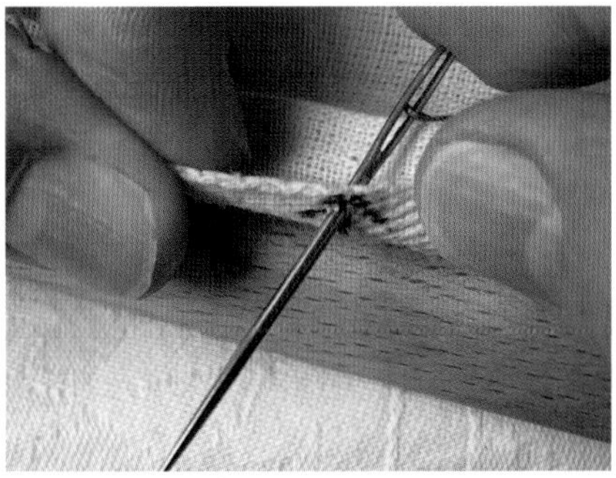

7. Thread up a long single length of strong linen or buttonhole thread in your chenille needle and put a knot at the end. We use a chenille needle as it makes it easier to stitch through the strong webbing. Starting in the centre of your webbing, secure the knot between the webbing and fabric.

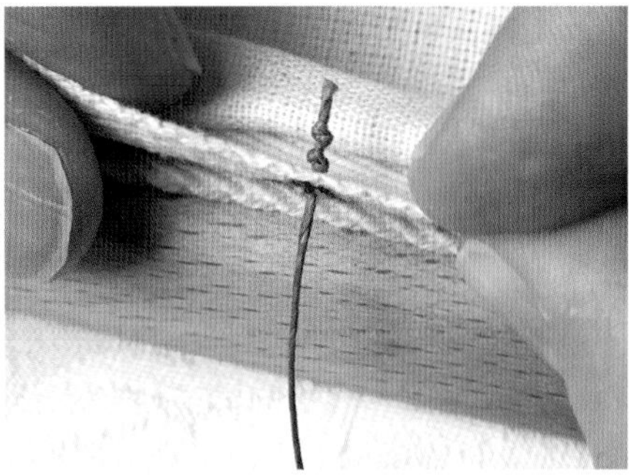

8. Showing the knot between the webbing and the fabric.

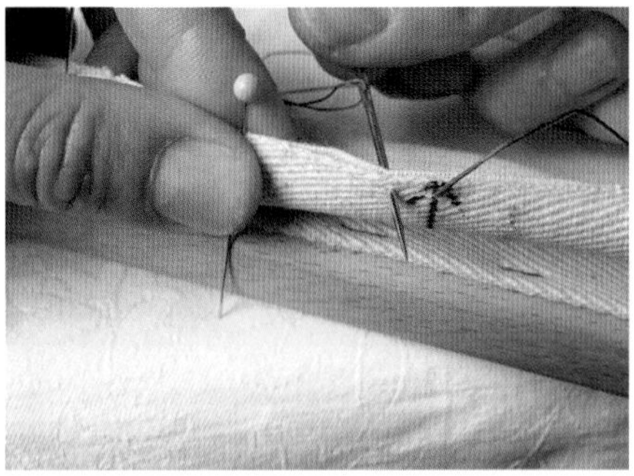

9. Now stitch the webbing and fabric together with a slightly diagonal over sew stitch working towards one end of the frame; these stitches are approximately 5mm apart.

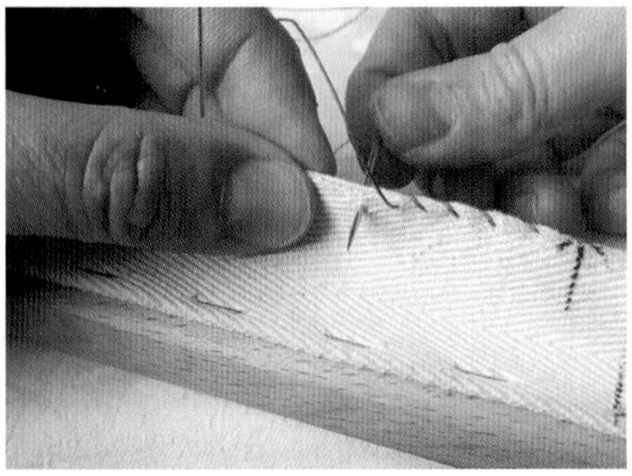

10. The stitches need to be small and tight. Do not try and get these stitches looking all the same and perfectly neat. These are functional stitches, if they are slightly different lengths it does not matter. You can check to see if they are working by trying to pull the fabric and the webbing apart where you have already stitched. If they are very secure and do not pull apart then your stitches are fine. If there are big gaps, then do your stitches closer together.

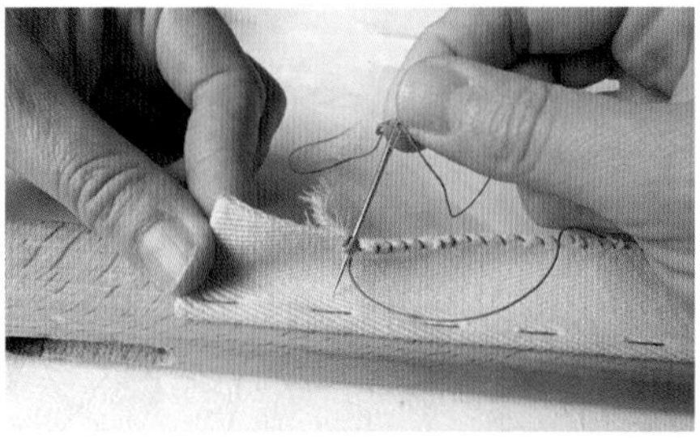

11. When you get to the end or run out of thread then work four over sew stitches on top of each other and cut your thread with a small tail. Start again in the middle and work to the other end. Repeat with the opposite side.

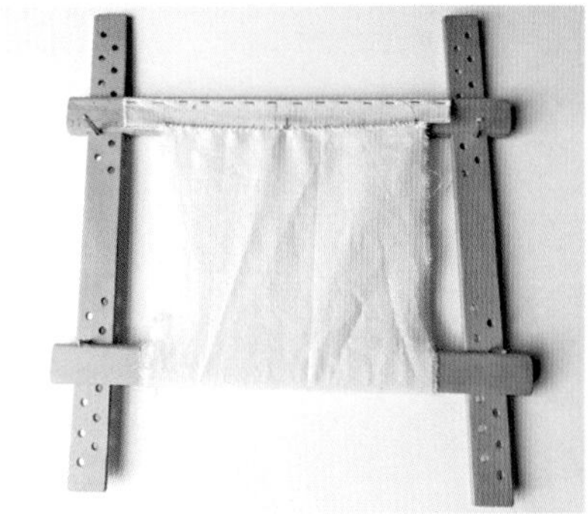

12. Now insert your arms in to the rollers and secure with the pegs. Count the holes in your arms and try and make the pegs match each side so everything is even. Do not stretch your fabric tightly at this point. You may wish to roll your rollers around a few times to get the correct size of fabric for working on. Try and roll the rollers equal turns if you do this. You can also roll the rollers after you have applied a top fabric, if you are doing so.

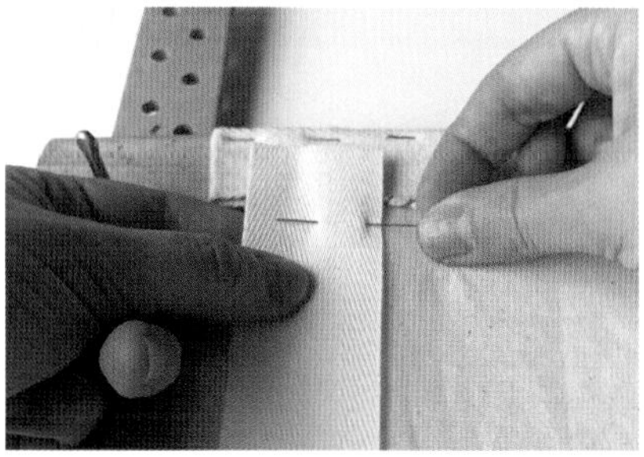

13. Cut a piece of webbing slightly longer than the fabric on your frame. Pin it in place; notice the pins are in a horizontal position.

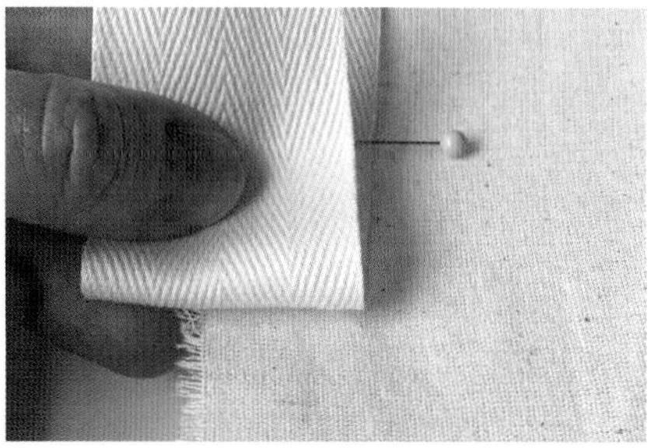

14. Two thirds of the webbing is on the fabric, one third is hanging off the edge.

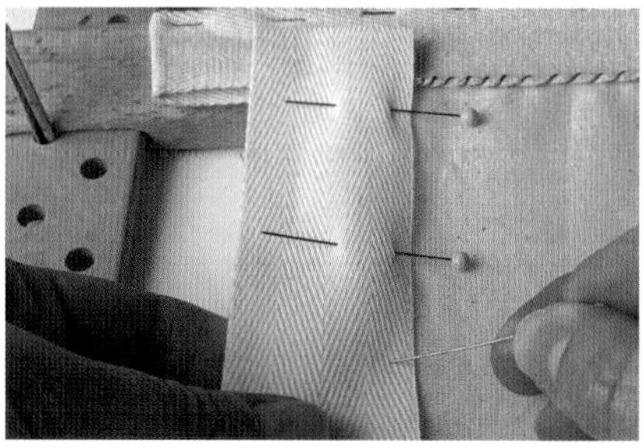

15. Try and pin the webbing so it is matching the straight grain of the fabric.

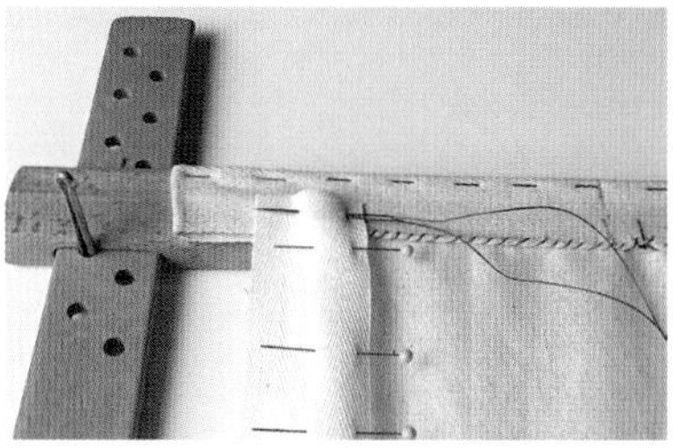

16. Thread up a chenille needle with a long single length of buttonhole or linen thread with a knot in the end. Starting at the very top of the frame, work a few over sew stitches on top of each other to secure the thread. Try and go through the webbing on the roller and the webbing you are applying so that it is really secure; if you miss this stage and attach the webbing to the fabric, the webbing may rip off the frame when it is pulled tight.

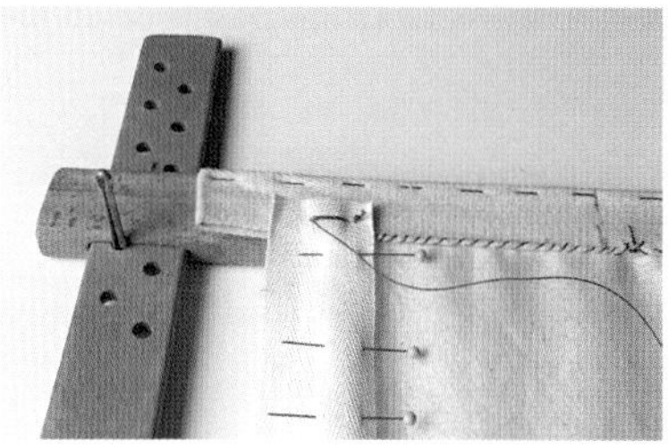

17. The webbing is now very secure to the roller.

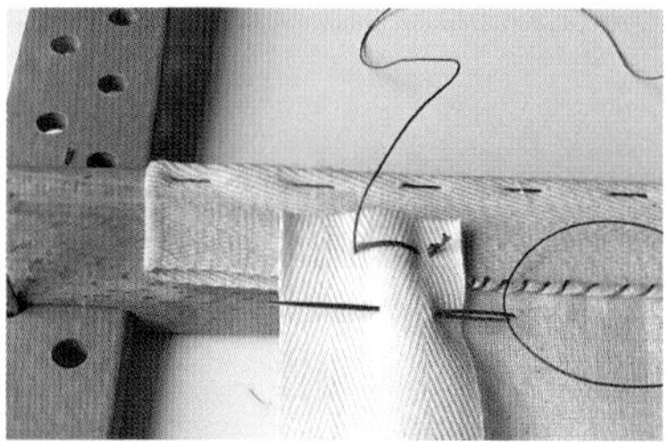

18. Now make a stitch with the needle horizontally so the thread creates a diagonal line; this is 'basting'. You are going through your webbing and your fabric.

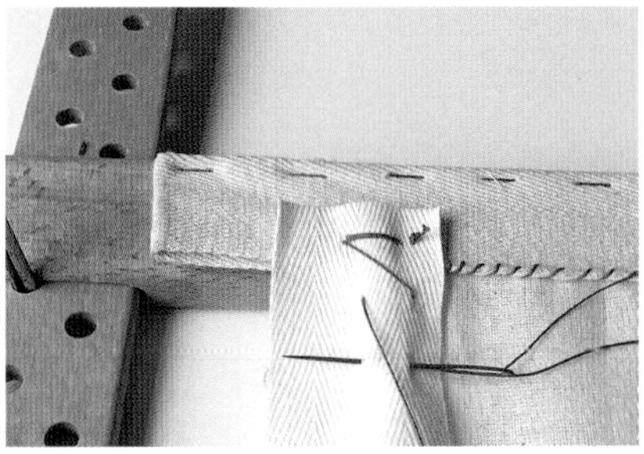

19. Repeat the stitch about 2.5cms from your first one.

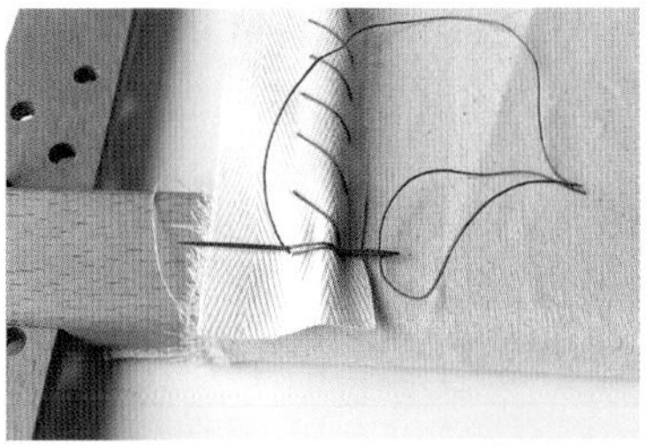

20. Work all the way down, pulling your stitches tightly; you need to have lots of these stitches. They need to securely fix the webbing in place. If the webbing buckles up a little it does not matter. When you get to the end or run out of thread, work a few over sew stitches on top of each other. Repeat with the other side.

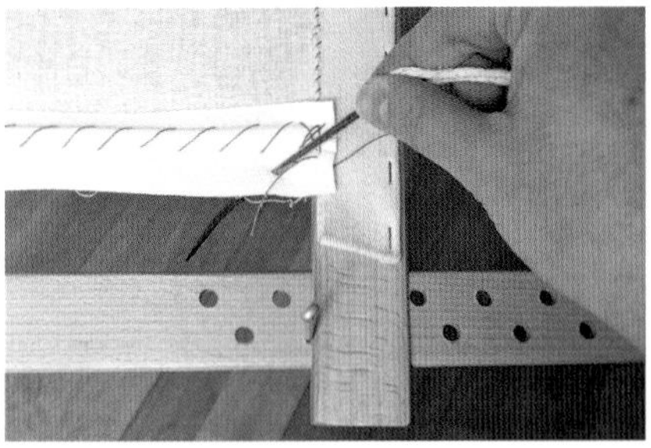

21. Now thread up your large needle with the string. As we don't know the exact length needed, it must be kept on the ball. Take the needle down into the part of the webbing that is hanging over the edge of the fabric. Pull through an amount of string to enable you to continue working and pull the string up over the arm of the frame.

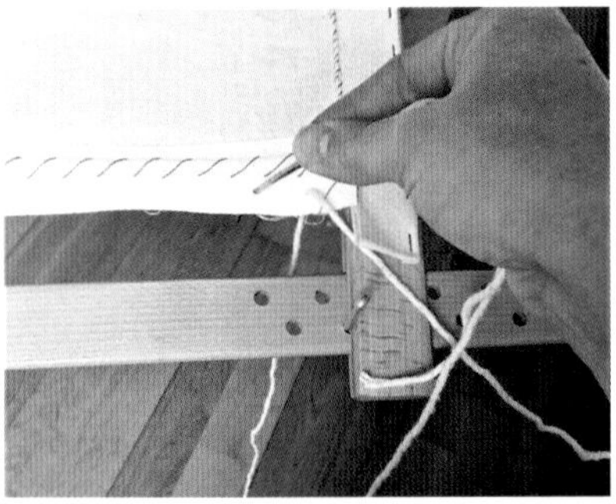

22. Moving along about 3cms, put the needle again down through the webbing and pull the string up and over the arm of the frame.

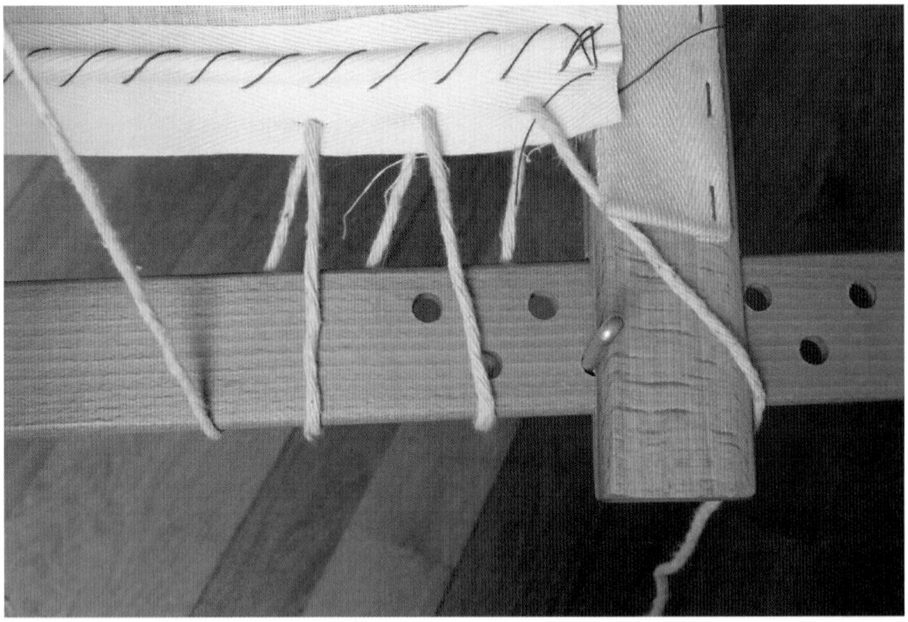

23. Continue this way all the length of the arm. Notice how the string enters the webbing in a straight line; this will ensure that the fabric is evenly pulled. You will have to keep stopping and pulling the string through the webbing every now and then. When you reach the end of the webbing, pull a bit extra off the string and cut the end. Repeat on the other side.

If you are not applying a fabric on top then you can now tighten your frame. It may be easier to stand on the roller part of the frame to get it as tight as you can. Move the pegs gradually each side so that the fabric is pulled evenly. Measure the distance between the arms with a tape measure to check it is the same. You may have counted the correct number of peg holes, but that doesn't mean to say the holes are in the same position each side.

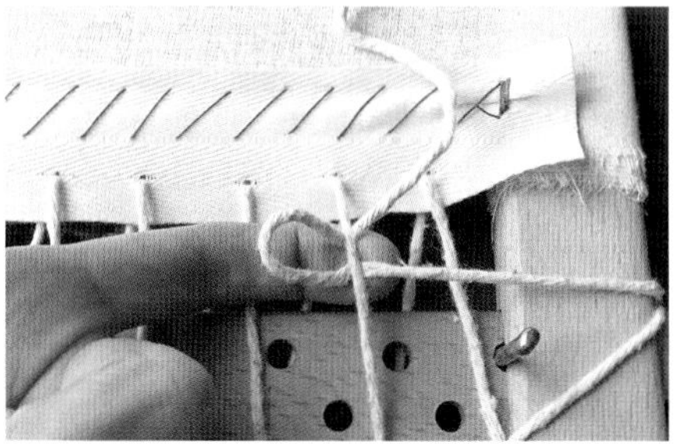

24. Now wrap the excess string around the end of the slate frame and secure with a slip knot. You need to be able to easily undo the string as you must tighten up every now and then while you work. Take the end of the string and make a loop under one of the strings as shown; keep your finger in place to hold it.

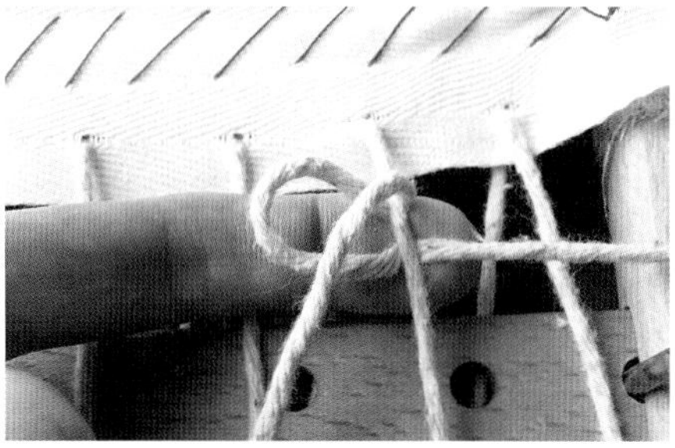

25. Take the end tail of the string and cross it over the front of the loop.

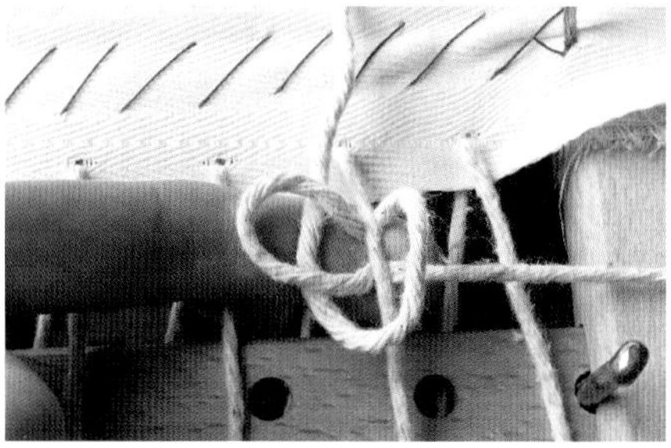

26. Then take this end of the string and pass it under the loop.

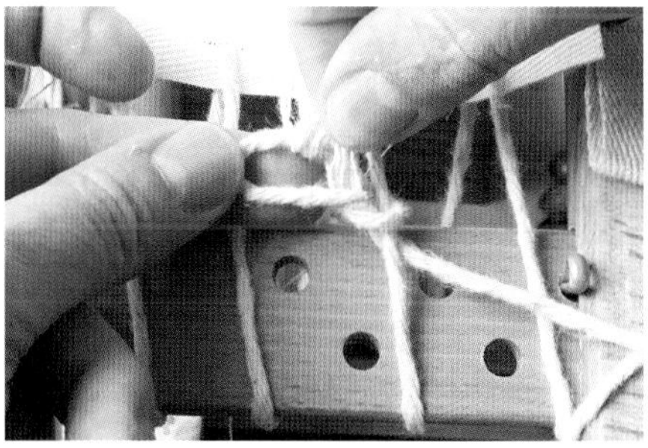

27. Pull the end tail through the loop you first created, to make another loop while letting go with the first hand you were holding the loop with. This takes a bit of practice!!

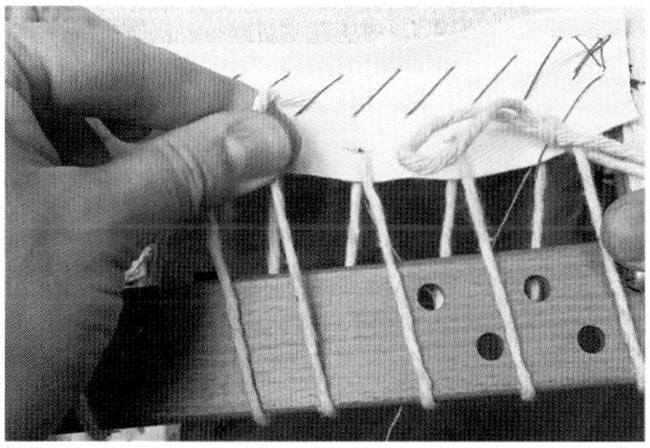

28. The finished slip knot shown at the top right of the picture. Now pull the string tight along the edge of the arm, from where you fastened your slip knot. Try and pull it so the webbing is in a straight line, which means the fabric is being pulled evenly. Wrap the excess around the frame; when you get to the end add a slip knot and repeat the opposite side. Now is a good time to attach tissue paper or a cotton wrapper to your frame to protect your fabric and your embroidery. It also means you have something to lean on while working.

Hints and tips

Keep the string from your frame for the next time you frame up. This way the string will be pre-stretched, and you will not have to tighten your frame up so much.

This preparation may seem long-winded, but it will help to get a good result with your embroidery. If you are going to spend lots of hours on a piece of work then preparation is the key.

Top Fabric Application

If you are using a silk or a thin fabric then you need to apply it to a backing fabric once it is in the frame if possible. This is to support it and help prevent wrinkles. The stitches we use to secure the two fabrics are a long and a short stitch – this is for two reasons. One, it means that as there are different length stitches, the grain of the fabric is not pulled purely in one place which can cause splitting of the top fabric. Two, you are always going *down* into the top fabric, pulling it slightly therefore making it tighter than your backing fabric, preventing wrinkles.

Materials:

- A slate frame or ring, framed up as before with a calico or linen, preferably white or cream and not too heavy a weight, without slubs or marks which can show through to the top fabric.
- Top fabric such as silk.
- Pins.
- Polyester or cotton machine thread in a colour to match your top fabric.
- Needle size 8–12.
- Scissors.

1. Make sure your backing fabric is not too tight in the frame. It should be a little bit bouncy. This is to allow us to apply the top fabric at a tighter tension to prevent wrinkles forming. Place your fabric (which is cut straight on the grain) onto the backing fabric. Think about where you want to place it. Do you need to work your design from both sides because it is too large or is it just being worked from one side? You may need to place your top fabric where you will be able to stitch it easily, so you can firstly see the design and embroidery but also be able to reach it without difficulty. Try and make sure the fabric is straight with the roller and arms of the frame.

2. Now pin into the top fabric vertically, starting in the centre at the top or bottom.

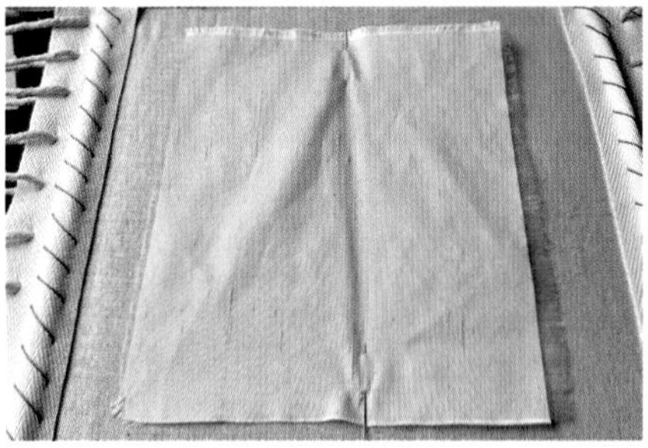

3. Now put a pin opposite the first one. Notice how the pin seems to be slightly pulling the fabric and creating a line down the centre. This is important. As you now pin around your fabric, you need to be pulling the top fabric slightly every time with your pins, so it is tighter than your backing fabric.

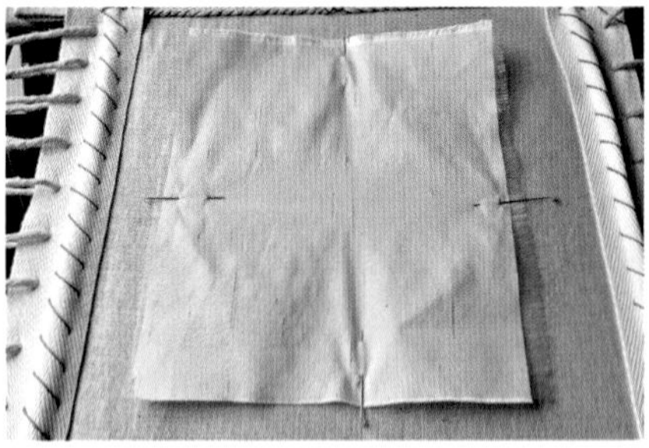

4. Next, a pin in the middle right and then the left. Each time a little bit of tension to pull the fabric tighter. You can now see in the centre of the silk it is beautifully smooth but not distorted, the edges of the silk are still straight. This is the effect you are trying to achieve.

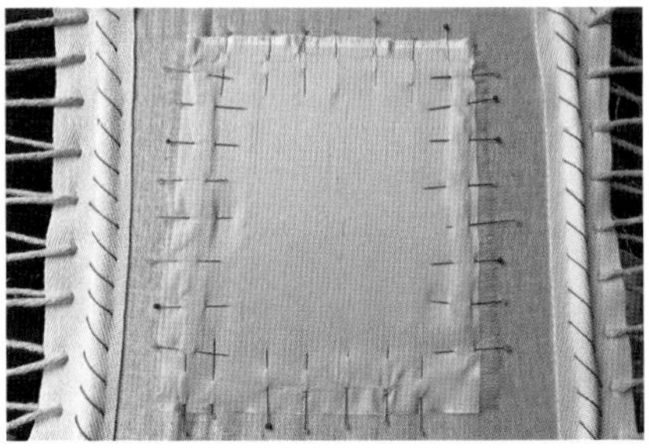

5. Now fill in all sides of the fabric with pins. Keep the edges of the top fabric straight as you pin. Do not over pull the top fabric so that it is straining. When you have finished pinning, the top fabric should be smooth and the edges straight. If you can see the edges waving or the pins buckling, then correct it now before you start sewing.

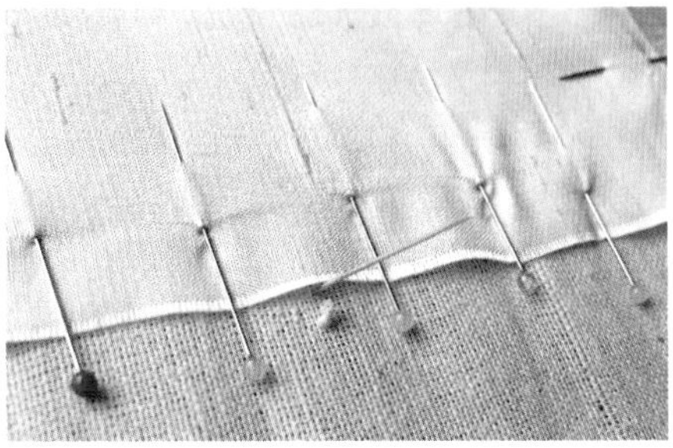

6. Thread your needle with one strand of thread and a knot. Start in the middle at the bottom and make a few stitches in your backing fabric with the knot on the top. Snip your knot off when the thread is secure. Bring your needle up in your base fabric near the edge of your top fabric.

7. Now take it down into your top fabric with a straight stitch. As you take your needle down you should pull slightly towards you with the needle to give the top fabric a tighter tension. Notice the angle of the needle in the photograph.

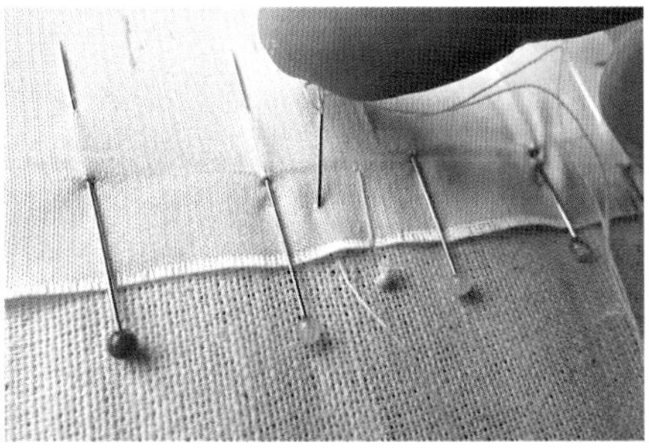

8. Now come up a little further along on the edge and take another stitch, this time half the size of the first one. Repeat in this way doing an alternate long and then short stitch. If you finish your thread, make a few stitches into your background fabric. Continue until you reach the corner. Come back to the middle and repeat to the other corner. Now stitch the opposite side starting again in the middle and then the two vertical sides in the same way. When all sides are secure, tighten your frame.

9. When your frame is tightened, it should look like this; string holes in a straight line, the webbing applied and pulled straight, the silk applied straight, the stitches even, the fabric smooth. A lot to consider perhaps, but worth it to prevent wrinkles and problems later.

Marking the Centre Lines

You may wish to mark the centre lines on your fabric so that you can line up centre lines on your design. This is purely a personal choice. Your design may not need to be centrally placed on the fabric for various reasons. You may have a mark or slub you are going to cover with your design for instance, or you may want the design nearer to you. However, if it is important, there is an easy way to mark them temporarily.

Measure the edge of each side of the fabric, attach a pin into the fabric, flat on the surface as you would pin your top fabric to your bottom fabric as shown to mark the centre measurement. Wrap a single thread of machine cotton around the pin a few times and then take the thread to the opposite centre pin and again wrap around a few times. If the thread comes from the right side of the bottom pin for example, it starts wrapping from the right side of the top pin.

Repeat with the other centre measurements.

This will make a temporary cross on your fabric which you can match up to the centre lines drawn on your design if needed.

Transferring your Design to the Fabric

The method you use to transfer your design is personal choice. Drawing straight on to the fabric freehand is fine if you are confident; however, if you go wrong you cannot just rub it out like you can a drawing on paper so think carefully before doing this option! You could use disappearing ink pen for fabrics but test them first. Once you are happy with the design, draw it in with a permanent method.

Tracing

A very basic and simple way of getting your design onto the fabric. However, for this to work you must be able to see your design through the material, using a brightly lit window or a light box. Dark and heavy fabrics are not suitable for this method.

Tape your design, which should be a photocopy or pen drawing (so as not to transfer pencil marks to the fabric), to a white table or paper, bright window or light box. Tape your fabric on top of this so that it is straight, smooth and flat. Line up centre lines if using. You do not want the fabric to move in any way. Using a hard pencil or ink pen, trace the design to your material using a fine line.

Prick and Pounce

A very accurate way of transfer but it does take more preparation.

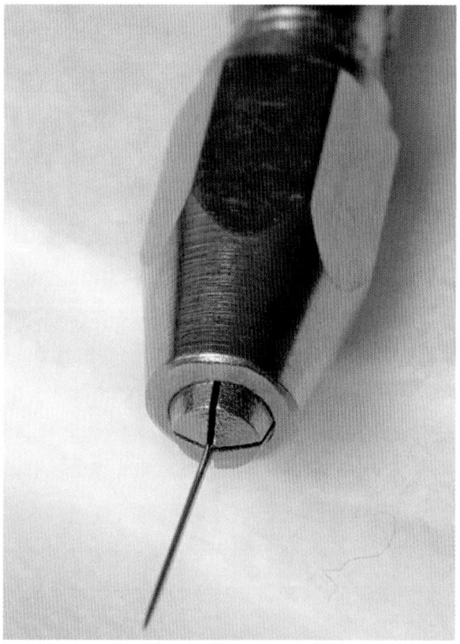

1. Trace your chosen design to thick tracing paper. Fit a needle to your pricking tool. Small intricate designs should have a smaller size needle, for example a 10–12; larger simple shapes could have a larger needle such as 5–9.

2. Place a soft pad (felt, towel) under your tracing and prick small holes into your tracing paper, close together.

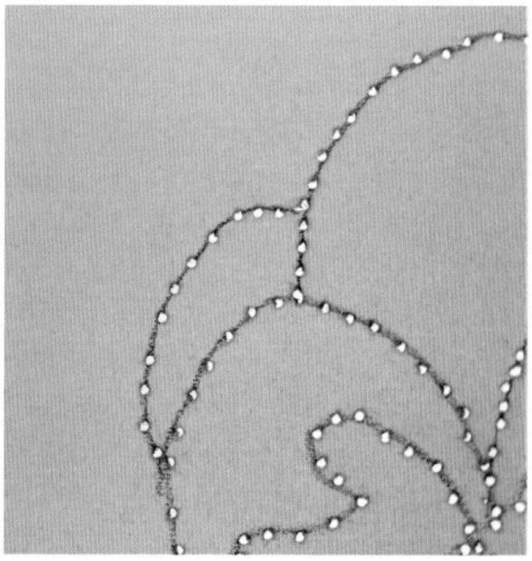

3. Hold your pricking up to the light at the end to check if you have pricked all the design. If you have a lot of lines very close together, you may wish to edit what you prick. If too much pounce comes through to the fabric, then it may be difficult to see which line is which.

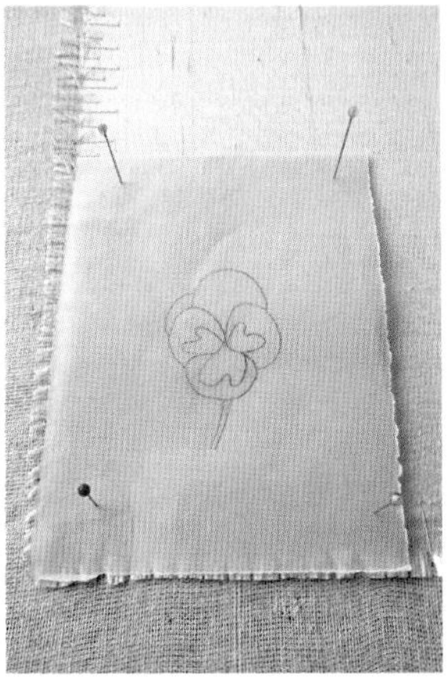

4. Place your completed pricking onto the fabric you are embroidering. It is best to do this when it is in the frame. Place pins vertically down in to the pricking, one at each corner should be enough. Too many pins could cause problems when being removed.

5. Using a soft pad, pick up a small amount of pounce in a colour that will show up on your fabric.

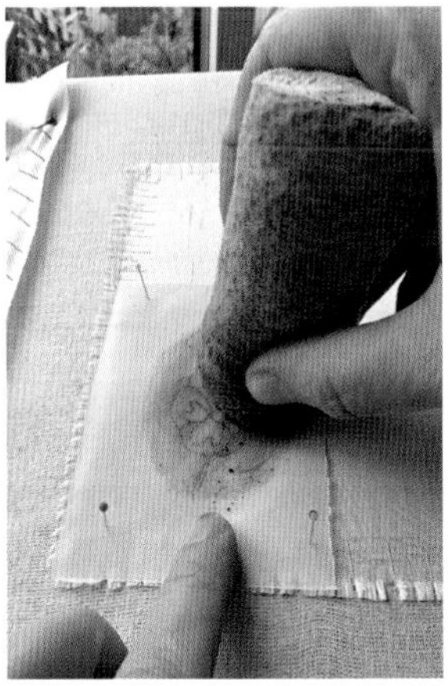

6. Gently rub over the pricking. *Do not* go over an area you have already covered to avoid double lines. Dip the pad into the pounce again if you feel it is running out. Try not to move the tracing paper about. You should be able to see where you have already covered.

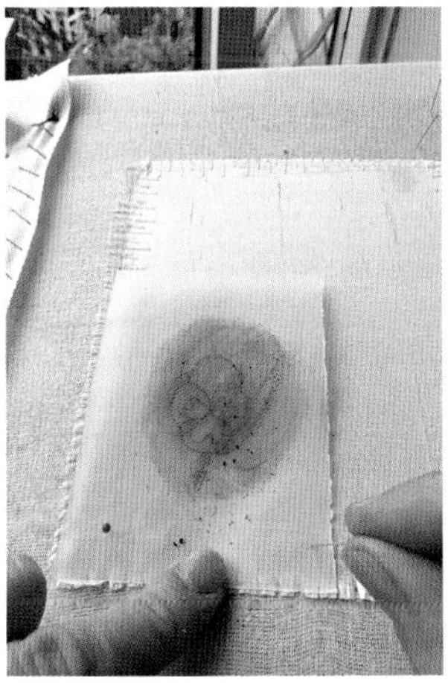

7. Remove the pins carefully from the fabric, trying not to move the pricking as you do so. Lift the pricking straight up into the air in one movement to avoid smudging the pounce. If you are happy with the pounce then continue to the next step. If something has gone wrong, turn the frame over, bang the back to remove the pounce and start again. You can also use a clean baby brush or cloth to remove excess pounce by flicking it away.

8. The design is now ready to be painted, inked or pencilled onto the fabric. When marking on the design, work in such a way that you do not smudge the pounce in areas you have yet to do. When painting, use a watercolour paint from a tube thinned with a little water and a very fine brush. Practise on the side of your fabric first, painting a thin, smooth line. Do not make the paint too watery or it will bleed, especially with thin fabrics such as silk. If the paintbrush picks up pounce from the surface of the material then clean it off with water. If the paint is too thick it will make a heavier line and when dry can flick off the surface of the fabric. When the design has been transferred successfully and your paint or ink is dry, brush away the excess pounce.

Hints and tips

- If your design is larger than the frame you are using, then transfer the design before putting it in the frame, weigh it down on a table, then weigh the pricking down on top. Clean tins of food make good weights.
- When you are painting on to your fabric make sure you cover everything up around the design so as not to accidentally get paint in the wrong place.

Transfer Paper

Another quick and easy way to transfer the design to fabric. This method can be used for all colour fabrics very successfully; it is easier to do before you put your material in the frame.

Attach your fabric to a table with tape, making sure it does not move around. Make sure it is smooth and straight. Place your transfer paper on top with the waxy powdered surface facing down. Choose a colour of paper appropriate to your fabric colour, so that it is easily seen, for example white for dark fabrics, grey or blue for light colour fabrics. Place a tracing of your design over the paper and secure with tape. It is useful for your tracing to be worked with a colour pencil so that when you trace it to the fabric, you can easily see where you have already worked. Using a ballpoint pen, trace over the design pressing down firmly. Try not to rest your arm or wrist on any areas outside of the design as the powder/wax can transfer. When you have finished remove your design and transfer paper. If your transfer paper is very powdery then go over the design with an ink pen or paint.

Transfer Pen

Transfer pen is another accurate way of transferring the design. It is permanent so make sure you test your pen first and make sure you are happy with your design before starting. This method only works with light colour fabrics as the pens are usually dark ink. Trace your design in *reverse*. This is very important, especially if you have lettering. Test your fabric with an iron to make sure it will take the heat stated, as some pens require a high heat for transfer. Iron your design onto the fabric as the pen instructions state, pressing firmly and not lifting the iron off the fabric too much as you may smudge the design and get a double line. Transfer pens vary in the required iron temperatures and length of time you need to press.

Transfer pencils are also available.

This shows the design traced onto tracing paper with a light blue pencil and then traced onto the white transfer paper with a black ball point pen; it is then clear which parts of the design have been transferred as it is hard to lift the paper up to check.

Tacking Method

This method is removable, so it is very useful for areas of your design that are not going to be fully covered with stitching. It is easier to do for simple designs rather than designs with lots of tiny little accurate details.

This method is also useful if you are unsure of placement of your design or you think you may change your mind about an element of your design once you start stitching. If you have a very delicate or fine fabric though, this method may make holes which may not be removable so do bear this in mind.

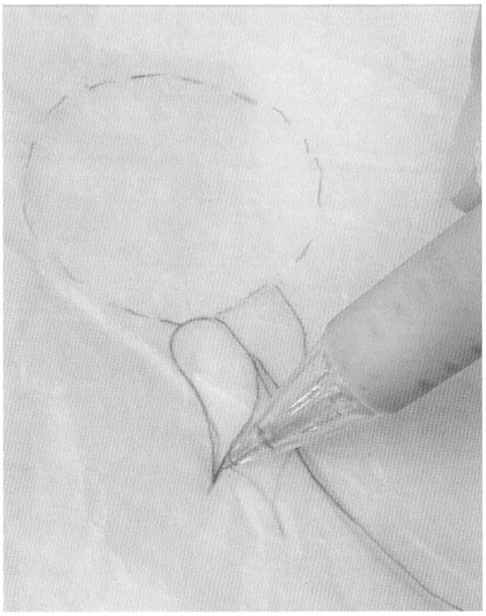

1. Trace your design onto white tissue paper. Do not use a very soft pencil as the lead may come through onto your fabric if it is a pale colour. A permanent ink pen or hard pencil would be suitable.

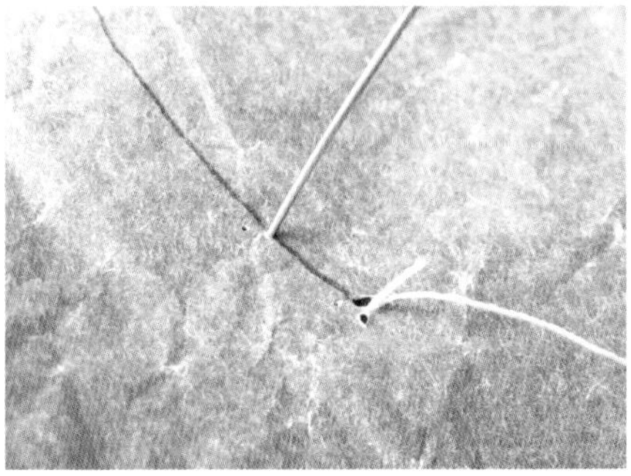

2. Pin or tack your tissue paper with your design on to your fabric in the correct position. This can be done on or off the frame, but you may find it gives you better tension in your tacking stitch if you do it when the fabric is taut in the frame. Make sure the tissue paper is secure and not flopping around, or the transfer may not be accurate. Using a polyester thread with a knot in it, in a colour that will show up on your fabric, make a small stitch at the start of a line. Go over this stitch a couple of times to make sure the thread is secure. If you have a large design, it is best to start in the centre and work out to the edge.

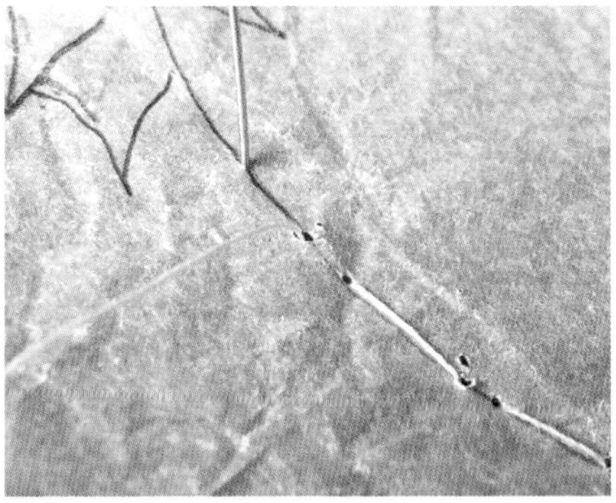

3. Now work a running stitch along the design line, with a large stitch on the surface of your design and a small stitch on the reverse of your fabric as shown. If you have too large a space between stitches on the front, much of your design will be missing when you remove your tissue paper. Pull the stitches firmly.

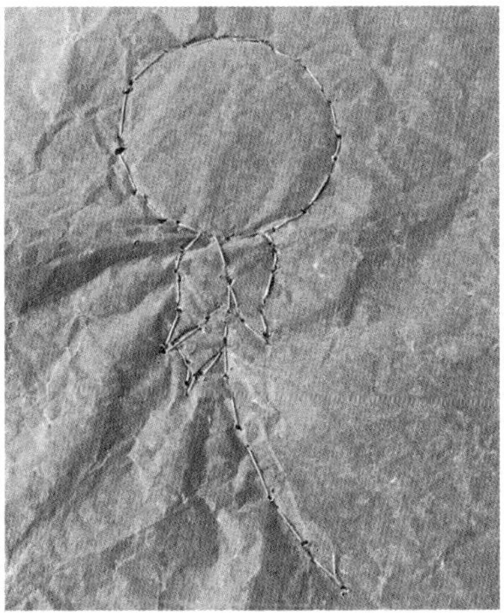

4. Work around all the design and then finish your threads securely by going over your last stitch about three times.

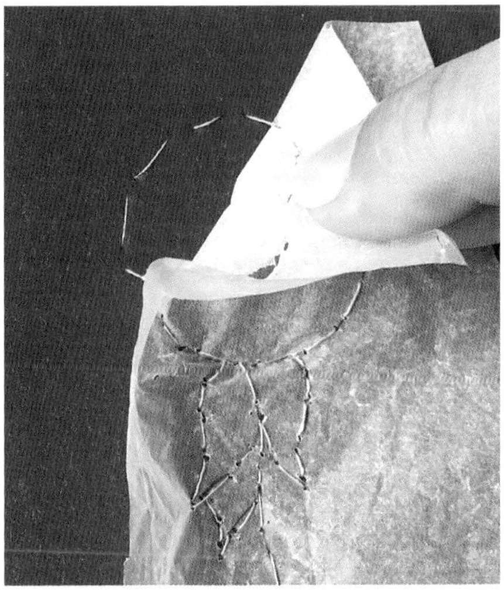

5. Carefully pull away your tissue paper to reveal your design. You may need to use tweezers to pull away the tissue from very small areas. As you work your embroidery you can remove these tacking stitches as needed.

MRD

CHAPTER 5

PRACTICE EXERCISES AND STARTING TO EMBROIDER

Long and short stitch is one of the most misunderstood embroidery stitches. Many instruction diagrams show it as a regimental ordered stitch with straight bands of colour and distinctive rows. The opposite is true. The beauty in this stitch is that there is a lot of freedom and you want randomness instead of order to get a natural-looking effect. However, it can sometimes be quite difficult to get randomness in embroidery; we are used to perhaps following stitches that are repeated and the same distance and same size over and over. Long and short stitch relies on the different sizes, colours and placement of stitch to obtain beautiful thread paintings.

Before attempting to embroider a picture in thread painting, practising long and short stitch is a good way to prepare. Most of the projects in this book are based on traditional long and short stitch. The others are just based on a straight stitch. These can be attempted without practising long and short samples, for example the felt beads, Venice scene and the Chinese embroidery sample.

The practice exercises help you get used to the construction of the stitch, how to turn angles and how to blend your thread colours. It is like learning scales on a piano; you want to play a tune, but you must first master the scales. You could jump in and start the projects, but you will understand them much better if you stitch these exercises first. A useful little thought to keep in mind; even though the stitch is called long and short, think of it as long and *longer* stitch. Short stitches in a row can make things much harder.

The one technique in embroidery that improves with practice is long and short stitch. The more you do the better you get. Practising close vertical stitches will make the tapestry shading projects look so much better. Practising turning angles will make the natural shading projects much easier to achieve.

You can use any thread you like to embroider the samples, just make sure you are using the correct size needle for whichever thread you choose. For example, a number 10–12 embroidery needle for stranded cotton and a number 5–7 embroidery or a chenille needle for wool or silk, size dependent on thickness of thread. All the samples have been stitched in one strand of thread on a silk dupion material, unless otherwise stated.

Use one big piece of fabric for these exercises and call it a sampler. Write notes on the fabric if you notice something important and want to remind yourself. If you repeatedly go wrong with an exercise, instead of unpicking constantly, try starting the exercise again. This way you can see improvement in your embroidery and you can see where you have previously made mistakes. The stitches will not be perfect first time, but that does not matter. It is a good way also to try out different threads and see which ones you prefer to use. Experiment and enjoy.

OPPOSITE: A blue tit embroidered in stranded cottons on a painted branch.

Threading a Needle

Big-eyed needle, thin thread – no problem. However, for the best results you do need to match your thread to your needle. A large needle is not always appropriate even if it is easy to thread. The needle section in Chapter Three tells you about the different types of needle for guidance. A common way to thread a needle is to fold the thread over and push this double thread through the needle; however sometimes an eye is too small for this technique, so follow the instructions below.

Start by cutting the thread very sharply, straight across. Any fluffy ends will make it hard to go through the needle, so you need a sharp pair of scissors for this.

Hold the end of the thread between your thumb and index finger so there is only a *tiny* portion of thread showing and you are squeezing it very tightly, so it is almost flattened. Then with your other hand hold the needle in position over the end of the thread as shown, almost touching it.

Keeping your needle still, roll your fingers upwards so the end of the thread glides into the eye of the needle.

This all sounds very easy and straightforward, but it does take practice with some of the thinner threads and smaller-eyed needles. If you have a long piece of thread and you are trying to get this through the eye it will not work; you need control over the thread, that is why there is only the very end of the thread held between your fingers.

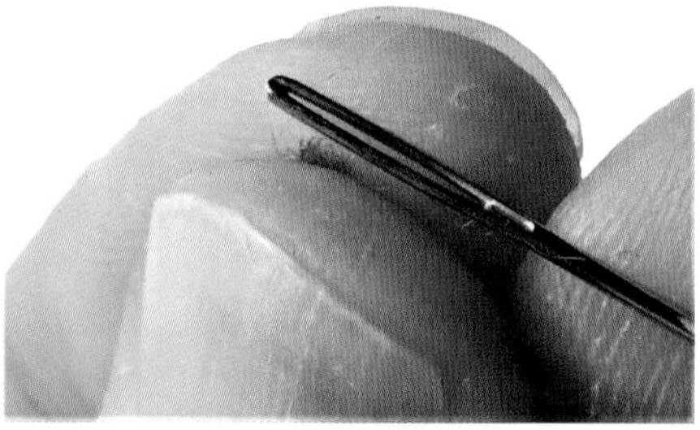

Squeeze the thread tightly so that it is almost flat.

Glide the thread through the eye of the needle.

Starting and Finishing Your Thread

You may be used to knotting your thread and putting the knot on the back of your work. This will result in lumps and tangles and the knot may get in the way of the embroidery, especially as it is so dense. Starting a thread with the knot on top of the work and then cutting it off may seem radical, but it leaves your work much smoother.

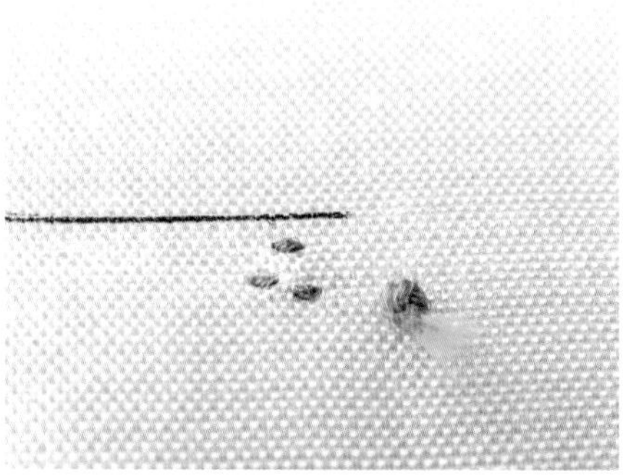

Starting the thread with a knot on top of the work will leave you with a neater result.

Make a knot in your thread and take your needle through your fabric so the knot sits near to where you want to start stitching on the *front* of your work. Make three tiny stitches close to where you are going to start stitching, preferably not on your design line, and in an area that will be later covered with embroidery. Now you can cut the knot off and your thread will be secure.

To finish off your thread later, when you have stitched an area and you are not going to use the thread again, bring your needle to the top of your work and make three tiny stitches just as you did for starting, bring your needle back through to the front again and then cut off your thread. If you have no room to do some tiny stitches, for example if you have finished an area, then take your thread to the back of your work and weave it through some of your stitches, making sure it is securely fastened.

This way you should not have to turn your frame over, unless you have a tangle of course!

Split Stitch

When embroidering, one of the trickiest things to achieve is a neat edge around your work. Split stitch is the secret way to create a very neat edge easily. It may seem pointless, as you will stitch over it and therefore it is hidden when you have finished. However, it is worth it. It can be used under the edge of long and short and satin stitch.

The colour you use for your split stitch will be one that will match the embroidery covering it. If you are using many shades, then use a medium tone for your split stitch.

1. Start your thread as described above and cut off your knot, come up at the end of your line that needs a split stitch, take a tiny stitch down on the line. The smaller and tighter your split stitches are then the better your embroidered edge will be over the top. If you have a thick line drawn, then stitch to the outside or top edge of it so it will be fully covered later.

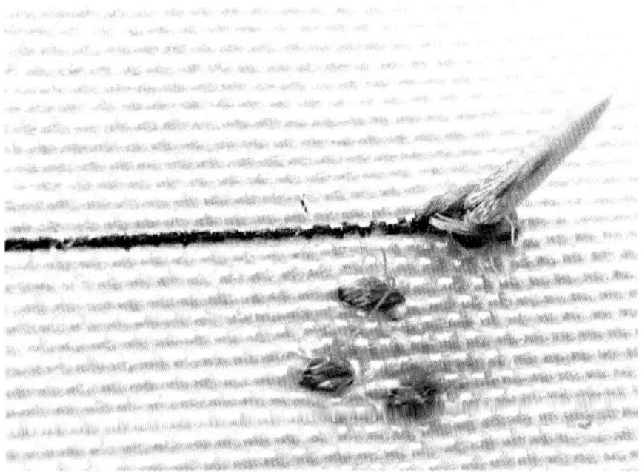

2. Come up through your stitch with the needle, splitting it (hence the name). Pull firmly.

3. Now take your needle down on the line a little further on to make another stitch.

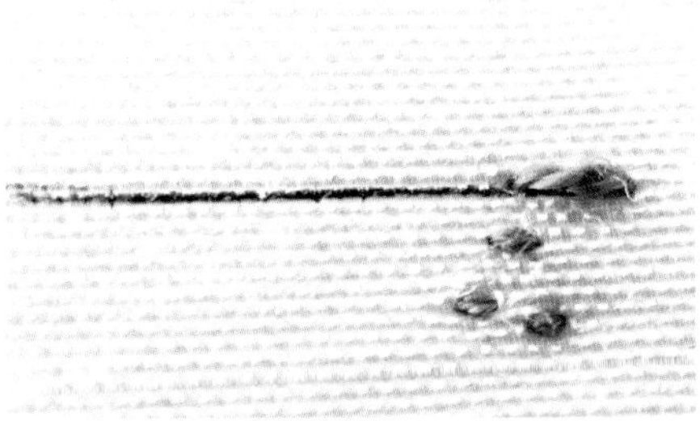

4. Pull this thread firmly.

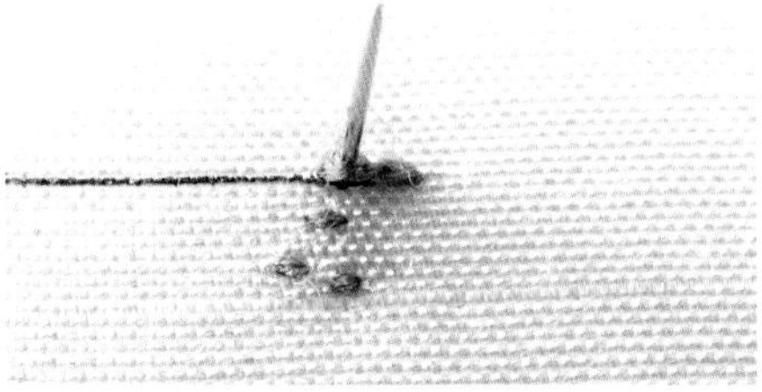

5. Come up in the middle of this second stitch just as before.

6. Continue in this way, with tiny tight stitches that are all connected to make a solid edge to go over. It is worth taking time to do this as well as you can. It makes all the difference to the finished look of your embroidery. Do not use the thread that you work your split stitch in to then stitch your long and short in. Split stitch is very wearing on the thread and you should always finish your thread off after your split stitch.

Tapestry Shading

Tapestry shading is long and short stitch that goes in a vertical direction only. It is appropriate for buildings and drapery, for example. You may find it useful to follow the grain of the fabric if it has a strong vertical weave to it and is straight in your frame. You may also want to mark vertical lines on your fabric with a hard pencil or air-disappearing pen to help you keep the direction. This sample has a different colour for each row; this is important, so you can see that you have the right placement of your stitch. It does not matter what colours you use but make sure they are all contrasting so you can check your progress.

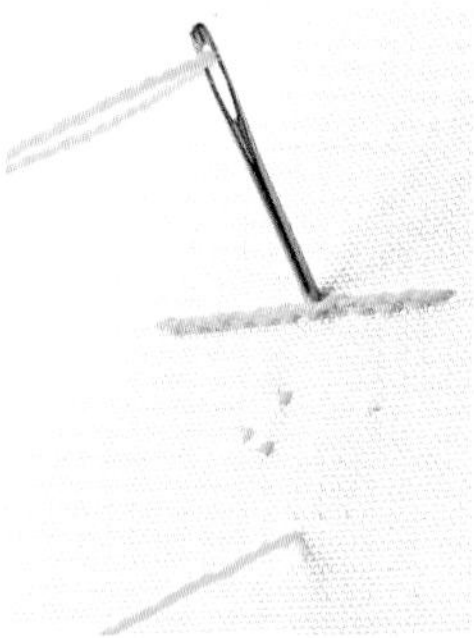

1. Embroider a straight horizontal line of split stitch on your fabric in the colour you are embroidering your first row in. Begin a new thread to start the long and short stitch. Bring your needle up through your fabric below your split stitch. Make sure you start in the middle of the area you are going to stitch; this makes it easier to keep the angle as you work to each side. There is no set length to long and short stitches. If your stitches seem a little loose and move around, then your stitches may be too long. The stitches in this sample range from 8mm to 15mm as a guide. Now take your needle down through the fabric directly above where you came up; it should form a perfectly vertical stitch, at a 90-degree angle to your split stitch. Rest your needle against the split stitch edge. You are not pushing the split stitch away; it is merely guiding you as to where to take your needle down. Pull your needle through to the back.

2. Now bring your needle up in the fabric again, this time a little below and to the left of where you came out for your first stitch; in the photo it looks as if it is directly underneath it but if you follow the grain vertically you can see it does not line up and is a couple of lines of the fabric to the left. This second stitch sits snugly up against the first stitch. There is no gap between them. This is very important. Take your needle down again against the split stitch. If you find there is a space between your first and second stitch, take out your second stitch and try again. As you get more practised you can just put an extra stitch between them perhaps, but as a starting sample try and get the stitches as close as possible, without filling in the gaps. Too many 'filling in the gap' stitches can result in an uneven edge.

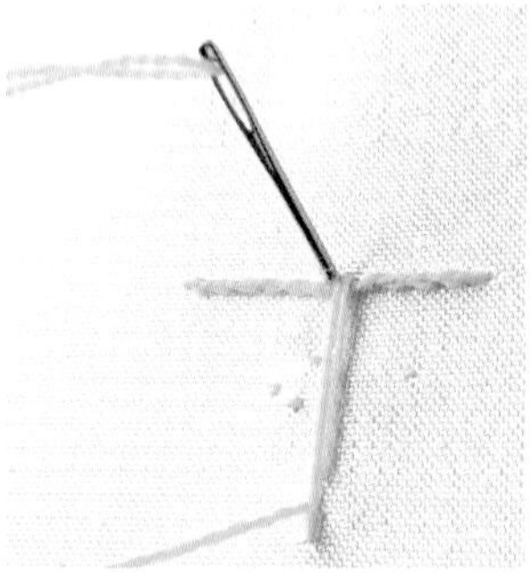

3. Now bring the needle up again in the fabric to the left of the second stitch, making sure it is not in the same position as the first or second stitches. All the stitches are slightly different lengths. Take your needle down over the split stitch as before. Check that it is as close as possible to the second stitch.

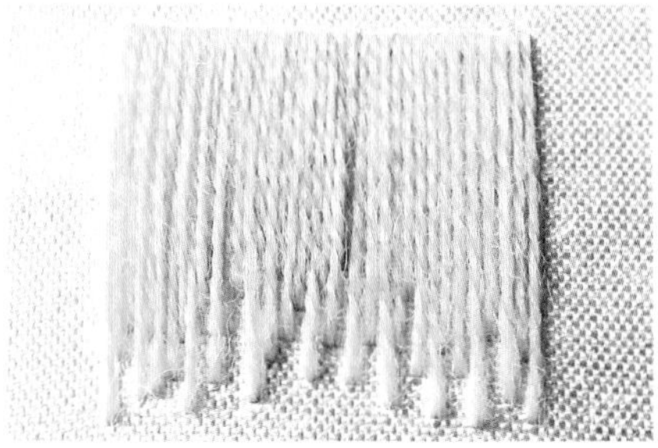

4. Continue working these stitches until you get to the very end of the split stitch. Finish your thread off, start a new one and start working from the middle going towards the right-hand side. Notice the stitches are *all* long (long and longer stitch!), but they are all different lengths. The bottom edge looks messy; this is correct. The top edge is neat and straight.

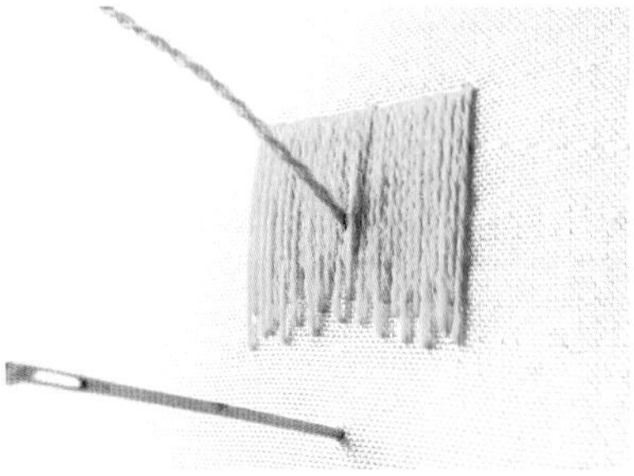

5. Thread up your needle with a contrasting colour and secure your thread as before. We are going to start again in the centre. Bring your needle up about a third of the way into your central stitch (or thereabouts) on your first row. You will probably split one of your stitches in your first row; this is correct. When you bring your needle up through your previous rows you should split most of your stitches – if you think you haven't don't worry, you will split the next one. Now take your needle down into the fabric directly below.

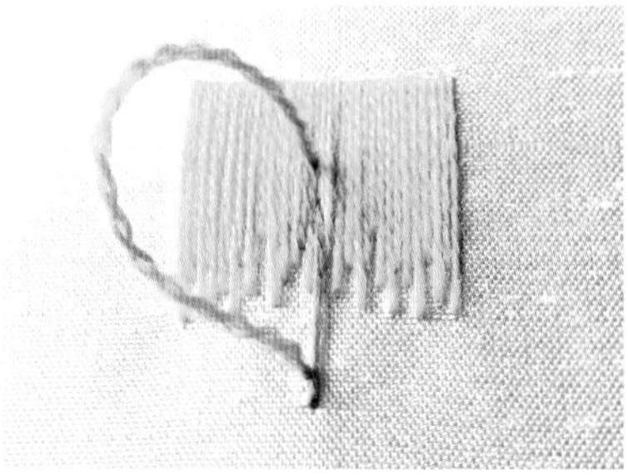

6. Now bring your needle up again into your first row; it may be a little higher or a little lower than your first stitch. It doesn't matter. All that is important is that it does not line up in any way with the placement of the first stitch. Notice that the second stitch came up a little higher in the first row so because of that, it comes up a little higher on the bottom. In effect these stitches are approximately the same length. *All* your stitches in this row should be about the same length. In this sample, the stitches are approximately 10mm.

7. Continue to embroider this row in the same way. All the stitches are the same length, but they vary in their placement. Notice how the top and bottom edges look uneven. This is correct.

8. Continue the next row with another contrasting colour, again bringing your needle up through your previous row.

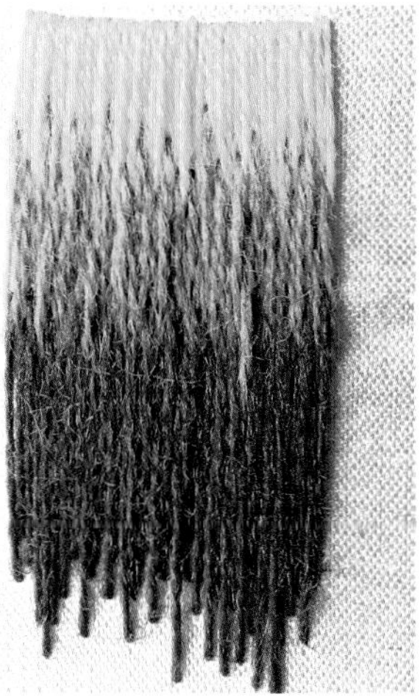

9. Practise this exercise until you feel you have achieved a neat top edge, completely vertical stitches, and a jagged effect between rows where they meet. Notice how there is about the same amount of colour showing from the first two rows. Notice that all the stitches on the last row are about the same length; they just vary in their placing.

NATURAL SHADING

Natural shading is long and short stitch that follows the form of the shape you are embroidering. Natural shading stitches change angle and can give the impression of curves and movement. It is useful for flowers and animals, for example.

The sample is a simple petal shape; it is worth stitching this a few times, to get used to changing the angle. Again, the sample is stitched in three colours, so you can see the rows of stitching clearly. The object of this exercise is to change the angle of your stitches smoothly, so that the rows look like they all flow into one another. The change is very gradual – this is the key to successful directional shading. Draw lines as instructed in the sample.

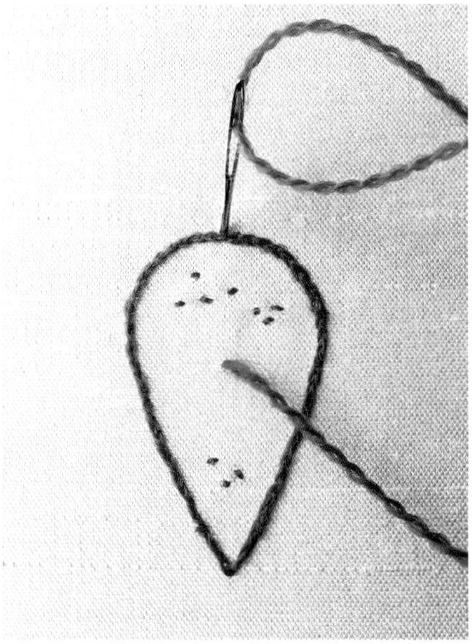

1. Start by split stitching around the petal shape in one of the colours – the shape is 25mm top to bottom as a guide. Finish your thread and start a new one for the long and short. Bring your needle up in the fabric as shown in the photo and take the needle *down* over the edge of the split stitch directly above where you came up. Be sure to start in the middle of the shape. It makes it much easier for keeping the correct angle as you work to each side. Angle the needle over the split stitch and rest against it. Do not push the split stitch out of the way; it is there to help you.

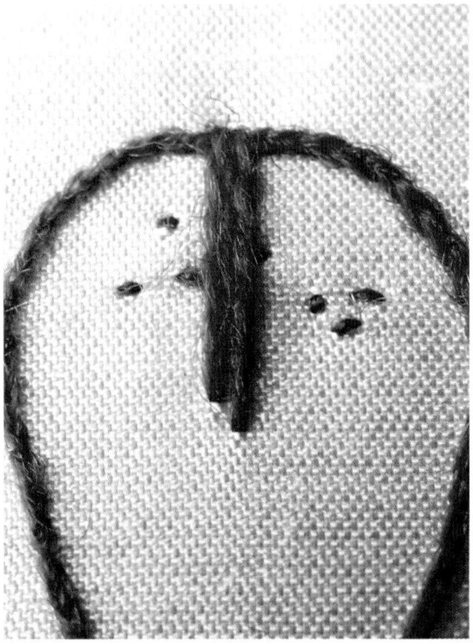

2. Do another two long and short stitches (long and longer!) to the left of the first stitch just like the tapestry shading, keeping them *very* close together, no spaces between them and all different lengths.

There are now three different ways of turning the angle of your stitching. You may find one works better for you than another. In the sample try all of them; it is better to use different ways of turning when you stitch, to keep your stitching more random.

METHOD ONE

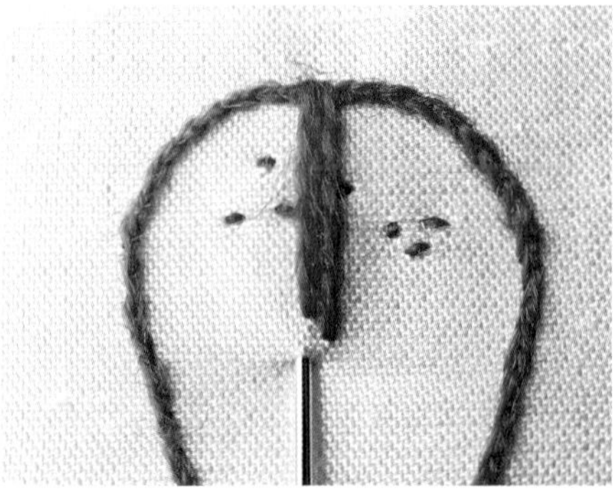

1. Bring your needle up directly *below* the third stitch as shown. It is a different length to all the other stitches so far.

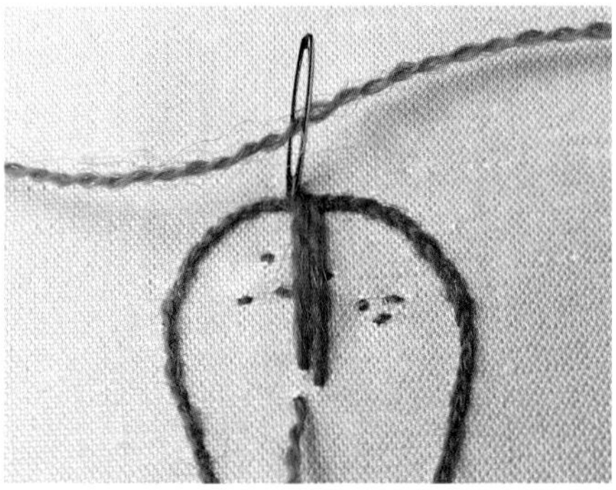

2. Now take your needle down over the edge just as before. This stitch will now lie at a slight angle alongside the previous stitch. It will *not* sit on top of your previous stitch – pull it firmly so that it is to the side. You have just turned a slight angle.

Method Two

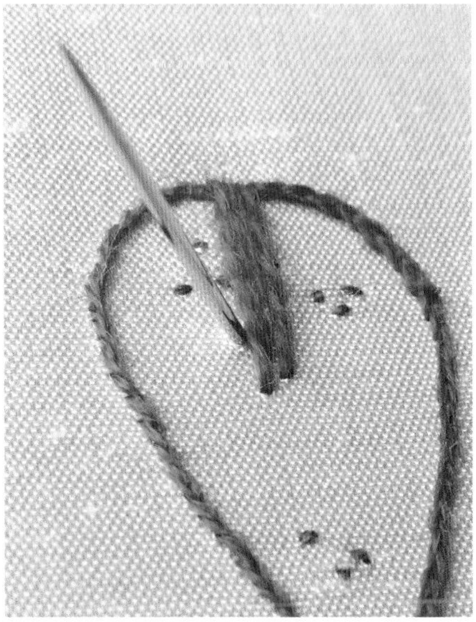

1. Bring your needle out at an angle from just under your last stitch, as shown in the picture. It is not pushing it out of the way but the needle is coming up in the same line of the fabric as the last stitch.

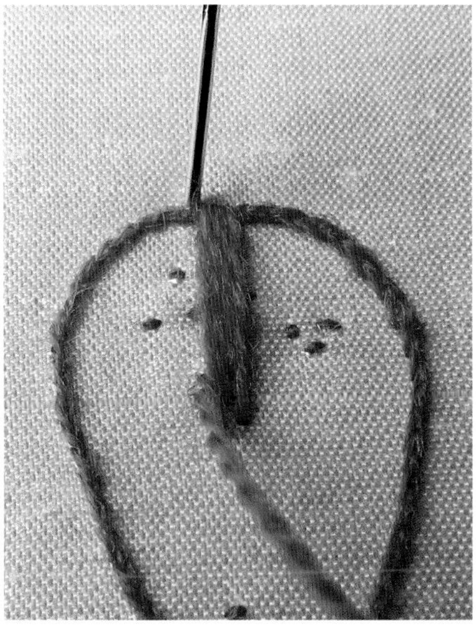

2. Now take your needle down just as before, again there will be a very slight angle change.

Method Three

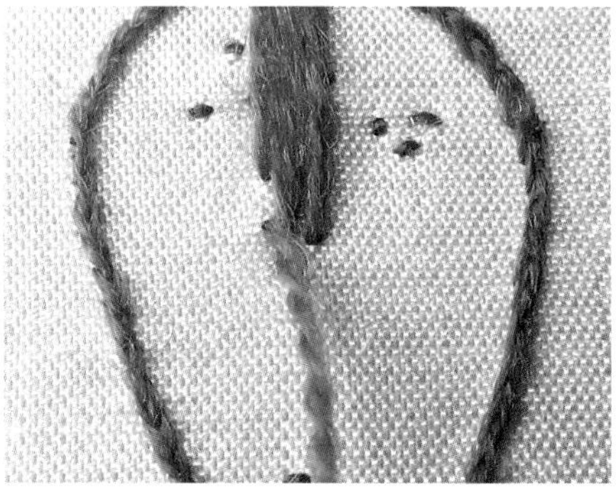

1. Bring your needle up *below* your last stitch, just as in method one.

2. This time when you take your needle down over the edge leave a *very* small gap between where you take the needle down and the last stitch. When you turn using this method, be careful you do not have a big space between your stitches. If you do, you can either unpick and redo the stitch or you can fill the space with another stitch, making sure the edge is neat. Sometimes when you fill spaces in your stitching you can get an uneven outside edge, so try to only do it occasionally.

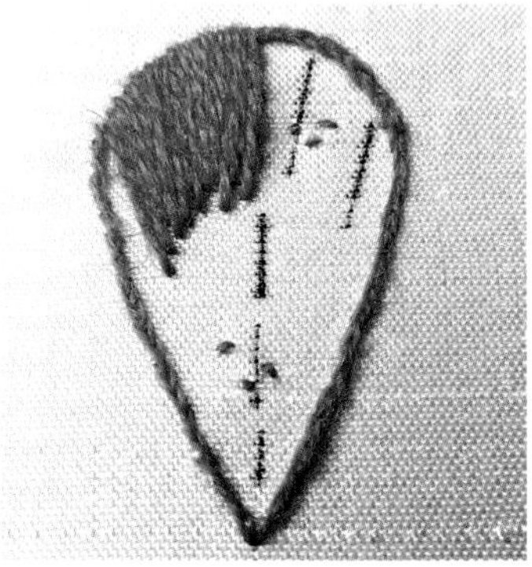

3. Stitch along the left side, turning your angle so it becomes almost the same angle as the edge of the petal as shown. If your angle does not match the one in the picture do not worry; if it is similar, it will be fine. Stop stitching before you get to the very edge, as in the photograph. Notice the bottom edge is jagged and the stitches are all long. It is very easy when stitching a shape like this to get very short stitches by the time you get to one side. Keep them long; if you have short stitches it means you have no choice in where to come up on your next row. If you find that by the time you have stitched to this edge your stitches are much shorter than when you started, it is better to take them out and redo. It will make the rest of the sample much easier. Now draw some lines on to your fabric if you think it will help. Lines straight down the centre and some lines on the right side to match the angle you have on the left side.

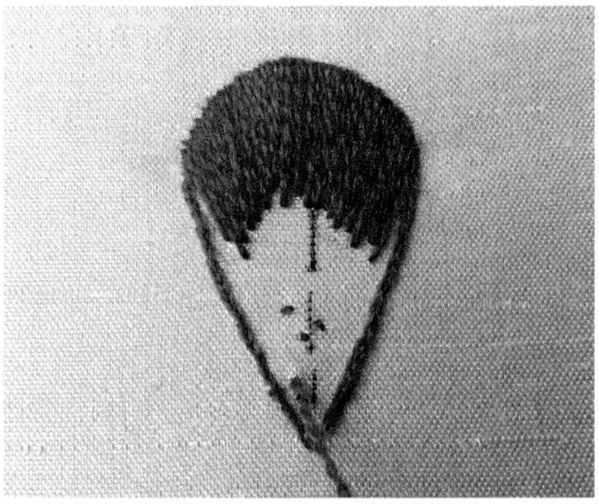

4. Stitch the right side in the same technique as the left.

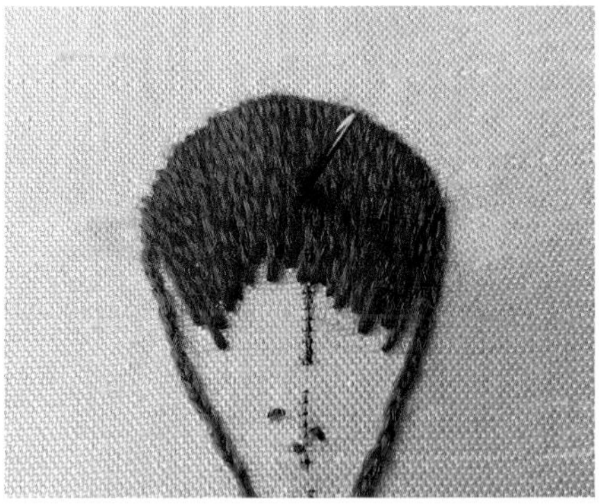

5. Now start your second row with a different colour, come *up* through your stitching about a third of the way through your first row, starting in the centre again, splitting a stitch if you can. Take your needle down through your fabric to make your first stitch.

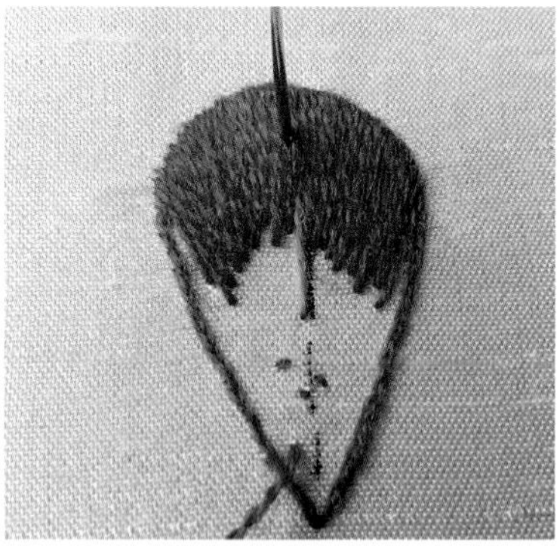

6. Now come up through your first row again fanning out a little to the left, making sure it is in a different position to your first stitch. There is a lot less space in this second row, so you do not need to come up through every stitch in your first row like we did in tapestry shading. If you did, your stitches would be sitting on top of each other and give a very bumpy appearance.

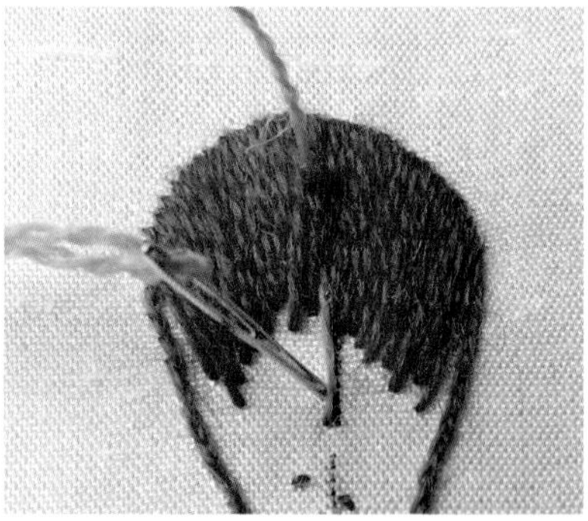

7. Take your needle down into your fabric, almost under your first stitch as shown in the picture; notice the angle of the needle – it is angling towards and under the first stitch.

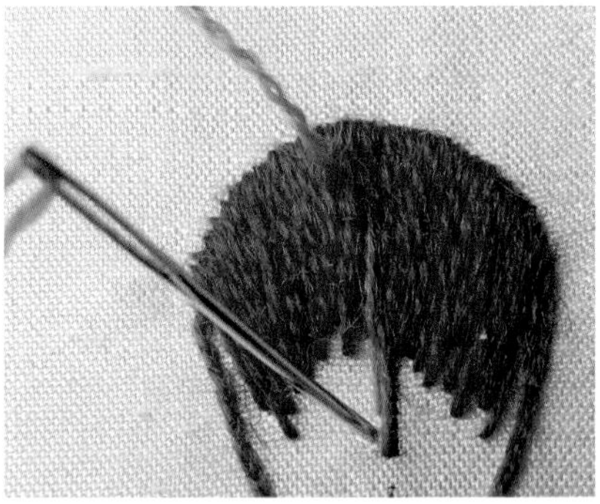

8. Now bring your needle up again in your first row in a different position, fanning out to the left, bring your needle down *very* close to your first stitch and below your second stitch.

9. Continue in this way, fanning out to the left, stopping just before the end of the first row. Notice how all the stitches are about the same length; they are not long and short anymore, just long, approximately 1cm in this sample.

10. Work the second row on the right side in the same way. Now go back to covering your outside edge, going over your split stitch as before with your first colour; it is worked in stages like this so you can make sure everything fits in.

11. Notice the angle of the needle as it goes over the split stitch edge. The angle of the stitch should be very straight against the side of the petal. You do not want it angling in towards the centre. Notice the bottom edge is still jagged.

12. Now go back to filling in a little of row two so it looks complete across the petal.

13. Cover the outside edge until you are almost at the bottom of the petal, repeat on the right-hand side. Now fill in the second row as before, keeping the stitches long and fanning them out. Notice how all the stitches angle very gently as they move down the petal. At the bottom you can go over the outside edge with your second colour if you wish. Notice the angle of the row at the bottom is the same angle as the outside edge, very straight and not turning in, almost sitting directly on top of the split stitch. The stitches are still long; do not do all the way to the bottom. Leave space as shown.

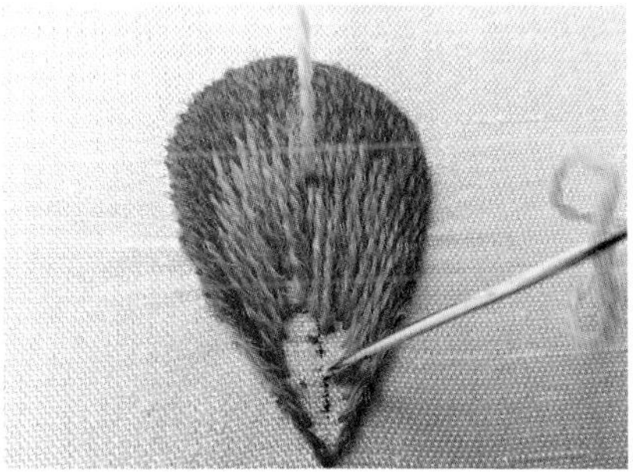

14. Now start your third row in the centre as before with your third colour.

15. Stitch the third colour as shown.

16. Now fill in the remaining space with just a few stitches following the angle you have already set. Take the first one all the way over the split stitch at the bottom in the centre.

17. Make sure you come up in some of your first-row edge stitches otherwise they will create a ridge if you do not split them, as shown in the photograph.

18. (left) The finished petal. No split stitch is showing. All the stitches flow gently to the centre. The edge is neat.

Repeat this exercise until you have a similar sample to the picture. It will help you when you are doing the projects from the book. The petal is not supposed to be symmetrical in colour or stitch.

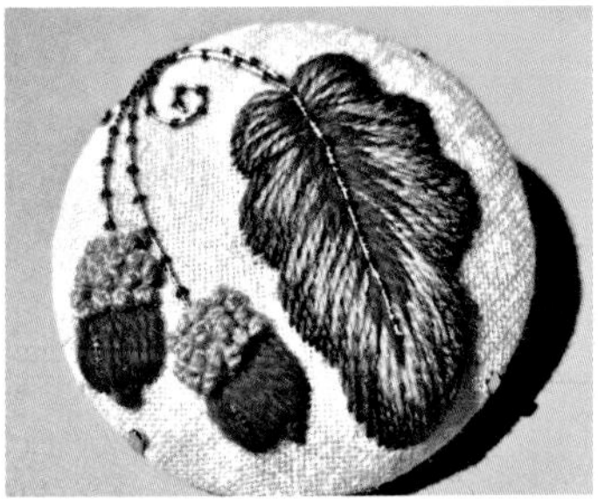

This little brooch has a long and short stitch leaf with satin stitch and French knot acorns and a couched leaf and vein.

Additional Stitches

Using other embroidery stitches alongside your thread painting is a great way to enhance your work. There are many different stitches that can be used to complement your thread painting; remember you do not want these other stitches to take away from the subtlety of your shading. Thread painting is for the most part very flat; adding a lot of surface embroidery can change the proportions and perspective of your work. Go cautiously, sometimes less is more in stitch additions to thread painting!

Stem stitch and couching for example are a good way of adding details on top of your embroidery or perhaps to add an outline in a contrast colour.

French knots are useful for adding texture, perhaps to the centre of a flower. They can be used singly or made into circles or clusters.

Beads can add texture in a similar way to French knots.

Satin Stitch

Satin stitch is a good filler for shapes which are perhaps too small for long and short or you want a flatter, unshaded look to an area. Although satin stitch looks very easy it can be tricky to create a smooth, even look with a neat edge. One tip is to use just one thread in the needle; this way you can control the thread so that it lies flat. Try to keep an even tension when working satin stitch. If you have some stitches tighter or looser, then the surface will be very uneven. Be careful that the shapes you satin stitch are not too big; too long a stitch will make the stitches loose. If this is the case you need to split the area up into sections or perhaps choose long and short stitch instead.

Always start in the centre of the shape you are going to satin stitch; this way it is much easier to keep the angle you require throughout the shape. Draw lines on your fabric if you need a guide.

The sample shows a circle being satin stitched – if you can satin stitch a circle then every other shape will be a breeze. As a circle is a symmetrical shape it is useful to put a stitch in each side alternatively, so you can make sure each side is equal. If the shape is small then use one thread as you will be crossing over on the back constantly; if the shape is big then use two threads and two needles to work the shape, alternating between the two otherwise you will create bulk on the reverse. This sample is 1cm diameter.

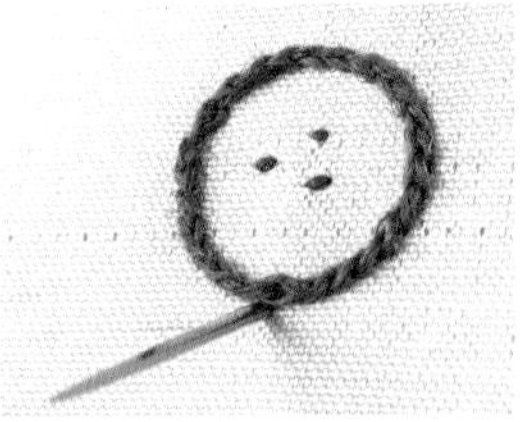

1. Firstly, split stitch around the design line of the satin stitch; this will give you a neat edge. Make the stitches small and tight. Bring the needle up at the *bottom* of the shape in the centre. Really try and get the centre correct on a circle, it will make all the difference. Notice the angle of the needle – it is coming up from under the split stitch, therefore the thread will 'wrap' nicely round giving a good edge.

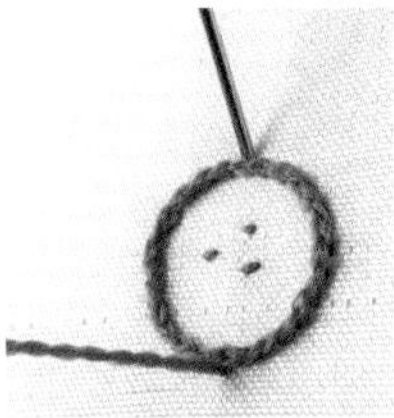

2. Now take the needle down over the split stitch. Notice the angle of the needle, resting against the split stitch, not pushing it out of the way. This first stitch should cut the circle in half exactly.

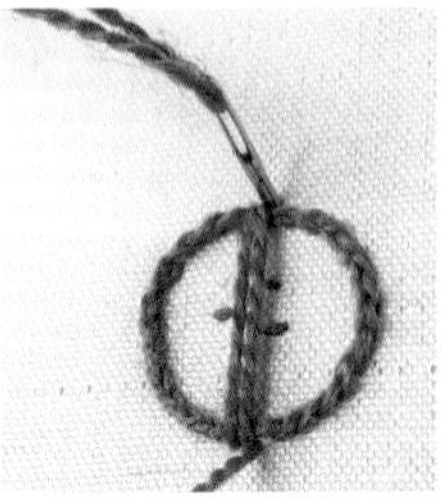

3. Now embroider another stitch to the left of the central stitch and then one to the right, in the same way. Try to get these stitches as close as possible to that first stitch. There should be no spaces between stitches and it is best not to add stitches to try and fill the gap.

4. Continue working back and forth, trying to get a symmetrical shape. If you think a stitch is too long or doesn't rest against the split stitch, then take it out.

COUCHING

Couching is a versatile line stitch. It is easy to work it in whatever size you wish, and it can be used to neaten edges, and as a decorative edging. The sample is shown with two contrasting colours, but it can also be stitched with the same colour in the needle as on the fabric. The sample is worked with one thread in the needle and *two* threads on the fabric.

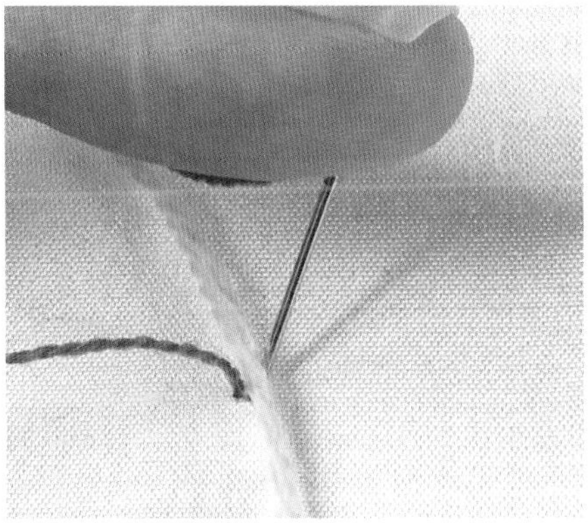

1. Firstly, cut a length of thread that will be long enough to cover the line you want to embroider plus a little bit extra for each end. Lay this thread on the line you want to cover leaving a tail of thread at the start. This is the light pink thread in the sample. Now fasten the thread you are going to stitch on top a little way along from the start of the line, stitch over the top of the thread you have lying on the fabric. Notice how the needle angles under the light pink thread; this will give a rounded effect and make sure the fastening stitch is not too big. If the stitch is too big, the thread on the fabric will move about. Try and make this couching stitch at a 90-degree angle to the other thread.

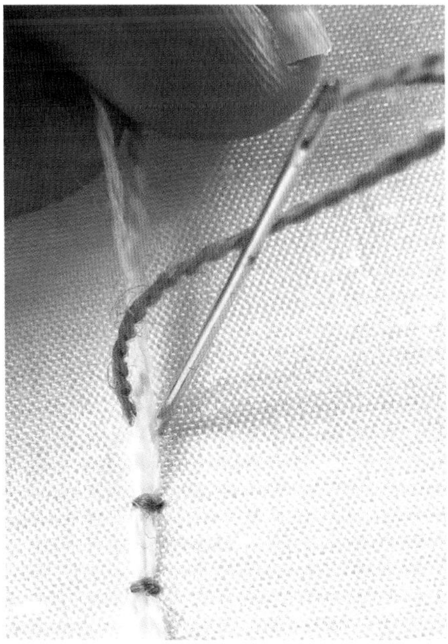

2. Now work another stitch a little further along the line; there is not a set distance to how far apart the couching stitches should be but too far apart and the thread will not be secure. Try and make them equally spaced, especially if you have contrasting colours. In the sample the stitches are 4mm apart. It helps if you have a little tension on the thread lying on the fabric, this will make the line smoother and stop the thread puffing out. Notice the fingers pulling the top thread to make it smooth.

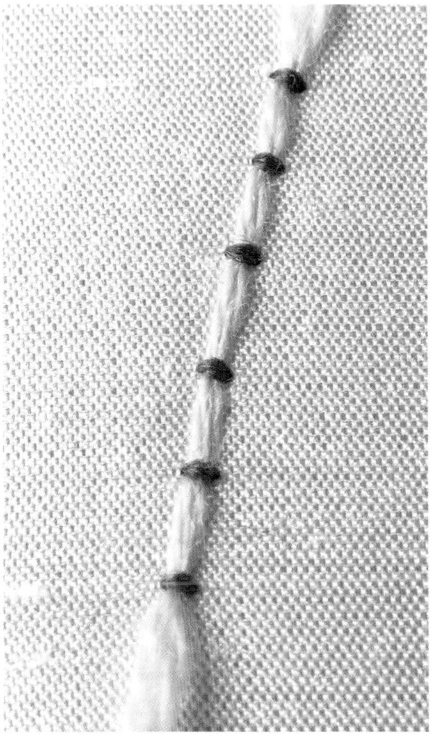

3. Try and make the stitches close together so that it follows the line you are covering exactly. When you have finished couching, take the ends of the thread lying on the surface of your fabric at the start and finish to the reverse and secure them by weaving them under some previous stitches.

Stem Stitch

Stem stitch is a great outline stitch. It follows curves well and can be made thicker easily by increasing the number of strands in the needle. It can also be used as a filling stitch by working many rows side by side. Even though stem stitch is straightforward, people do struggle with it if they are going around curves or changing direction. Try it a few different ways to get used to its structure. If it looks different to the photograph, then the loop is on the wrong side.

The sample shows the stitch being worked in an upward direction. Remember the word 'upright'. This will remind you to keep your loop to the right when you work the stitch in this way. If you are working the stitch down towards you, the loop is on the left-hand side.

If you are going in a curve, then the loop changes direction as you move around.

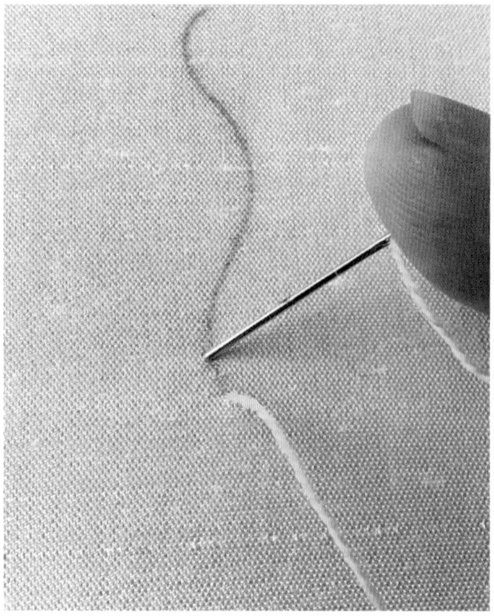

1. Bring your needle up at the bottom of the line you are going to cover and take it down 3–4mm along the line to make a stitch; do not pull the thread all the way through, leave a loop on the top of your fabric.

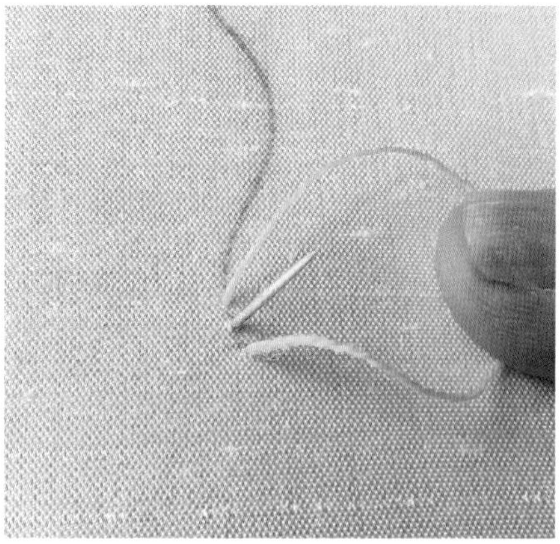

2. Holding the loop of thread away to the *right* side of the line, bring your needle up in the middle space of your last stitch as shown.

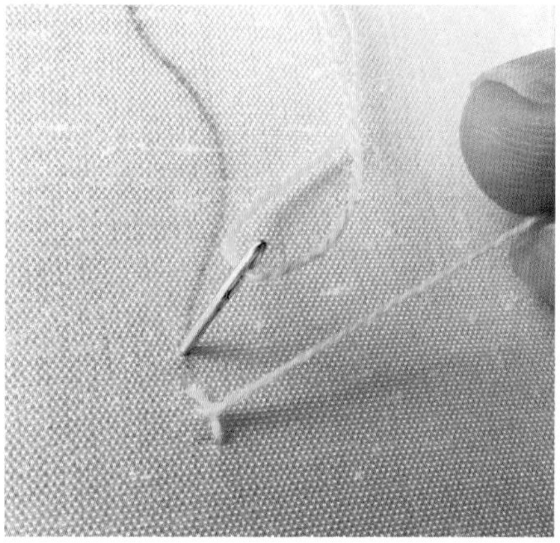

4. Now make another stitch the same length as the first, keep a loop of thread on top of the fabric as before to the right-hand side.

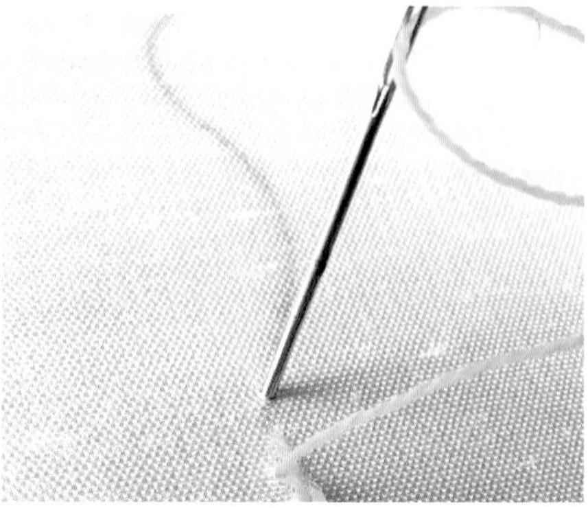

6. Make another stitch again further along the line, holding the thread to the right of the line as before and repeat as above.

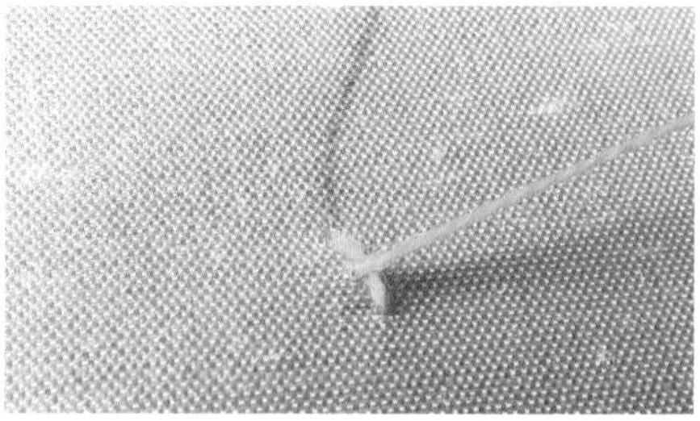

3. Now pull tight and it should look like the picture; stitch to the right, working thread to the left.

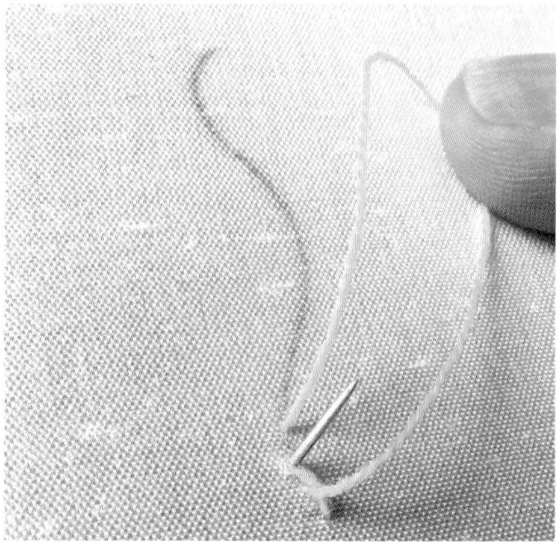

5. Now bring the needle up through the fabric where the previous stitch ended. They share the same hole. Notice the loop of thread is being held to the right again. Pull the needle all the way through.

7. The finished line. Notice the stitches all slope the same way. If you are going around a lot of curves you may need to make your stitches slightly smaller to stop the stitch looking spiky.

French Knots

French knots can add a great dimension to your thread painting as they have so much texture. It is useful sometimes if you are working flat long and short stitch to add a textured stitch such as a knot. They can be worked singly, in clusters or in a circle. They can be made bigger by using more threads. They can also be shaded by having different colours in the needle. They are very useful for the centre of some flowers. Think of a daisy; the centre is crying out to be stitched in French knots.

Try and use an embroidery/crewel or straw/millinery needle for French knots rather than a chenille needle. This is because a chenille needle gets a lot thicker at the eye and can make it hard to pull the thread through. A longer needle such as a darner can also be helpful if you are just starting to practise French knots.

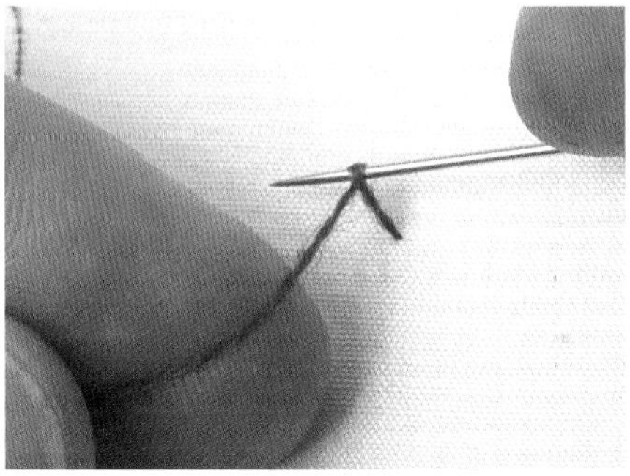

1. Bring the thread fully through the fabric and wrap the thread *once* around as shown, it does not matter in which direction. Wrap the thread around the needle close to where the thread comes through the fabric. Keep the needle still and just move the thread.

2. Now take the needle down very close to where it came up. Notice the excess thread is pulled a little taut while the needle is being pushed into the fabric.

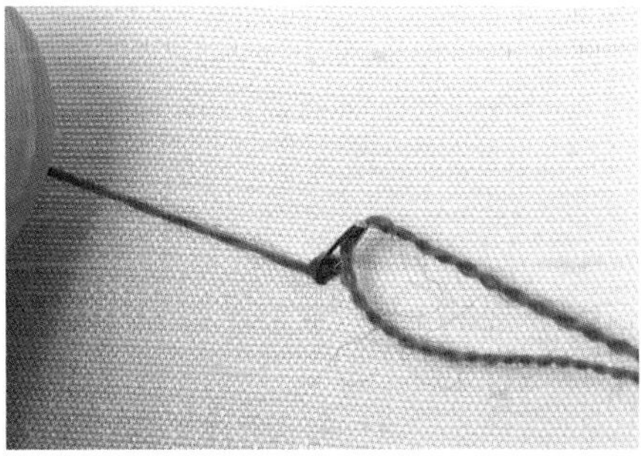

3. Pull the needle all the way through, keeping the excess thread taut.

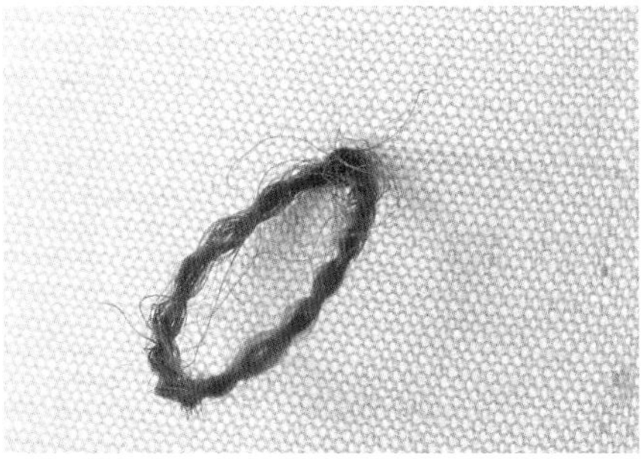

4. Once the needle is through to the other side, you can let go of the excess thread you were pulling taut and finish pulling the thread all the way through.

5. The finished knot. If you wrapped the thread around the needle more than once, you would get a wobbly knot. If you want bigger knots use more strands in the needle, that way they will always be neat.

6. A central French knot surrounded by other knots to make a circle.

Making a Sharp Point In Long and Short or Satin Stitch

It is very easy to 'round' off a point in embroidery. Following the instructions below, you will always get a sharp point to your stitching.

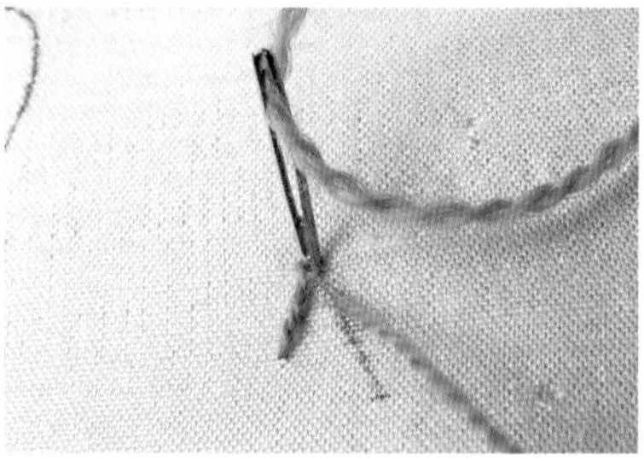

1. When split stitching for a point, work right up to the point and then split the stitch by going down into it from the other side as shown, otherwise your stitch may keep coming undone at the point.

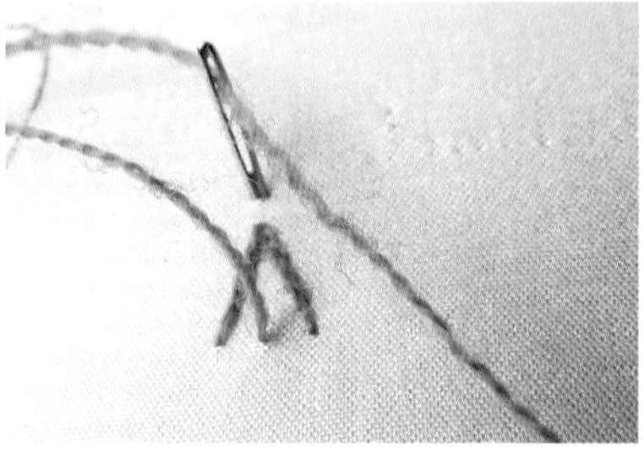

2. Always stitch the centre of the point first, come up in the fabric and then take your needle down a little way beyond the split stitch; a few millimetres is sufficient.

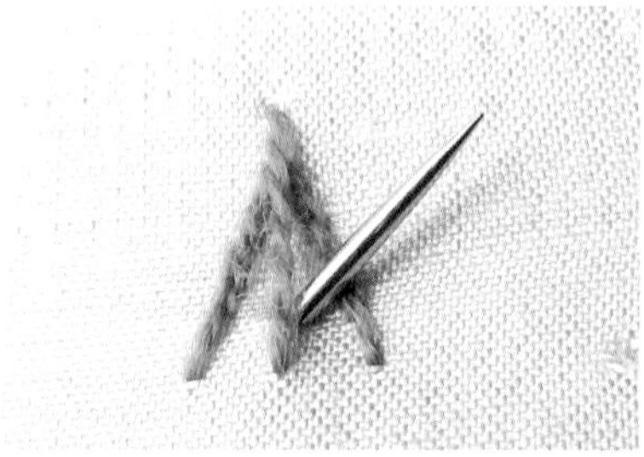

3. Now bring your needle up on the right at an angle from almost underneath the first stitch as shown.

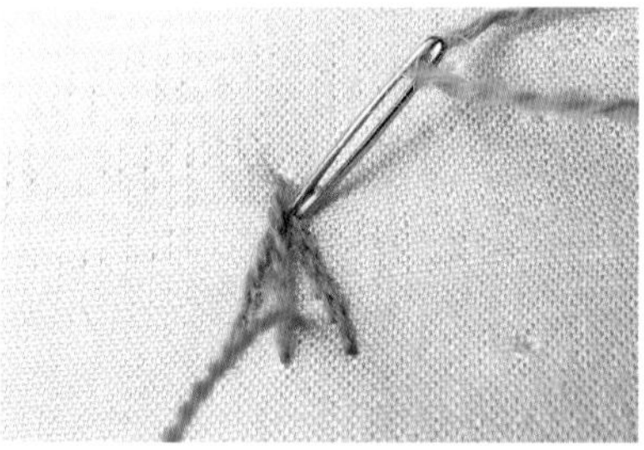

4. Now take the needle down against the split stitch on the right-hand side of the first stitch at the point of the split stitch. Notice it is not pushing the first stitch out of the way.

5. Now repeat this on the left-hand side.

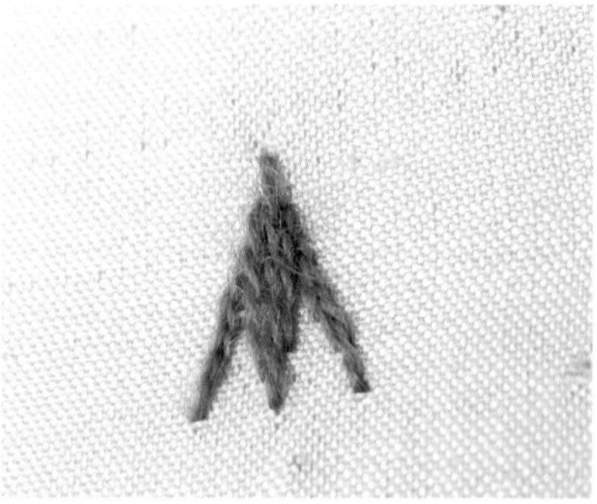

6. The completed point. The shape is now ready to be long and short stitched in the usual way.

Stab Stitch

If you have used two layers of fabric on your frame it is vital that you secure them together throughout the design *before* you start your embroidery. This helps stop movement between the two fabrics as you embroider, which can cause wrinkling on the fabric. This will spoil the effect of the finished embroidery, which is a shame when it can be avoided by a small, easy step in preparation.

If you are working a very small design and/or working in a small ring frame, this step is not necessary. If you are working on a slate frame with two layers then it is necessary; even if your frame is super tight there will still be movement between the fabrics.

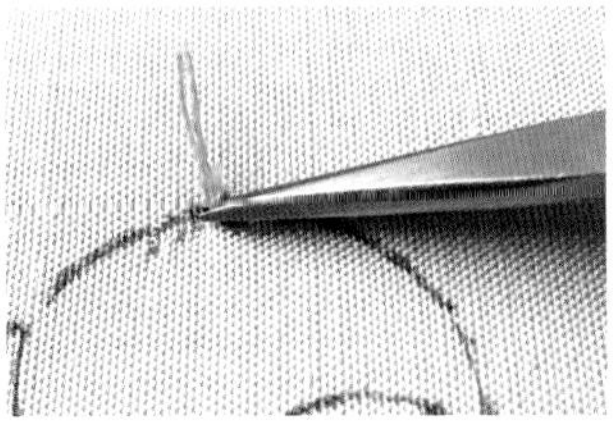

1. After you have your design on the fabric and tight in your frame then you can stab stitch. Using a polyester thread that matches the colour of your top fabric and a fine needle, start your thread off with a knot on the top and work three tiny 1–2mm stitches. Then cut your knot away.

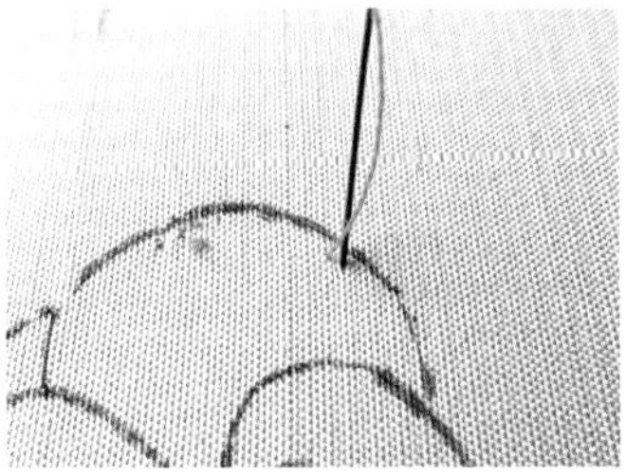

2. Bring your needle up about 1cm away from where you started and make a tiny 1–2mm stitch just inside the design line. Pull your stitches quite tightly and they should just disappear into the fabric.

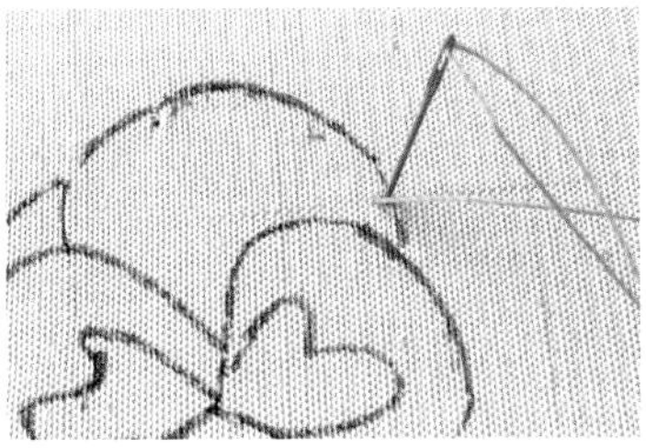

3. Bring your needle up again 1cm away and repeat.

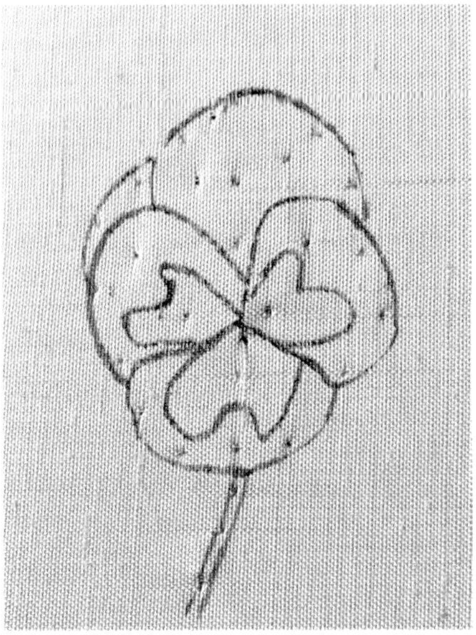

4. (left) Work the stab stitches throughout your design. It is less important to fill the middle of your embroidery with stab stitches. In the photo you can see the centre of the pansy does not have many stitches, but the outer edge and stem have. Wrinkles may appear on your work even if you do this step. That may be down to your fabric not being tight enough, or too tight a stitch tension.

Stitch Direction Plan

Stitch direction is vital for thread painting and natural long and short stitch. Tapestry shading stitches are all vertical, so you do not need a direction plan for this technique. Very often the original source picture can help you with your direction plan. For example, animals and birds will have a natural direction from how the fur or feathers lie, flowers will often have stripes or veins. Use this as a starting point for your stitch plan. Use a pencil to start drawing your stitch direction on to a copy of your design, so you can erase any lines that do not work. It is useful for the lines to be a similar size to the stitches you are going to embroider.

Think of the pencil marks as the rows of stitches. Do the rows flow smoothly into one another? Are some of the angle changes impossible to recreate in stitch? It is important to try and visualize how you will recreate these lines in your embroidery. The direction of your stitches is vital to a successful embroidery.

A simple stitch direction plan for a pansy.

Colour and Shading Plan

A colour and shading plan is another important stage in starting to work on your embroidery as discussed in Chapter Two. Make sure you have worked your own colour version as an exercise before starting your embroidery, so you are familiar with colour placement; this will also help with choosing the correct thread colours. The same goes for a shaded tonal version of your design so you know where the light and dark tones are. This will help you separate different areas of the design.

A colour version of a pansy for stitching.

A tonal version of a pansy for stitching.

Order Of Work

An order of work plan is also vital before you start stitching. Long and short stitch is always worked from the areas in the background first to areas in the foreground last. Therefore, the areas are giving the impression that they are overlapping one another. Number the area in your stitch guide, with where you are starting from as '1' and then work out the order from there. You may like to mark on this plan where your split stitch needs to go if needed and which area it belongs to. A dotted line is useful for this; mark out the split stitch line just before you embroider it, so the dots do not get too confusing.

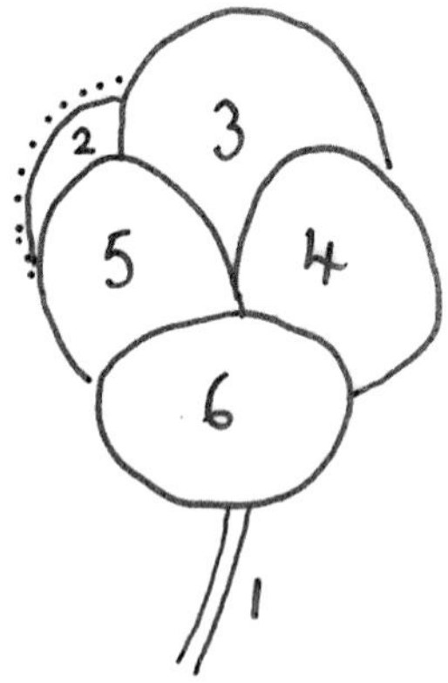

Order of work for a pansy with the first row of split stitch marked in a dotted line.

Shading and Blending Colours

Blending your colours successfully is key to creating a natural-looking embroidery. We do not just finish with one colour and start the next one. There is a certain amount of blending that must happen so that the colours mix together invisibly. That is why it is helpful that your colours are not too contrasting. We also usually have quite a few needles on the go at once all with differing colours in them, so you can pick up and put down the colours as you need them.

This pansy design demonstrates how to blend colours simply and how the overlapping of each separate area works. It starts on the outside of the petal and works towards the growing point; this is usually the case on natural shading. The colours have been chosen to be contrasting, so the process is clear to see. This is not a step-by-step project, so the template is not included in the book; it is an example of how an embroidery is worked.

1. The stem was stitched first then petal 1 was outlined in split stitch just on the outside edge, then filled in with dark satin stitch as it is too small for long and short stitch. Notice how the angle slightly turns at the bottom.

   Petal number 2 is outlined in a medium purple as that is the colour that will be mostly used on the first row. It is only the outer edge that is split stitched, the lower edges belong to other petals so they will be split stitched later. This is important; only split stitch the area you are immediately going to work. You can see that as the split stitch comes alongside the first petal it overlaps a stitch at the top slightly. This is because there is a stitch sticking out from the first petal. This is to make a smooth split stitch edge.

   The new split stitch edge will sit very close alongside the first petal. There should be no space between the first petal and the new split stitch. If the new split stitch overlaps some of the long and short stitch from previously worked areas to create a good edge, this is fine. However, it is better that it just rests up against it, so you do not get big bumps on your split stitch. That is why it is always good practice to finish areas neatly on the design line, so you do not have to compensate with split stitching over it to make a neat edge later.

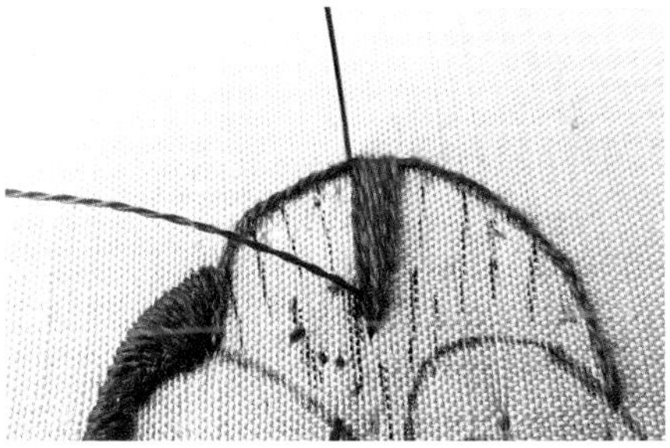

2. Petal 2 has been started off in the centre with a medium colour purple and the angle is starting to change; a new darker colour is introduced by just working one stitch of it and then parking the needle nearby. Do not leave any threads dangling on the back of the work, they will just get tangled up. Any threads you are not holding in your hand need to be brought up to the top of the fabric, preferably near where they are needed next. When you need it again try and go back down the same hole by pulling it a little and putting the needle in the hole formed – however, that does not happen every time and you will just get a tiny stab stitch forming. This is correct as you will see throughout the book, lots of little dots on unworked areas.

   After the one dark stitch the medium colour gets used again, as shown in the photograph.

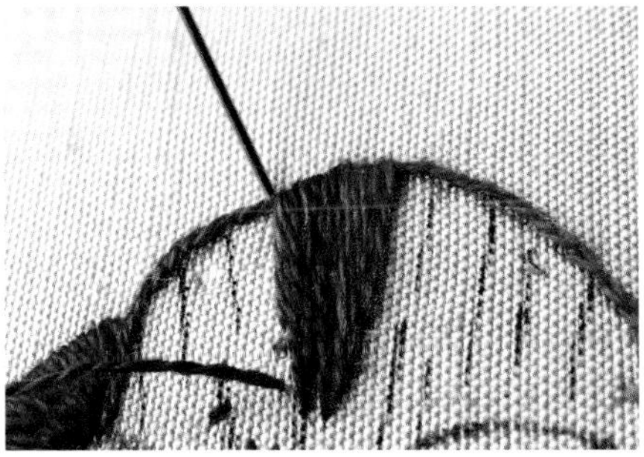

3. (left) The stitches now alternate between the medium and dark colours, sometimes one stitch of the medium colour then one stitch of the dark, or perhaps two stitches of medium colour and one or three of the dark. There is no set rule. If the colours are very contrasting, then you need more blending. You need to decide how much blending is needed to make a smooth transition between colours. If the colours are very striped, you may need more colours in your embroidery to create a smoother effect.

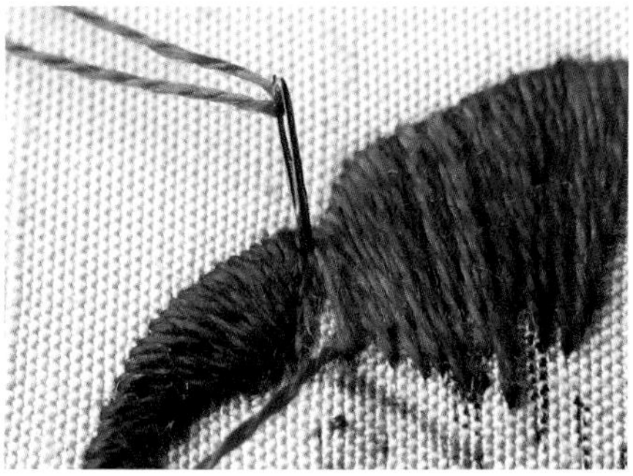

4. Where one petal overlaps another, there should be no spaces between them, the angle of the needle is still against the split stitch just as before. Try and ignore the previous long and short area and try and create a neat edge on the part you are working. This will take a little practice. It can be difficult as you have previous embroidery that you may feel gets in the way, but if you finish each area neatly on the design line then this should help.

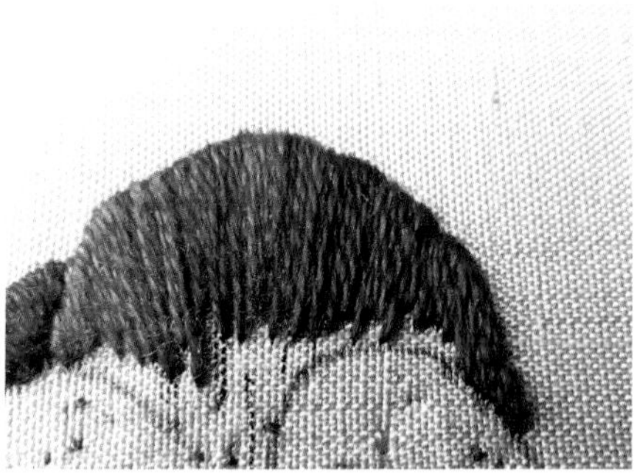

5. The first row is complete. The far left and right of the petal is just worked in satin stitch, as there is no room for long and short stitch. The colours are blended with the right side of the petal much darker than the left.

6. The second row has been stitched with the two original colours and a lighter colour, alternating between them all. The third row has just been stitched in a light lilac colour.

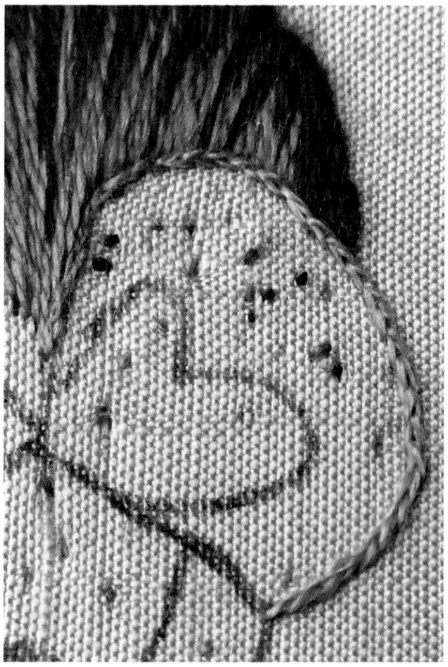

7. Petal 3 is now split stitched, again very close to petal 2, occasionally overlapping the ends of some of the stitches to create a smooth line for working over. Notice the lines that have not been split stitched; this is because they belong to other petals, the petals that are overlapping petal 3.

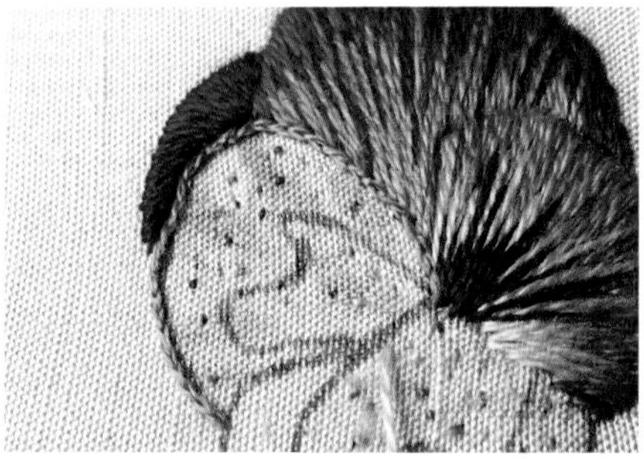

8. Petal 3 embroidery completed and the split stitch for petal 4 completed. Notice the smooth shape of the split stitch and no spaces between the petals.

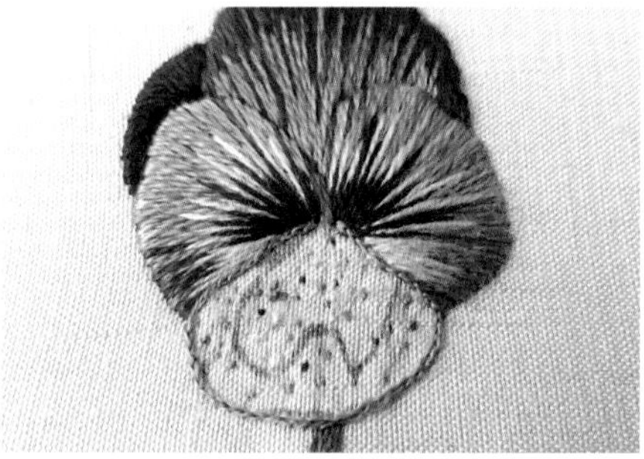

9. Petal 4 completed, notice how there is a slightly darker area on the bottom left of petal 4. Flowers are not symmetrical so not every petal is the same. Petal 5 overlaps everything so it has split stitch all the way around it.

10. (left) Completed pansy.

Threads

The threads you choose are personal to you for each project. However, there are a few pointers to help give a good result.

Make sure you have enough threads to complete a project. This may seem an obvious point but sometimes you can use up a lot more threads than you imagine you will, especially if you are using more than one strand in the needle. This is especially important if you are using antique or hand-dyed threads, as you may not be able to get any more once they have run out.

Threads may have different dye lots. This means that you may have two threads that have the same reference number but can look very dissimilar colours. Check before you start.

Condition and Storage Of Threads

Check that your threads are in good condition. Skeins that may have been in your stash for a while can be hairy or knotted. Antique threads may be prone to breakage and knotting also. If your threads are in bad condition it will show in your embroidery, especially in long and short stitch where you are trying to get a smooth result.

Try to keep your threads in good condition, once you purchase them. If you can, keep threads you are not immediately using out of the light. They may say that they are fade proof but that is not always the case.

If you are using stranded cottons, try not to keep them in one big bundle, for example in a bag. They will tangle and the threads themselves fluff up where they rub up against each other. You want as much as possible to keep them smooth. Many people wind them onto card bobbins. This is personal choice; if you do, make sure you do not wind them too tightly so that you get a kink in them. Make sure you write the number of the colour on the card for future reference. Wrapping them around wooden pegs may look pretty but the varnish can stain them.

If you use wool threads do check them occasionally for moths. Moths eat threads as well as clothes and carpets. Store a moth repellent in your wool storage area. Preferably an unscented one so your embroidery does not become scented!

Silk threads are very prone to tangles. Never leave a long thread hanging off a silk bobbin. Always wind back what you don't use.

If you have a large amount of threads it can be useful to store them in colour order to make it easier for choosing colours for a project. It makes it much easier if you can see all the options for one colour range immediately.

Keeping Things Clean

Wash your hands before you start and after that sneaky bit of chocolate, cover your work when you have finished or if an area is not being worked on. If you wear make-up don't touch your face; if you wear hand cream only put it on the back of your hands before you start stitching.

All this may sound a bit like school rules, but it is so much better if your embroidery does not have to be washed at the end of stitching. The beautiful, natural sheen of many threads and that of some fabrics is lost by washing. Silk embroidery especially does not like to be washed so if you can, keep it clean!

Embroidering With Two Hands

Stitching with two hands at once is a skill every embroiderer should master, not just professionals. It is worth it; your stitching will be at a much more even tension plus you will stitch must faster as your hand will not have to continually keep moving to the top of the frame.

However, it will feel awful the first time you try it. *Do not give up.*

This will only work if your frame is clamped or held by something. You cannot hold your frame in your hand and stitch two-handed, obviously.

The general rule is that your dominant hand is *under* the frame and your less dominant is *above* the frame (so you can see what it's doing!). In some specific embroidery disciplines the opposite of this is true.

When you start stitching in this way your dominant hand will keep trying to come to the top of your frame to stitch automatically. You will also start with good intentions and then forget and realize you are back to stitching with one hand. This is all completely normal. Leave a note on the side of your frame to remind you, until you are stitching two-handed automatically. It is amazing how quickly you will get used to this, especially as it seems so strange to start with.

Sometimes you do need to bring your dominant hand to the top of the frame if you have a tricky angle or you are working a French knot for example, but otherwise get into a smooth rhythm by stitching two-handed.

CHAPTER 6

TAPESTRY SHADING

Tapestry shading is long and short stitch in which all the stitches are vertical. This results in a similar appearance to a woven tapestry, hence the name.

There is no angle change; everything is straight down. Some consider this to be an easier technique to learn than natural directional long and short stitch. However, although you do not have to think about angle turns and direction, the skill in tapestry shading is the ability to keep your stitches truly vertical. Sometimes a fabric with an obvious grain can help with this. A linen for example, where you can see the weave, can be followed to help with placement of stitches. For this to be successful, you need to make sure your linen is evenly woven and that your fabric is straight in the frame.

Tapestry shading was used extensively in Victorian England in the stitching of figures. Saints that were stitched for church hangings have fantastic robes embroidered in jewel-like silks. The embroiderer's skill created pleats and curved folds to the drapery, even though all the stitches were vertical – again the placement of stitch and colour in tapestry long and short is vitally important.

OPPOSITE: One of the twelfth-century Lewis chessmen. Originally carved in walrus ivory and whales' teeth, this king piece has been embroidered in seven colours of stranded cotton. It is worked in tapestry shading with additional French knots and couching for details.

Tapestry shading is very useful for stitching buildings and landscapes. Shadows, and details such as windows and architectural motifs, are much easier to work in some cases if all the stitches are vertical.

As with all long and short stitch, the background areas are stitched first coming forward to the foreground area last. You *do not* split stitch the vertical design lines in tapestry shading as the stitches would get in the way and force you to have a slight angle change as you go over them, or force you to stitch on top of them giving you a ridge. See the London skyline project as a clear example of which lines to split stitch.

Many of the techniques described in this chapter can also be used for natural directional shading, for example shading in the needle, outlining, voiding and so on. Do use these across your embroidery projects, not just tapestry shading.

This detail of drapery shows the amazing effects that can be created with just vertical stitches. The stitches are worked to give the impression of curved fabric folds and the narrow band looks very three-dimensional, even though all the shading is relatively simple and a minimum number of colours have been used. The fringe in contrast is stitched in rows of split stitch that are not vertical and follow the movement of the garment. (Royal School of Needlework, RSN1968)

This embroidery design was inspired by the seventeenth-century topiary garden at Levens Hall in Cumbria, a yew tree crowned with a little bird and a base of allium flowers.

Topiary Tree

This design is an introduction in how to gradually shade your colours so the transition between shades is smooth. The tree has a rounded effect, as there are no big jumps between colours. It shows that a successful shaded effect can be achieved with only four colours, which are well blended in the embroidery. The light is gently catching the left of the tree with the darker colours on the right and the bottom sections of the tree. For the sample the colours have a slight jump between them so that they are clear for the photograph – you may want to have a subtler change.

Most of the rows are photographed individually so you can follow every row and see how the stitch placement works with what colours and what proportion the stitches take up of each area. Read through *all* the instructions before you start so you get a feel of what you are trying to achieve.

The sample was stitched on a printed cotton with one strand of fine crewel wool.

Materials:

- Fabric with the design transferred, a backing if required, stab stitched if necessary.
- Frame and scissors.
- A range of fine crewel wools that blend together smoothly with no big jumps in colour; very dark green, dark green, medium green, light green, one pink any shade, one brown any shade.
- Chenille needle appropriate to your wool; size 24–26.
- Embroidery needle; size 5–10.

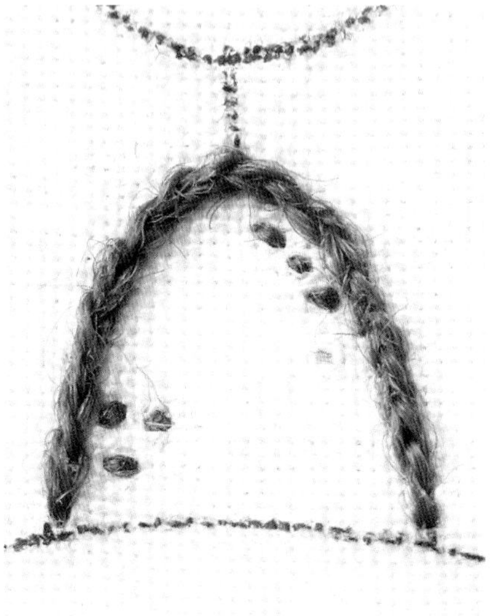

1. Split stitch the first shape with one strand of your medium shade of wool. Make sure the stitches are small and tight as the split stitch goes around the curve. This shape is first as it is underneath all other areas.

2. Starting in the centre of the shape, work long and short stitch in your dark green shade of wool. Keep the stitches nice and long, and angle your needle over the split stitch to give a neat edge. As you work towards the outside of the shape bring in another colour, medium green on the left and very dark green on the right. Alternate your colours as you bring in a new colour. Do not just finish one shade and start another, this is easier to see in the next photograph. *Do not* shorten your stitches as you start getting nearer the outside edge. This shape only has two rows of colour so make sure you leave room for a second row.

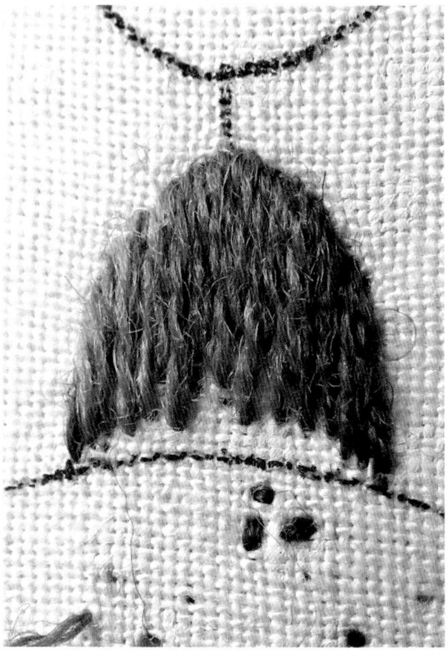

3. Completed first row; the colours are blended together by working alternate stitches of each colour where they meet and not jumping from one colour to another. This is important so as not to get blocks of colour and gives a more natural effect.

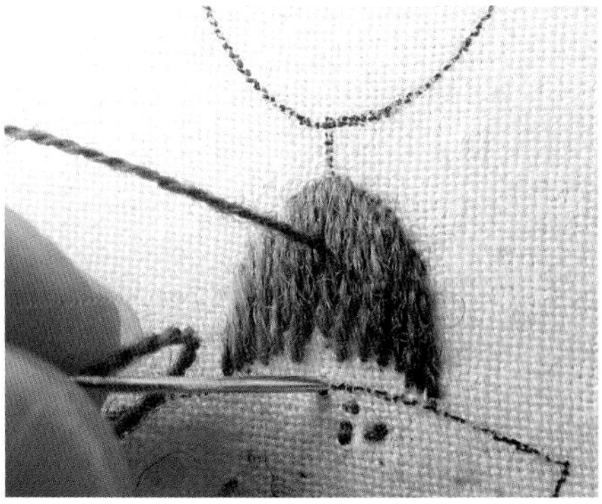

4. Starting again in the middle of the shape, bring your needle up in your first row with your very dark green splitting a stitch. Take the needle down on the line. Do not go beyond or before the line, as you will make a messy bottom edge. Fill in this row with long and short stitch just in the dark green wool colour, varying where you bring the needle up.

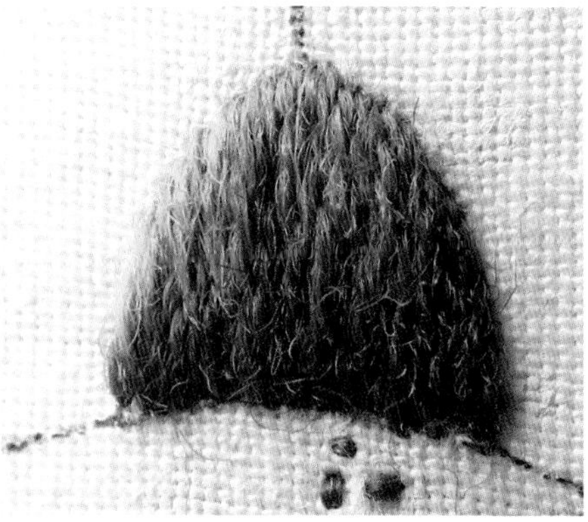

5. Completed second row; the dark green stitches in the second row vary where they come up in the first row. You do not want a straight line where all the stitches come up in a similar place. They all end neatly on the drawn line.

6. Split stitch the second shape in your medium green colour. You want the split stitch to sit alongside the end of the previous shape's stitches. *There should be no space* between the split stitch you are doing now and the row of long and short you have just completed. If some of your split stitches overlap the previous stitches a little for you to make a neater edge, that is better than leaving a space.

7. Starting again in the middle of the shape, work your long and short stitch in the medium colour. Angle your needle over the split stitch trying not to go through your previous stitches unless absolutely necessary. You do not want to pull against the split stitch and distort it. Try and make this top edge as neat as possible.

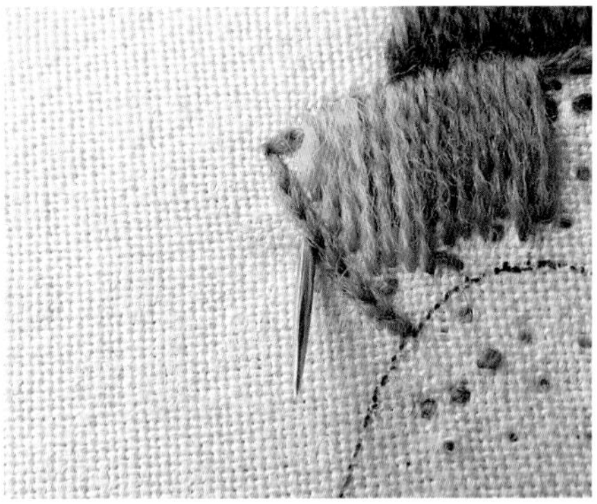

8. As you stitch towards the left-hand side, bring in the light green colour; stitch these colours alternatively to blend them smoothly. When you get to the end you will have to make your stitches a little smaller to fit in. The very last few stitches will be satin stitches. This is because there is no room for long and short stitches. Bring your needle up from under the curved split stitch edge of the shape, angling the needle towards you.

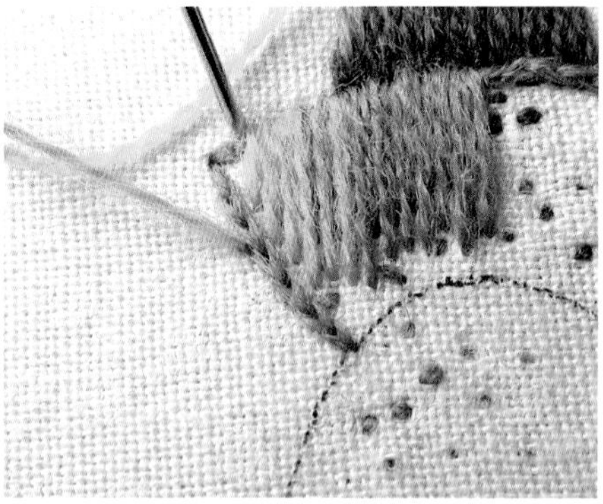

9. Take the needle down over the top of the split stitch to make a satin stitch.

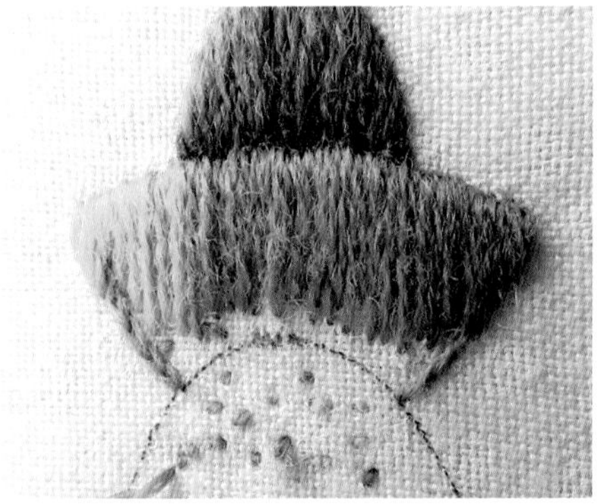

10. Finish this row with smaller and smaller satin stitches. Repeat this process on the right side working from medium green to dark green. Notice the stitches are all long and longer!

11. Work the second row of this shape in dark and very dark green, blending the colours as before. Using the brown wool, satin stitch the trunk and little bird twig in a vertical direction. No split stitch is needed for the trunk as your stitches are vertical. Split stitch the curved part of the main tree and the bird in medium green wool and the base of the tree in very dark green.

12. Embroider the first row of the main tree in light and medium green, blending the colours where necessary. As you have more space here the stitches can be longer and the area where the two colours mix can be larger. Again, do not be tempted to sew shorter stitches as you get to the edge of the shape. If your stitches seem to be loose then they are too long; make then smaller until you have a smooth effect.

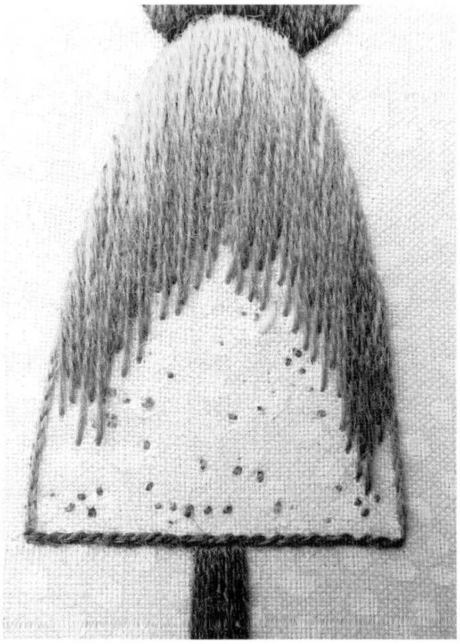

13. The second row of long and short stitch is worked in medium and dark green. Notice that you add more stitches to the outside edge as you work down the tree. You do not have to stitch all the outside edge at once.

14. The third and fourth rows of long and short are worked in dark and very dark green. If you find you have more space to fill and therefore more rows than the sample, do not worry, just fill them in with the appropriate colour.

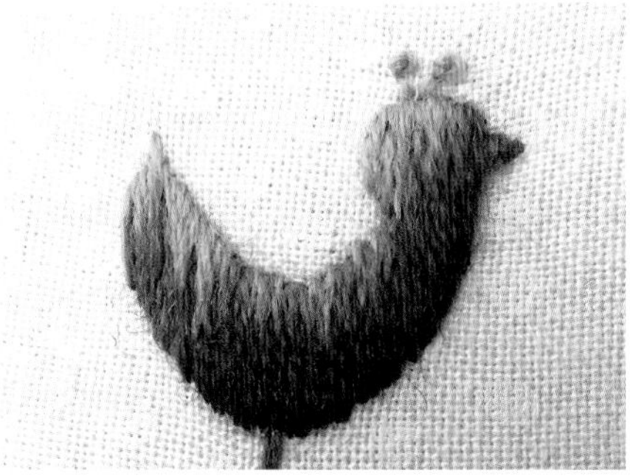

15. Stitch the bird in the same way as the tree but your stitches will need to be shorter and there are a few areas of satin stitch. Add a couple of straight stitches and French knots above the head for a little crest.

Embroider French knot circles in pink at the top of each stem and embroider stem stitch in one of your greens for the stems and ground.

Shading In the Needle

Having more than one colour in the needle can be an interesting way of shading colours for embroidery. You need to be aware of the tension of your stitches as they can work against each other with one thread loose and one thread tight, but when stitched correctly it is a useful technique to master. It can be an easier way to learn about shading as in some cases you will have two colours in your needle, therefore the threads shade for you.

It is important that the threads in the needle are of the same type when you are learning this technique. You can run into problems if for example you have one cotton and one wool. As you get more experienced, having two different types of threads can add an extra texture to your stitching.

When you thread up your needle with more than one strand of thread, gently stroke all the strands together, so they are all the same tension before you start stitching. As you embroider you may have to repeat this, especially if one strand gets wrapped around another and causes a twisted effect. You want the strands to lie side by side on the fabric. Use two separate strands in the needle, do not cut one and double it over in the needle.

Differing heights of embroidery can be achieved in one design if areas are embroidered in differing amounts of thread. If you are embroidering a piece like this, it is important to plan and sample first, so you know exactly how many strands you are using in all areas.

If you have many threads in the needle, then a chenille needle will help the threads go through the fabric and your embroidery stitches lie smoothly as it has a larger eye and therefore makes a hole, so less friction is placed on the threads.

Adding Additional Stitches to the Surface Of Your Long and Short Stitch

Using other stitches on top of your long and short stitch is a great way to add texture to your embroidery that you may not be able to achieve otherwise. You need to make sure that the additional stitches are not distracting and are also the correct dimension for your design.

Remember when adding stitching on top of your long and short, you do not want to disturb the embroidery that you have already completed. So, go carefully through your work. Try and hold the needle in a vertical position as it goes through your embroidery and fabric to prevent catching on your work. If you are not confident in French knots for example, then sample them first until you are well practised. Therefore, you do not have to take them out and potentially damage your embroidery. If you are unsure then it is probably better to leave them off.

If you have a pattern to follow when adding additional stitching on top of your embroidery, then you may want to transfer the lines with the tissue paper method on top of the embroidery you have already worked, as any design lines will be covered up. This way you have an exact line to follow when stitching. You then remove the tacking lines as you go.

This wild rose embroidery has tiny French knots for the centre of the flower. If they were padded any more than this then they may look out of proportion, as the petals are simply shaded and quite flat. French knots are also very useful for the ends of stamens as seen here. Remember that additional stitches can be shaded too, just as in your long and short stitch.

This face has additional stitching in the beard area and for the crown. It was important to use additional stitched lines on this face as the beard would not have this effect if just long and short stitch was used.

Fly agaric (or *amanita muscaria* to give it its scientific name) is one of the most eye-catching fungi, with its beautiful red or orange cap and its scattering of white spots, a perfect opportunity to use French knots to create texture.

Fly Agaric Fungi

Although it is highly poisonous, fly agaric was often found on Victorian and Edwardian Christmas cards as a good luck symbol. It also often appears in fairy tales and the mushroom Alice ate in Wonderland may well have been one of these.

The sample was stitched in one strand of very fine wool in the stalk and frill and two strands of very fine wool in the toadstool cap. This means that the embroidery on the toadstool cap looks slightly padded compared to the rest. The foliage is stitched in one strand of wool; the backing is a silk dupion. This sample could be stitched very easily in one and two strands of stranded cotton.

Materials:

- Fabric with the design transferred, backing if required, stab stitched if necessary.
- Frame and scissors.
- A range of very fine crewel wools that blend together smoothly, for the cap; dark coral, coral, dark gold, yellow. For the additional parts; white, light grey, grey, dark grey, light green, medium green, dark green.
- Chenille needles appropriate to your wool size 24–26.
- Embroidery needle for the French knots size 7–10.

1. Split stitch the stalk with one strand of any grey. Just stitch the two vertical sides of the stalk, which have a slight curve to them. Split stitch the top of the cap with the gold or a coral colour in *one* strand of wool. Even though the cap is embroidered in two strands of thread, the split stitch is still only worked in one strand. The bottom of the cap and frills are split-stitched later.

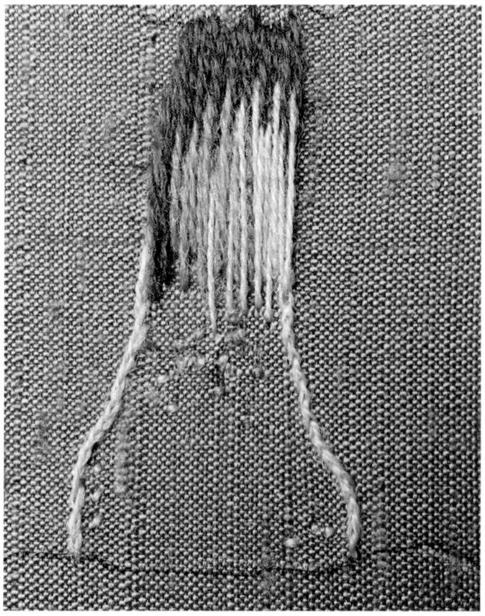

2. Embroider the stalk in one strand of wool starting at the top and working down. Create a dark shadow at the top by just using the darkest grey under the frill. Then introduce the other two greys and white before ending up with mostly the darkest grey on the last row at the bottom. Make your stitches smooth and long. Shade between the colours as necessary as shown by stitching with them alternately. Notice the white and light grey colour are alternately stitched in the centre of the stalk but the dark grey is not mixed with another colour. This will create a strong shadow. Make sure you are coming up in the stalk and down over the split stitch edge; notice on the right edge a stitch has gone down into the split stitch edge – this is fine if it is straight and fits in with the other stitches. Follow the main photograph for colour placement.

3. Split stitch only the left-hand part of the frill as shown with white as this part is underneath. Make your stitches very small as they create the frilly edge.

4. Stitch this part of the frill as shown, making a shadow at the top and right side with the darker greys before bringing in the light grey and white. Again, blend the white and lighter grey. Split stitch the right-hand part of the frill as shown, again with very small stitches. The split stitch edge goes alongside the long and short stitches at the top of the stalk.

5. Stitch this frill as shown making sure you use the darker greys for a shadow underneath the cap and using the white on the left-hand edge, so it stands out against the other frill. Try and carefully go over the split stitch edge so you create a good frill to the bottom as it goes over the stalk.

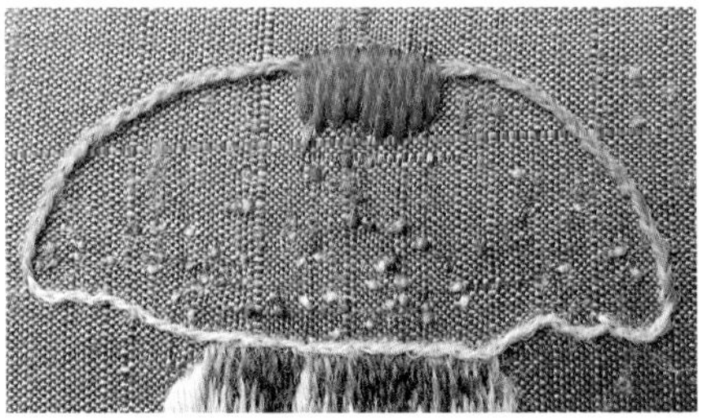

6. Split stitch the bottom part of the toadstool cap in one of your lighter shades.

   Now start using two strands of wool in your needle. Cut two separate strands – *do not* cut one strand and double over in the needle – make sure they are pulled through the needle evenly.

   You are going to use two strands of the darkest coral in the needle and embroider one row of long and short stitch in the very top centre of the toadstool cap as shown. The stitches are only in the middle; do not work more than shown in the photograph. As you stitch make sure that the threads lie side by side, they may tend to twist around each other spoiling the effect of the long and short. Make sure that the threads are of an even tension so that one is not looser than the other when you stitch. If you think the stitch is not lying flat, try pulling your stitches a little tighter to see if that helps.

   Notice the length of the stitches in comparison with the size of the cap. There are many rows of colour in this cap, so make sure you leave enough room for them.

7. Now thread up with one strand of the dark coral and one strand of the coral in the needle. You are going to surround the first row of stitching with this combination of colours. Start in the centre of the cap, coming up through the first row as usual and work towards one side. When you have no more of the dark coral stitches to come up into, take a few stitches over the top edge of the cap covering some more of the split stitch, so you have almost a curved row of stitches. Go back to the centre and work to the other side of the cap as before. The photo shows the second row completed and there is only a small amount of the first row showing; a little circle of dark coral at the very top in the centre.

8. Next, work a row of just the coral colour in the needle and surround the previous row as before. Then move onto one coral and one dark gold in the needle. The picture shows one coral and one gold in the needle making a curved shape to the row by working a few stitches over the top edge. Each time you start a new row, you will be working further out to the side of the cap. Each row you stitch surrounds the previous row.

9. Continue across and down the mushroom cap working through the colours, one row in a single colour and the next row in a mix of colours. When you have worked through all your colours you may have some spaces left, as shown in the photograph. The cap is not symmetrical, and you may have varied the length of the stitches, so fill in any spaces with the yellow or a combination of yellow and white.

10. Using the greens, embroider some straight stitches from the stems and add a few French knots to the ends. Stem stitch up the main stems to finish the sprigs.

    Add clusters of French knots to the base of the toadstool with your greens to create a mossy effect.

    Then add clusters of French knots to the toadstool stalk and cap. Be careful that you are not disturbing your embroidery, bring your needle vertically up and down to prevent damage to your work; if your needle is angled you may catch on your stitches. You can add French knots in a single colour or you can have two strands in your needle such as a grey and a white and add shaded knots. These will also be a little bigger. Remember only once around the needle. Use the main photograph for placement.

Intricate Patterns

Sometimes you may have a very definite pattern or markings to follow that need to be very clearly defined. Working long and short stitch in the normal way would cover up all your design lines as you usually vary the placement of stitches. How do you know where to bring up the needle to give you the exact pattern you have marked on to the fabric if your stitches are covering the lines? Long and short stitch in this case needs to be altered slightly to accommodate the need of an exacting design.

Your working design for this type of embroidery must have all the design lines marked clearly and transferred to the fabric. For example, if you were doing a portrait you need all the information on your fabric for a successful embroidery, rather than just guessing where specific areas are.

This swallowtail butterfly (stitched in natural shading but it is the same principle) has exact markings that are then repeated on the other wing. It was important to make sure all the markings were in the right place and the correct size for it to be an accurate representation. Notice the direction of the stitches follows the direction of the shapes to make the stitching easier to achieve and create a natural flow. The butterfly is embroidered in one strand of stranded cotton and the background is sateen cotton fabric, painted with acrylic paint.

This design is based on a seventeenth-century marbled paper. It is called 'nonpareil' and very often seen on end papers in antique books.

Marbled Paper

Normal long and short stitch would cover the design lines and make it impossible to create such a crisp pattern. You could argue that this could be successfully stitched in satin stitch blocks, but then the areas would not interlock and create this lovely flowing effect.

The sample was stitched in one strand of stranded cotton on a fine white linen. The template for this is only a few rows of the pattern, so either repeat the pattern in your tracing or add your own rows to the design.

Materials:

- Fabric with the design transferred, backing if required. Stab stitch is not necessary as the embroidery is in one solid block.
- Frame and scissors.
- A range of stranded cottons in contrasting colours. To create the marbled design successfully, the colours need to be repeated in at least two rows. Make the colours all very different for the best effect.
- Needles size 10–12.

1. Starting at the top of the design, split stitch around the very top edge shapes with your first colour using one strand.

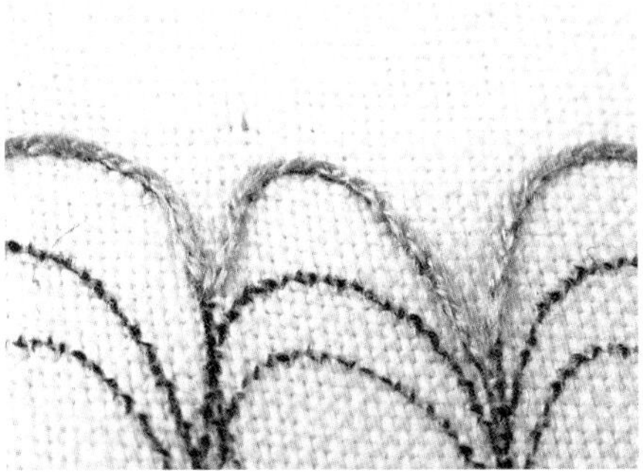

2. Notice how the split stitch does not go too far down the vertical line between the shapes, it is purely the top edge. Small, tight stitches are vital to get the smooth, curved shape.

3. You can begin stitching on any shape in the top row, but you may find it easier to start in the centre of each curved shape to try and keep a true vertical stitch. Bring your needle up just below the design line of the shape below. Notice it is about a needle's space below the line.

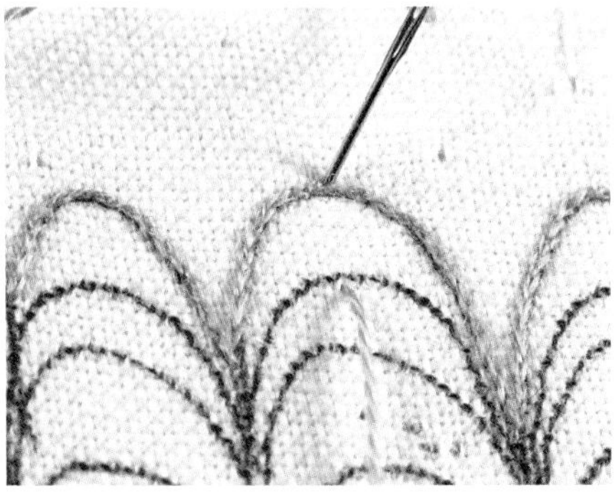

4. Now take your needle down over the split stitch edge, angling it against the stitches to create a smooth line.

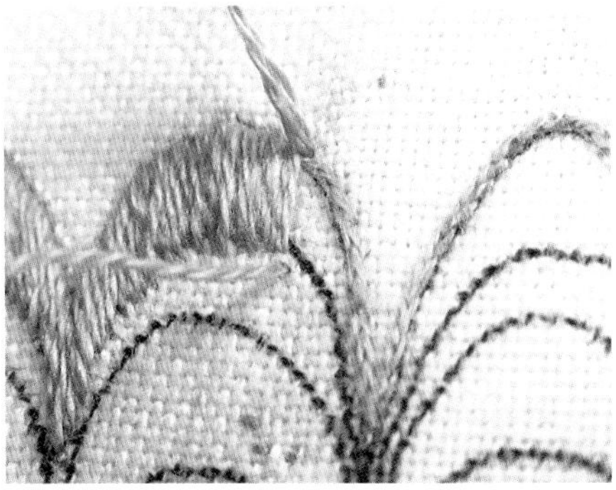

5. Work stitches along this top edge in one colour. Although this really is not a row of long and short stitches, notice that the stitches differ very slightly in length. Sometimes the needle comes up one width of a needle away; sometimes it comes up two widths of a needle away from the design line. The bottom edge that you can see in the picture is a little uneven. This is important to prevent a solid ridge forming.

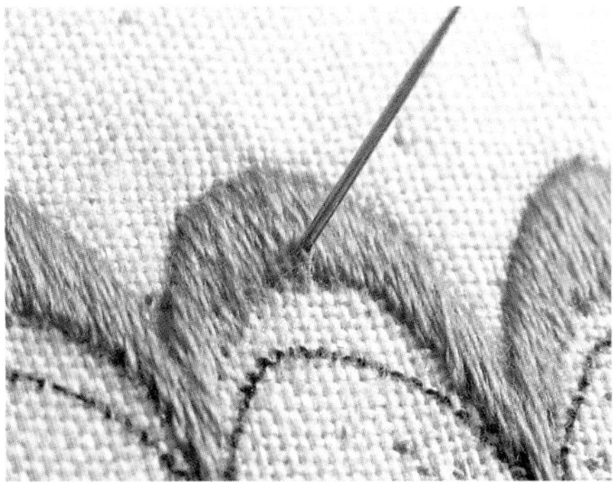

6. Now start your second row in a contrasting colour. Bring your needle up, starting in the middle of the shape and just a fraction into the last row. Almost biting into it. This way your needle comes up approximately on the design line you have drawn. It helps with this type of embroidery where the design placement is important to try and bring your needle up perfectly straight, as shown in the photograph.

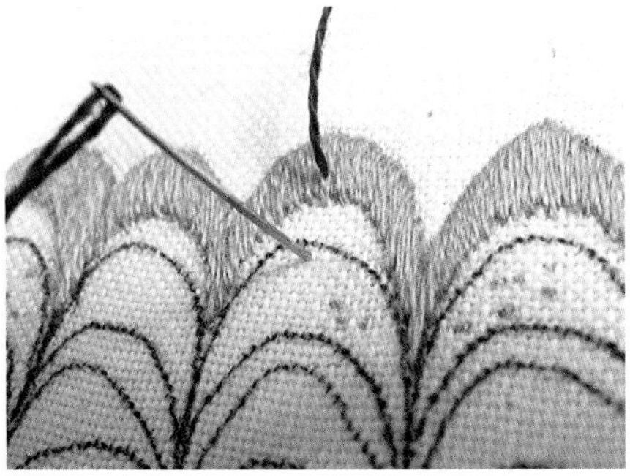

7. Take your needle down just below the design line on the next row just as before.

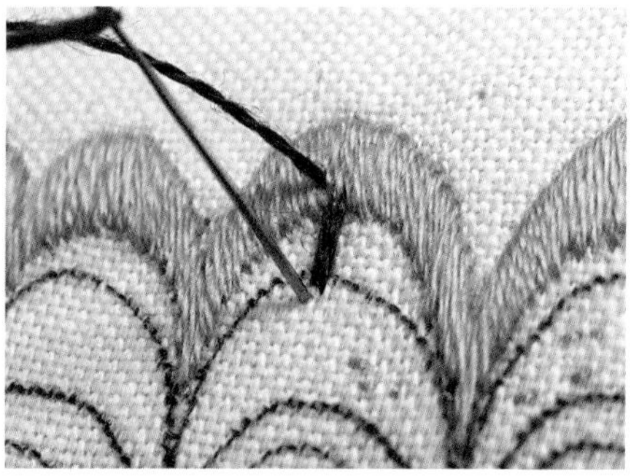

8. Continue to bring your needle up in the first row very close to where your previous stitch came up. Use your previous stitch placement as a guide to help you. You are not trying to create an uneven top line; you are trying to create a smooth line along the top edge of these stitches. The needle will still create a slightly uneven bottom edge, though.

9. Continue to fill in the rows, working your way across and finishing one colour before moving on to another. Notice the careful placement as the needle comes through the stitches so it just drops a little below the previous stitch to create a smooth, curved line.

   This embroidery looks very simple to do, but takes a little practice to create a smooth, accurate line on each row. It is however a good exercise in improving the accuracy of your stitch placement.

Outlining and Voiding

Outlining your embroidery can be a useful way of tidying up if you have a less than neat edge, although the trick is that you want as neater edge as possible so that way you have the choice to outline if you want it. It can also be a good way of bringing attention to certain shapes and making them more dominant.

If you want to outline your embroidery then try it out on your colour plan first – remember outlining does not have to be in a dominant colour, as this could just appear heavy and unsophisticated compared to your embroidery.

This elaborate crest has very dominant outlining on the grey mantling sections. The thread is a heavy twisted cord with stem stitch on the outside of it just for good measure and as well as going around the outline, it also goes on top of the embroidery to separate the differing sections. If the long and short embroidery was shaded more skilfully to show shadows and highlights successfully, then such a heavy outline would not be necessary.

The badge has a red tapestry shaded background with a natural shading lion. The crown and knight's head are in metal thread embroidery. The ermine is in white tapestry shading with little black patterns stitched over the top afterwards and the feathers are a mix of stem and satin stitch.

Voiding areas in your embroidery, to create shapes that are not stitched, creates interesting effects. You need to treat the voids just the same as an outside edge and make them as neat as possible – they are in fact holes in your design.

They can create very interesting effects in contemporary embroidery so are a useful technique to use.

An ornate crest illustrating the use of outlining to define specific areas. (Royal School of Needlework, RSN 1219)

Hints and tips

If your edges are not perfect and you want to cover them, you could always stitch an outline in the colour of your background fabric so that it 'disappears'.

London skyline

The sample was stitched with one strand of stranded cotton on a silver lurex and white silk fabric, with one strand of number 50 black machine thread for outlining. Some of the stitches in this project are not true tapestry shading as they are not vertical, but as there are mostly vertical stitches it is included in this chapter. This design would work equally well in just one range of colours instead of four as the buildings are mostly separated by outlines; add additional ones as needed.

As this is a simply shaded embroidery, follow the photograph for all the colour placement and outlining.

This graphic imagined view of four iconic London landmarks with an obligatory crane shows that a simple range of colours can be brought to life with some partial outlines in place. Even though there are outlines, they are very thin, so it is important to get neat edges even though some of them are covered with a line.

Materials:

- Fabric with the design transferred and a backing if required, stab stitched if necessary. Use a fabric colour that is very contrasting to the thread colours used as you want the voids in the embroidery to stand out.
- Frame and scissors.
- Stranded cottons, three shades for each building from the same colour range, light, medium and dark of each colour.
- Black or navy machine cotton or polyester or a very fine embroidery thread.
- Embroidery needles size 10–12.

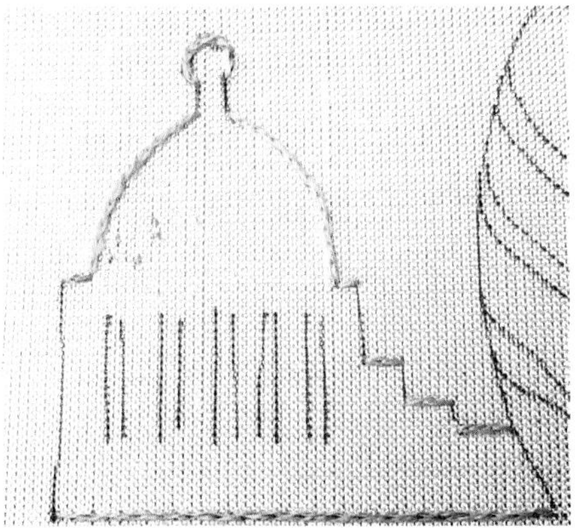

1 Even though parts of the embroidery are going to be outlined, it is a good idea to split stitch the edges of the embroidery to make them neat. It means you can work a very thin outline to contrast the embroidery rather than having a thick one to tidy up. Starting with St Paul's Cathedral on the very left, split stitch with one strand of stranded cotton on the horizontal and curved edges. The windows are very narrow so may not need split stitch at the top and bottom. Try and get a good circular shape on the tiny circle at the top of the dome.

2. Using the darkest shade of the colour you have chosen for St Paul's, stitch all along the top edge. You will need more than one row of the dark colour in the dome area as shown in the photograph. Make the stitches shorter on the right-hand side so you have enough room for three rows of stitching and therefore three colours.

3. Next, stitch with the medium colour. Leave little voids for the windows where they are marked on the fabric. Try and create a smooth and even edge. You may want to stitch the window edge first where there is a vertical line on the fabric and then fill in between. This way you do not lose the pen line on your fabric. The very last row at the bottom is the light colour. Bring your needle down neatly over the bottom edge.

4. Next is the Millennium Wheel. Split stitch alternate boxes on the wheel. You may find you only need split stitch on the longer side of the box, as it will be curving. As the boxes are small you may only get two of your colours in. Or you may want to have one row dark and one row with a mix of medium and light. The stitches change direction as they move round the wheel shape.

5. Work long and short stitch on the struts of the wheel. No split stitch is needed. Start with the darkest shade at the top, going down to the light at the bottom. These stitches are diagonal in direction. Split stitch the little circle on the top and satin stitch it with the lightest colour. Work the crane in the same colour as the wheel; all stitches are vertical.

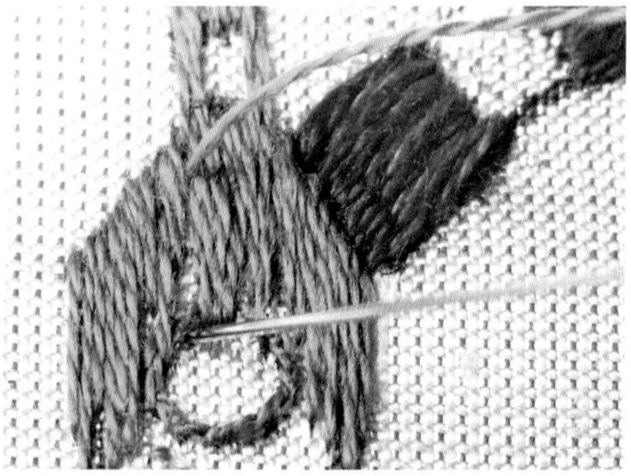

6. Split stitch Big Ben and the Houses of Parliament in the same way as St Paul's, with extra split stitch going around the clock face and the horizontal parts of the windows as they are larger. Start at the top of Big Ben in the darkest colour and work down. Take extra care around the clock face to create a perfectly circular voided shape as shown in the photograph. Really tuck the needle under the split stitch.

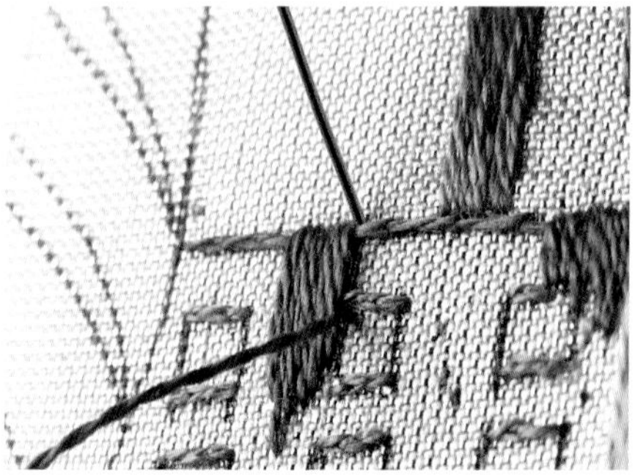

7. The part above the windows can be worked in satin stitch. Come up from under the split stitch in the window shape as shown and take your needle down over the split stitch edge on the top. This will then create a beautiful, even line all the way along the top edge. The spaces in between the windows can be normal long and short. Finish with your medium and light colours, as for St Pauls.

8. Split stitch the Gherkin as shown, paying attention to the curved shapes; they should be very smooth. Notice not all the sides of the Gherkin have split stitch. This is so the voided areas can just have a black outline and also, we don't split stitch vertical lines in tapestry shading.

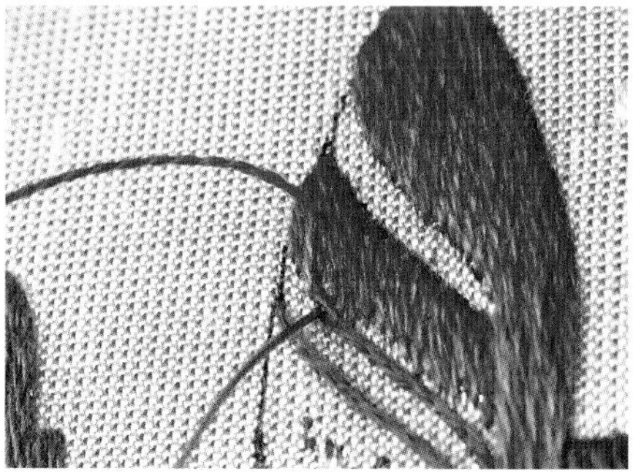

9. Stitch the Gherkin from the top starting with the darkest colour again. Pay attention to the voids, getting them as neat as possible on the edge. Really tuck the needle smoothly against the split stitch.

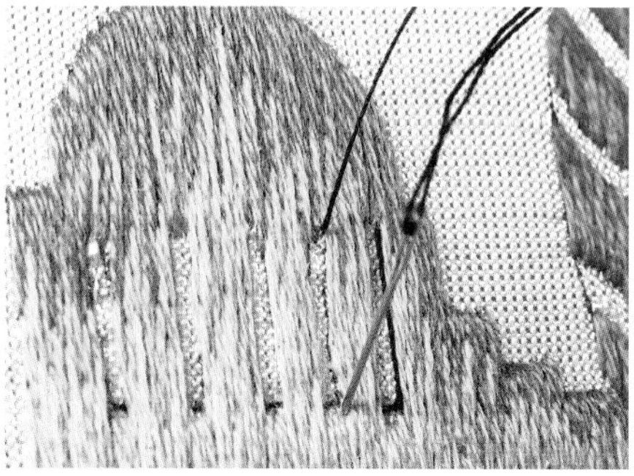

10. Using one strand of black thread, you can now accentuate some of your stitched areas. The windows in St Paul's just have black stitched on the right and bottom of them; this creates a shadow effect. The stitch is just one long stitch from the top to the bottom of the window. Pull these stitches firmly. They do *not* go over your previous stitching, they lie alongside.

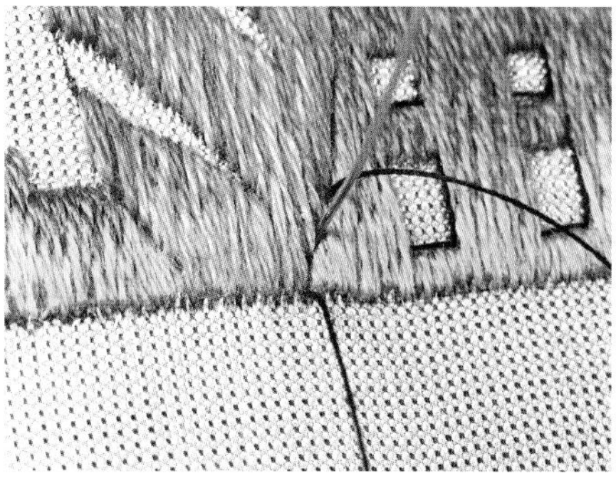

11. Some of the buildings have an outline to separate them; this is worked in stem stitch. The stem stitch will naturally fall between the two stitched areas. Again, they do not sit on your previous stitching.

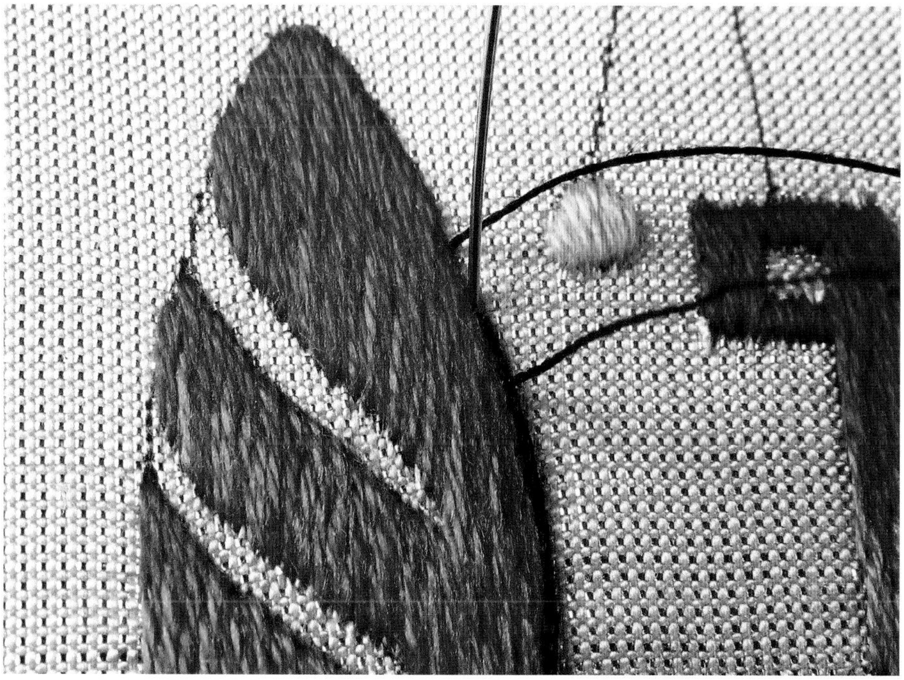

12. The picture shows the stem stitch 'hugging' the edge of the embroidery. Notice how the neat edge of the embroidery makes it easier to work the stem stitch.

CHAPTER 7

NATURAL SHADING

Natural shading is – as its name suggests – used to portray the natural form in long and short stitch. Also known as directional long and short, it relies on the direction of the stitch and the change of angles in the rows to suggest texture and movement within the stitching, as well as using shading within the colour ranges.

Traditionally this type of long and short was used for flowers. Pictures, clothing and home furnishings have used this type of embroidery as decoration, bringing the garden indoors. Natural long and short stitch enables the embroiderer to attempt botanical studies with thread in an equally beautiful way to painters. You can capture birds and animals with lifelike accuracy and create texture in a way that no other medium can.

Natural long and short stitch needs very close observation of the object you are embroidering. Looking at an object and working out direction can be daunting but breaking it down into sections and looking at any natural lines that are already present will give you all the information you need to work your embroidery. Stitch plans are essential in natural shading. You must work out all the directions of your stitches first before starting.

Again start at the back of the subject and work forward, outlining each section in split stitch. Unlike tapestry shading, all edges of natural shading are outlined, except perhaps stems on flowers.

OPPOSITE: A long-tailed tit embroidered in stranded cottons.

This iris brooch is only 5cm in diameter, so it was essential the angles suggested the petals' positions and separation from each other. There were limited rows stitched as the subject was so small.

TURNING ANGLES

Turning angles smoothly is one of the challenges of long and short stitch. To be successful the angle change needs to happen very gradually and smoothly. It is important to work through the angle change samples in Chapter Five first or at least understand them fully before attempting the projects in this chapter. Draw lines on your fabric to help you aim for the right position of your stitch. If you think the angle looks wrong, then it probably is. Take it out and try again. You can fill in gaps in the row with extra stitches if they occur when turning the angle, *if* they fit in. Do not just fill the gaps in and think you can correct it or cover it up on the next row. This will usually cause more problems and a messy effect.

Practice makes perfect when turning angles; draw the angles out on a piece of paper first before starting the projects so you have gone through the construction of each section in your mind.

Striped Feather

This first project in natural shading gives you the chance to stitch an embroidery without the need for neat edges or subtle shading. No split stitches are needed on the outside edge at all. A feather has naturally uneven edges, so your focus is on changing the angle as you work down the feather. Do not worry if your feather has more or less stripes than the sample picture or they get thicker or thinner, you are aiming for gentle turning of angles. A tiny European jay feather (shown in the sample picture) inspired this design.

The sample is worked on a yellow flat silk, using one strand of stranded cotton.

Materials:

- Fabric with the design transferred, a backing if required and stab stitched if necessary.
- Frame and scissors.
- A range of stranded cottons; light two shades, medium two shades, dark one shade, black. Any colour range you like can be used for this.
- Embroidery needles; size 10–12.

This design based on a jay feather is a good exercise in changing the angle of your stitching.

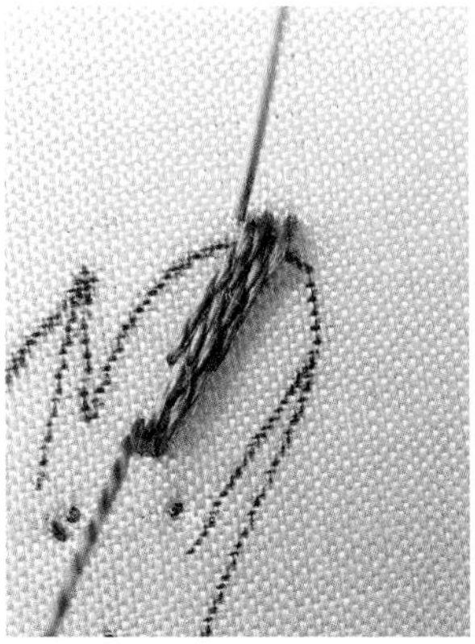

1. Add direction marks on to your fabric to help you keep the right angle, use the photograph as a guide. As a feather has uneven edges no split stitch is required. Thread up one strand of your dark colour and starting at the top and in the middle of the feather, work a row of long and short stitch over your design line. Make the edge as you take the needle down into the fabric slightly uneven and 'messy'. This will give a feathery effect. Make sure your design line is covered.

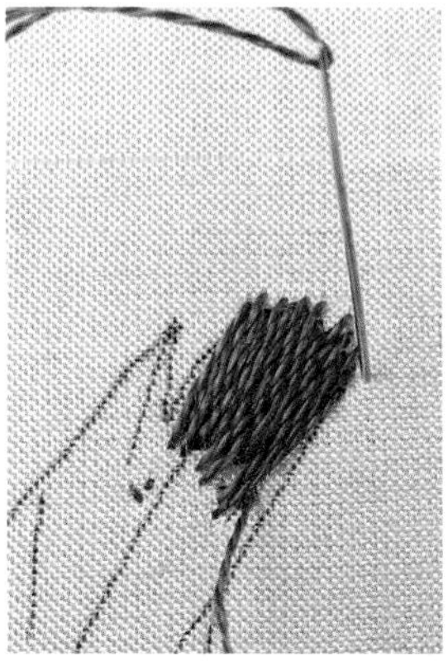

2. Make sure you go well over the design line occasionally to give points to the feather. As you can see from the photograph the far right- and left-hand sides of this row have slightly turned their angle. This is not vital for the first row but if you can, just try and turn the last couple of stitches slightly. You can see the needle comes up *very* closely to the last stitch at the bottom of the row and then spaces out a little at the top, therefore causing a slight angle change.

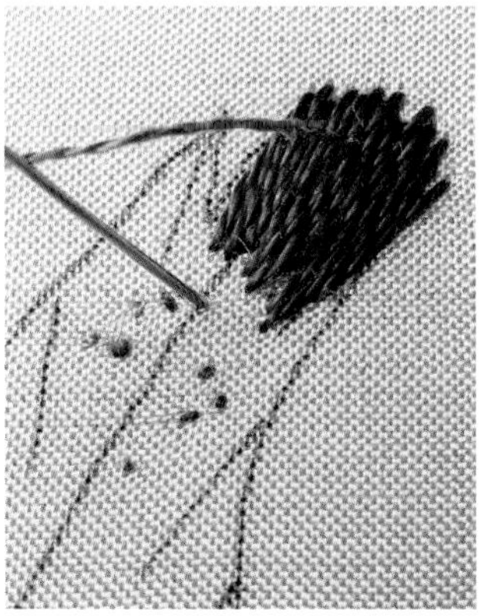

3. Once your first row is complete, thread up with your two medium colours in two separate needles. Starting in the centre of the feather come up through your stitch, splitting it if you can and down into the fabric to embroider your second row.

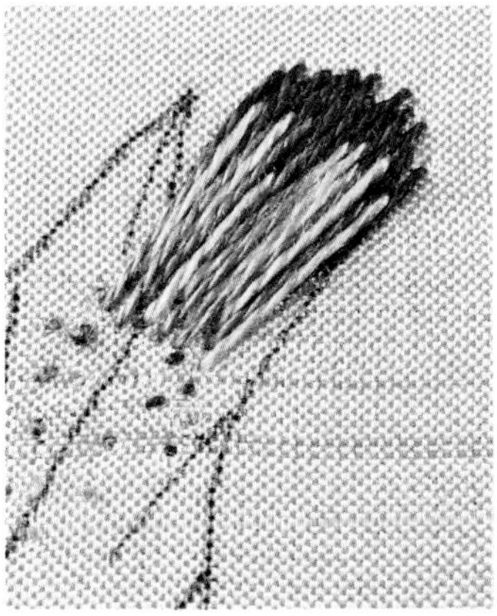

4. In this row vary the colours you use to give a shaded effect. Keep your stitches nice and long and vary where you come up through your row so there is a slightly zig-zag effect. Turn the angle at the end of the row.

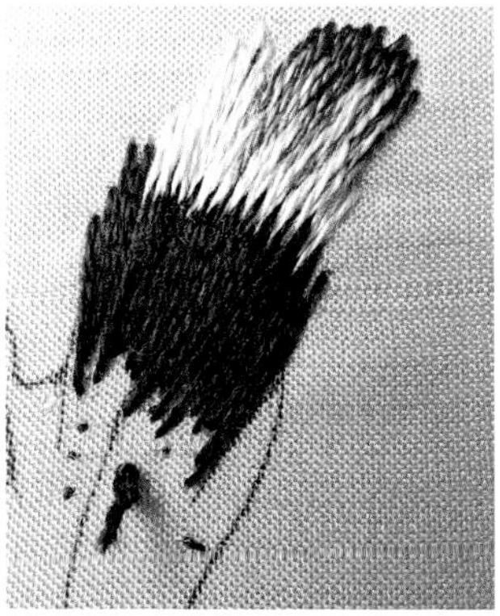

5. Keep working your way down the feather, changing colour with each row. The third row is worked in your light colours and then there is a row of black. Try and keep all the bands of colour the same size. You will need to change the angle of your stitch as you work down the feather; at the top of the feather it is straight in the centre and then gradually turns as it reaches the edge of the row. The black stitches on the edge here show a very slight change of angle to the other stitches in this row.

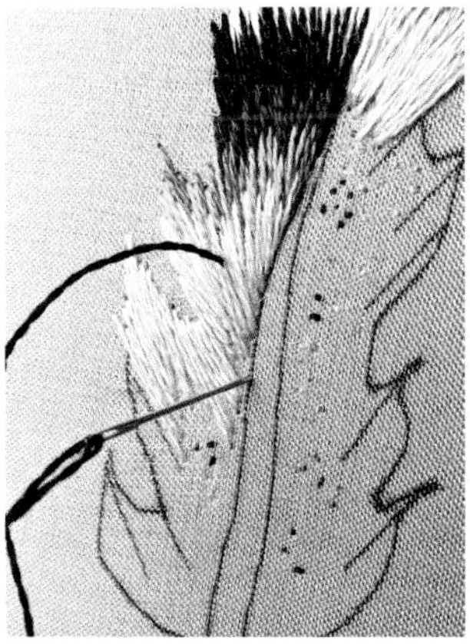

6. When you reach the spine, work down one side of the feather only and finish the edge of the spine as shown in the photograph. The spine is stitched last, so we must leave a space for it. Take the needle neatly down on the design line of the spine. Remember to keep turning your angle as you work down the feather. The centre stitches of the feather now have quite an angle change compared to the top of the feather; it changes a little bit with each row. Do not worry about getting the same angle as the sample, just try and change your angle gradually as you work down. It should flow very gently.

7. Repeat the same stitching to the other side of the feather.

8. The rest of the feather is stitched in stem stitch. Work the curly lines at the bottom first. This stem stitch must have short stitches to keep the curved shape. Then embroider the outside of the spine in a black stem stitch on both sides, as shown in the photograph.

9. Work a line of stem stitch in the centre of the spine in a light colour. Fill in around this with lines of stem stitch in your medium colours.

Flowers

One of an embroiderer's favourite subjects. Well, traditionally anyway!! Flowers lend themselves to thread painting especially well. The effect of a flower in long and short stitch often looks like a painting.

There are a few pointers to look out for when choosing a flower to embroider in long and short stitch. Flowers with many tiny petals can be a challenge as the rows would be so small that your embroidery may look very textured and messy. So, for example a flower like a dahlia or chrysanthemum must be made bigger so that you can fit your stitches in; edit it so you remove some of the petals or zoom in so that you are only stitching a section.

Also, flowers with many complex coloured markings, creases and turnovers in their petals can be quite difficult, you must make sure the markings look natural and flow with the rows and contend with the shading to create separation between the petals and turnovers. You may end up with a confused piece of embroidery if you don't simplify or enlarge your design.

A flower and its leaves will often have veins and markings that will help you to plan the direction of your stitches. It is easier to try and make your stitches flow the same way as the markings if possible so that you can incorporate them into your long and short stitch rather than add them on top later – they can look a little 'stuck on the top' if added.

To embroider a flower, you always start as usual in long and short stitch from the back and work forwards. So, your underneath back petal or leaf is first, and you work towards the front. Petals and leaves are always worked from the outside edge towards the growing point. This is often an easier way of working anyway as a lot of the time there are less stitches in each subsequent row, which makes stitching it easier than adding stitches for the beginner.

Again, observation is the key; try not to choose your colours from one range, do not presume that the shadow a petal casts is the darker version of the main colour in your subject. Use browns and greys and perhaps a navy to add a shadow, it can look a lot more natural and it helps to create depth if your main colour range does not go as dark as you would like. Black for shadow is probably too strong and not very natural. If your black thread comes in a few shades and you really wish to use it, then choose the lightest version as it can overpower other thread colours and if you are using it for shadow then you obviously want it to recede.

Where petals overlap one another, you need to have good separation by colour and/or very neat split stitch-covered edges, preferably both. You do not want one petal merging into another, so editing may be required if you are working from a photograph to make sure this doesn't happen. If you have very strong or large shadows on your picture you might need to edit them somewhat as they may look odd worked in the embroidery. Do so carefully; flowers will have natural shadows and highlights, so they are needed but if you find half your flower is dark and you are unable to see the colours clearly you may want to choose a different image, so it is easier to embroider.

Turnovers

Petals and leaves often have a natural turnover in them. They present their own challenges as sometimes they can be very small and look unnatural when embroidered. It can also be difficult to work out what angle your stitches should be.

If the turnover is too small in your original source, either remove it or make it bigger so it is easier to stitch. If you can get two rows of stitching in it then so much the better, as you can then shade it and create a shadow as it turns away from the petal or leaf. Do not be tempted to pad the turnover; i.e. you should be able to give the effect of a turnover without it. Padding will often look unnatural. If the rest of the petals or leaves are unpadded, it will look very disjointed.

To work out the direction of your turnover, draw the petal or leaf in question on a small piece of tracing paper without the turnover, i.e. in its full form, unfolded. Draw direction lines on it and then fold the tracing paper over as it is shown in your design. This will then give you the correct angles to work from.

This little leaf has a turnover at the top. You can see it has two rows of stitching and has been shaded to suggest it is turning away. There is also a slight shadow underneath it. Notice the direction of the turnover compared to the main leaf.

Leaves

Leaves often have sharp points at the end of them and in fact many petals do too. It is important not to 'round' off the points. Always extend your first stitch over the point beyond the split stitch, and then the other two stitches alongside that first stitch can rest against the split stitch. Therefore, leaving that first stitch to stick out. *See* Chapter Five.

Stems

Stems are very often straight and therefore *do not* need a split stitch on the outside edge. If you have a split stitch running down a stem there is a tendency to turn your stitch angle to cover it rather than flowing straight down; you will then end up with the outside edge of slightly diagonal stitches and the middle of the stem with straight stitches. Rather like we do not use split stitch on vertical lines in tapestry shading, it is the same principle. *See* the poppy project to see how this works.

Thistle leaves have very sharp spikes, so it was vital that all the spikes were pointed and not rounded off in this embroidery. That is also true of the flower; the top of each part of the flower is just one stitch, no split stitch was used at all on the flower head. Remember only use a split stitch if it will help you achieve the desired effect.

Centres of flowers

The centres of flowers and their stamens are a chance to be a little creative in your embroidery. French knots, tiny beads, couching, stem stitch and padding can all be used. There needs to be a little constraint though as you do not want the centre of the flowers to be out of proportion with the flatter long and short stitch. You can pad the centre with a layer of satin stitch in the way the Japanese flower project is created, by padding the front only. It is the beautiful shading on your flower that should stand out, not lots of padding.

Holes and brown bits!

Flowers are natural forms; there may be a bit missing from your petal where an insect has munched it, there may be a leaf that has started to go brown on the edge. Leave all this in your design, it is what makes a design look interesting and natural. If there is a still a caterpillar eating one of your leaves in your design... embroider it too!

Materials:

- Fabric with the design transferred, a backing if required, stab stitched if necessary.
- Frame and scissors.
- A range of stranded cottons or fine silks, two or three of each, dark, medium and light shades for the flower so you will be using approximately nine shades for the petals – if you have slightly more or less it does not matter. The sample is pink, but you may like to use another poppy colour such as red or blue, the principle is the same. Try and get the colours to blend smoothly to make the shading easier. Four green shades for the stalk from light to dark, plus an extra light colour if you wish to add spikes to the stalk.
- Embroidery needle size 10–12.

Poppy

This poppy embroidery project gives row-by-row instructions on how to complete a flower. It is important to notice the length of the stitches that are in the photographs and use these as a guide. Try and get the same number of rows as in the sample. If the stitches are too long you will not have enough room for all the colours. If your stitches are too short, you will have too many rows and the petals will be lumpy.

The sample has been stitched in one strand of stranded cotton on a silk dupion.

The colours and petals of this poppy have been stylized to make it simple to follow in terms of light, medium and dark colours, and the formation of rows. The angle changes start easy and then progress to harder in the bottom petals.

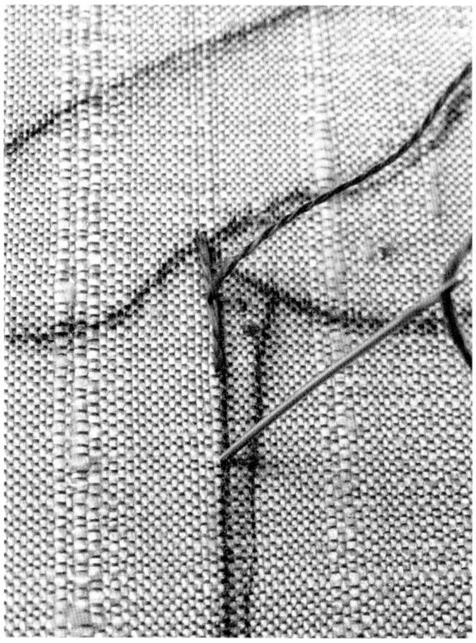

1. The stalk is underneath the flower so that is started first. No outlining is needed as split stitches would get in the way of making a smooth line flowing down the stem; you want to keep them straight. Using your darkest green, start on the left side of the petal stitching a row of *long* split stitch all the way to the bottom of the stem. If you think about the construction of long and short stitch, it is made up of split stitch so for narrow areas like a stem it is easiest to work in long, vertical rows.

2. Now work a row of the dark colour from the bottom back up to the top next to the first row. No space should be between the first and second row. Try and make sure the placement of stitches is staggered so the position of split stitches on the first row is different from the second row. This should happen naturally if your stitches are all slightly different lengths. Work a third row of dark now from the top a little way down the row, then change to a slightly lighter colour as seen in the picture; take this colour to the bottom, then back up again, stopping before you reach the top. You want a row of stitches running all along the top row to be dark, so it looks like a shadow.

3. Add a row of light stitches almost all along the right-hand side so you have a definite highlight. Fill in any gaps you have in the stem with a medium or light colour.

4. Add one or two rows of medium or dark to the right-hand edge and add straight stitches with a light colour to give the look of spikes. Having a slightly darker edge to a stem will help give the impression it is rounded. The light hits the centre where it is highest.

5. Split stitch around the outer edge of the back petal in a dark shade. Start in the centre of the petal and work a row of long and short stitch in your darkest shades. As you get near to the other petals on this first row, there will not be enough room for long and short stitch so just finish this first row in satin stitch. Tuck your needle against the split stitch as shown to create a smooth edge.

6. Create a second row with your medium and dark shades, making sure your needle goes down neatly on the line. Notice how the first row has just very dark stitches on the right-hand side.

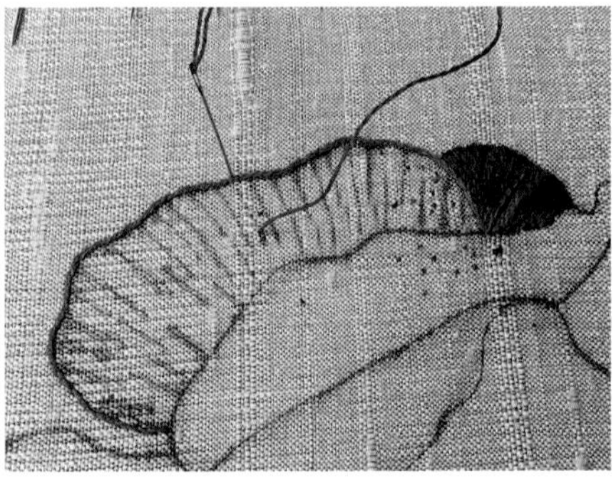

7. Split stitch around the next petal in a medium shade. Draw your angles on the petal so you know where you need to start turning. Again, beginning in the centre of the petal start to work a row of long and short with a mixture of your darkest shades. Work one stitch next to another with no gaps between them. If you see a gap as you turn the angle then fill it in at the time. Try and change colours as often as possible, so that you do not get solid blocks of colour.

8. As you get to the end of this first row start to bring in the medium shades; blend them in gently. Notice in the picture that the very darkest colour has been dropped from the row before bringing in the medium shades. Then at the end of this row it is just the lightest of the medium shades so it stands out against the back petal. Notice the direction of the stitch at the end is almost vertical and it again ends up by being a satin stitch, by bringing the needle up on the drawn line and down over the edge of the split stitch.

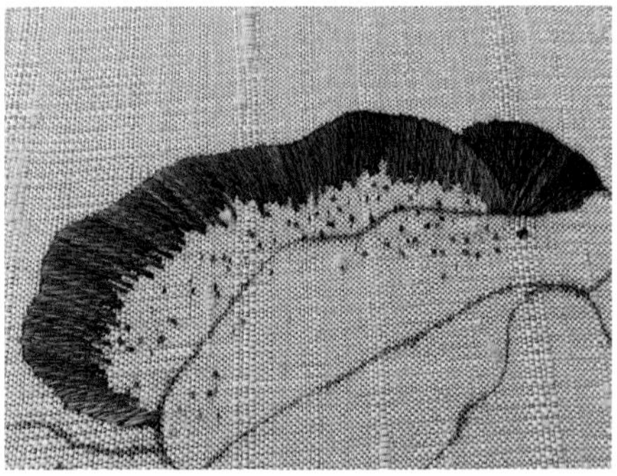

9. The completed first row, showing mostly dark shades and a little medium colour towards the far right and left. Notice the proportion the first row takes up of the petal. It is important to make the stitches long enough. Remember that a lot of this row will be covered by the next row. Notice the very gentle turning of this row; you have lots of space to turn the angle from the centre of the petal out to each side so there should be no sudden changes of angle.

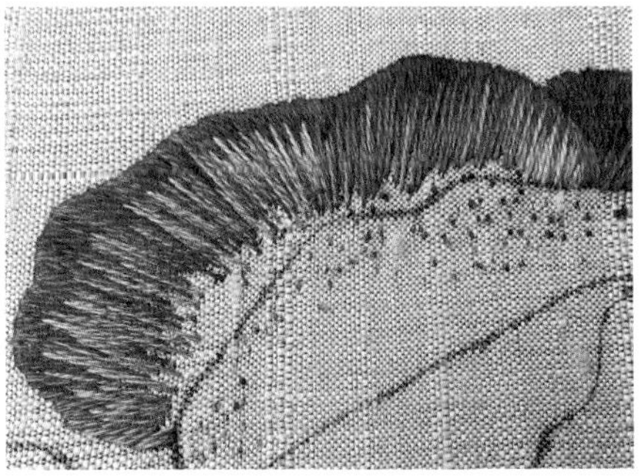

10. Starting again in the centre, stitch your second row using your medium shades. Make sure you vary where you bring your needle up and down to create a jagged effect.

11. Complete this petal with a third row in your lightest shades. Make sure the stitches end very neatly on the design line. This will make it so much easier to work your future petals' split stitch.

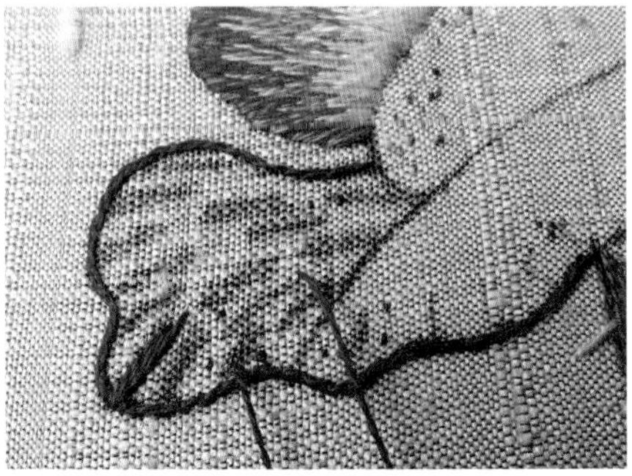

12. Next partially split stitch the next petal as shown up to the stem in a darker shade. Part of this petal is underneath another and part of it is on top of another, so it must be worked in two separate stages. Start the first row at the position shown in the photograph with your darkest shades. Draw the angles on to this petal carefully; the angle turns quite quickly so make the lines as accurate as possible.

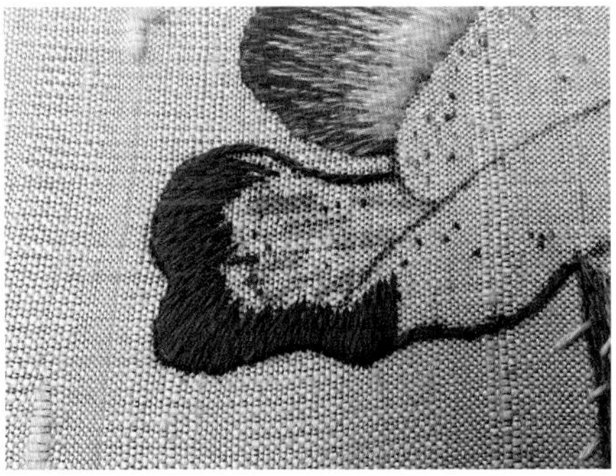

13. The first row completed in the darkest shades. Notice the angle turns quite dramatically in a small space, but they all flow very smoothly. If you think you have the wrong angle, unpick before you start the next row. You cannot correct it by covering it up.

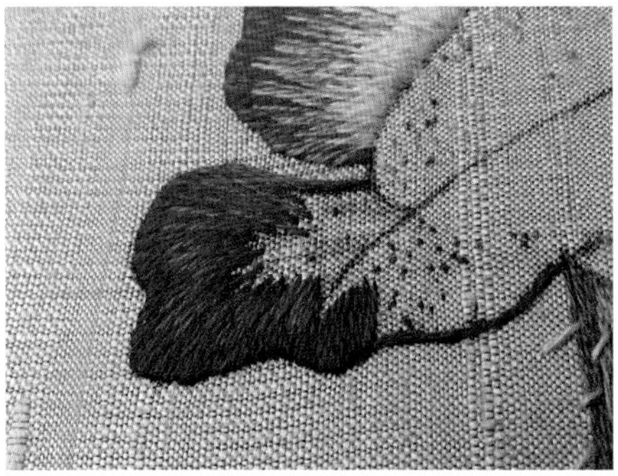

14. The second row is stitched in medium shades; the space here is much smaller than the first row, *do not* crowd too many stitches into this area it will just create lumps. Notice how the angle is very sharp towards the top edge of the petal. Remember to come up in the fabric and down over the split stitch edge when working this part of the petal.

15. The third row is worked with light and medium shades, but not the very lightest. To help the angle turn towards the bottom, notice how the stitches get a little bit shorter. Again, do not crowd too many stitches in.

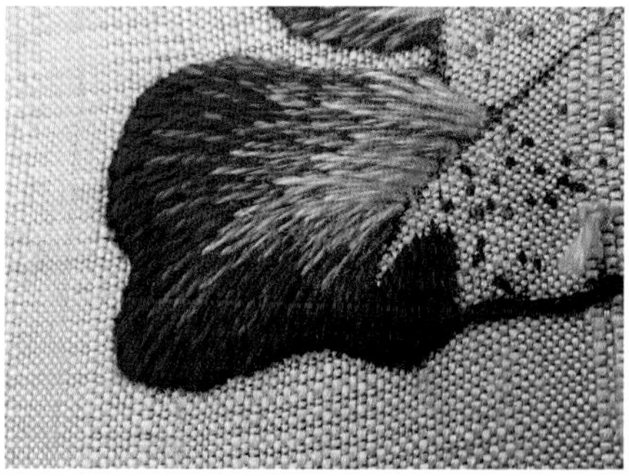

16. Finish the petal with your lightest colours, turning the angle a little more if you can. If you feel that you cannot turn the last row any more or it will look out of place with the rest of the rows, then keep it the same angle as the one before. Try and end the last row as neatly as you can on the line as this will help greatly with the impression of the turnover of the petal later.

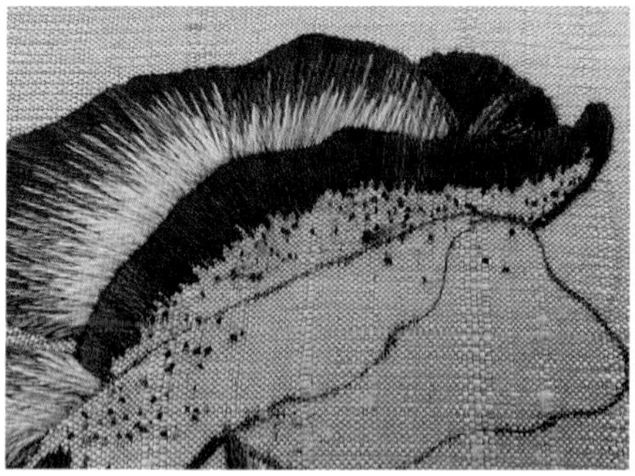

17. Split stitch the next petal along the top edge. Make sure there are no spaces between this petal and the previous ones. Make sure the split stitches are close, and almost overlapping the previous petal. If you feel the edge of the previous petal is messy then take your split stitch a little way over the last row to ensure a neat edge. It is better to try and work neatly in the first instance but this can help tidy the edge until your stitches improve. Embroider this row of long and short in mostly your dark shades and a few patches of medium.

18. A close up of this row showing that there is no space between this row and the previous one. It is vital that the petals do not have a space between them. However you do not want the stitches overlapping the previous row either; this will give a bumpy effect to the embroidery.

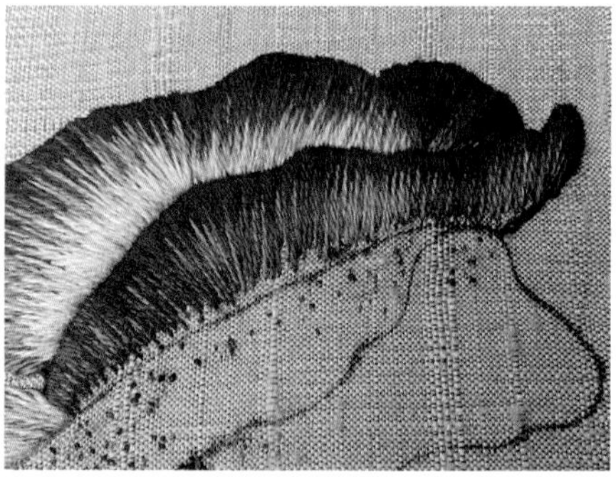

19. Stitch your second row, in the medium colours. The row almost but not quite reaches the design line – make sure you leave room for a third row of stitching.

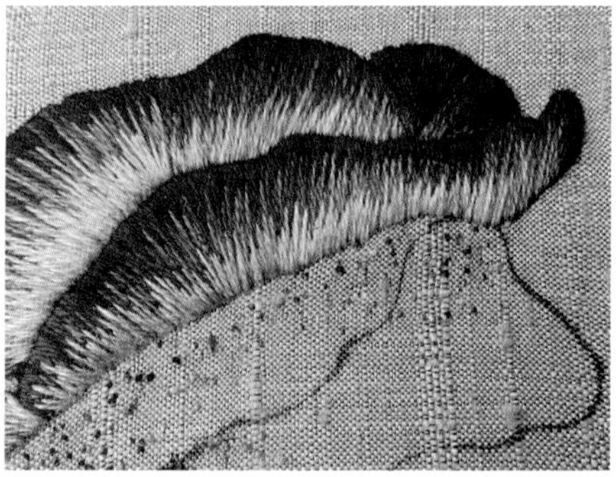

20. Finish this petal as before with your lightest colours. Notice that the light, medium and dark shades/rows have an equal amount of colour showing on the completed petal.

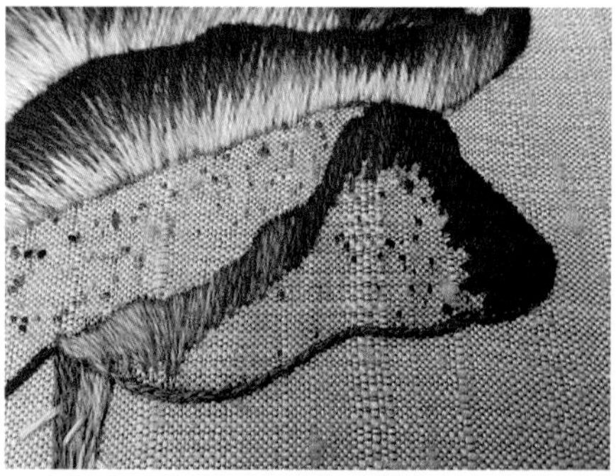

21. For the next petal, split stitch round the bottom right-hand side and the top, just where it overlaps the previous petal in a medium colour. The top left of this petal has no split stitches under the first row as it is overlapped by the top petal. The first row of long and short stitch has almost all the colours present in it. Start at the point where it overlaps the previous petal with the darker shades and work round the right-hand side edge to the bottom, turning the angle until it is almost horizontal as shown in the photograph. Then come back again to the overlap and work from your medium to your lighter shades on the left. Do not use your very lightest colour in this row.

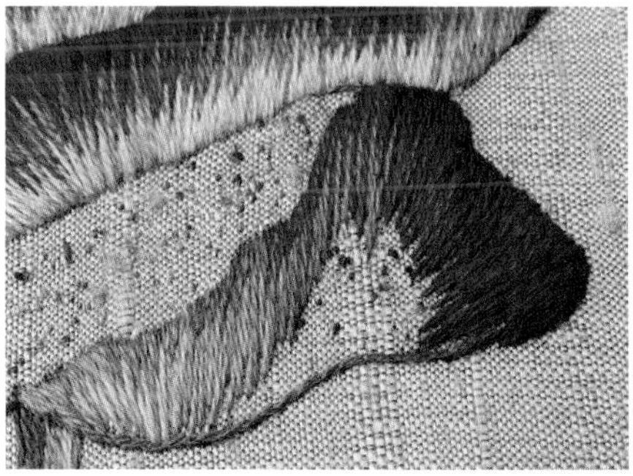

22. Now work the second row of long and short stitch with slightly lighter shades than the first row. Make sure you carefully turn the angle as shown in the photograph. Notice how the stitch on the bottom far right is outside of the split stitch to round the edge off. You may need to try and place this stitch a few times so that it fits in with the rest of the petal; you want to achieve a nice, smooth edge.

23. Finish this row by using lighter colours and really tucking the needle under the split stitch.

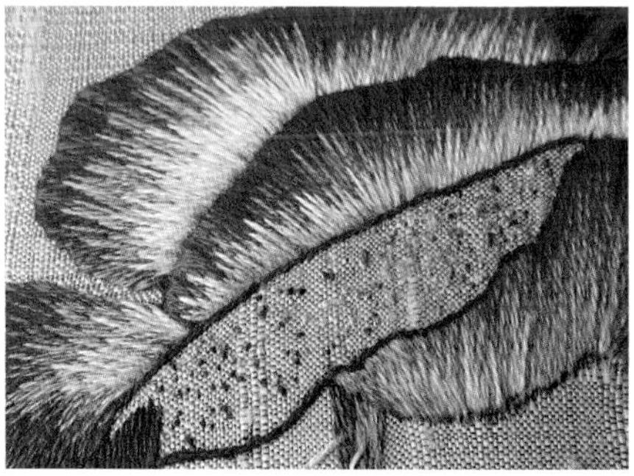

24. Split stitch all the way round the final petal in a darker shade. This petal sits on top of everything else so therefore it has a split stitch all around it.

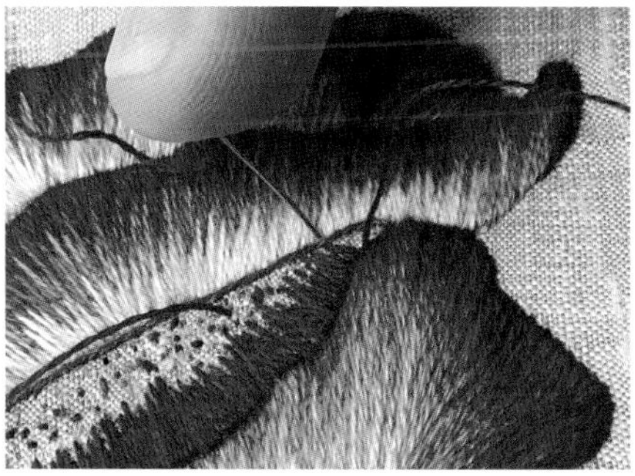

25. Stitch the first row of this petal in your darker shades starting in the centre as before; the bottom edge of this petal is the outside edge, so it is stitched first. At the far right of the petal you have a satin stitch, in this case come up from the bottom of the split stitch and go over the top to make a neat edge as shown. Notice how the angle changes at the very end.

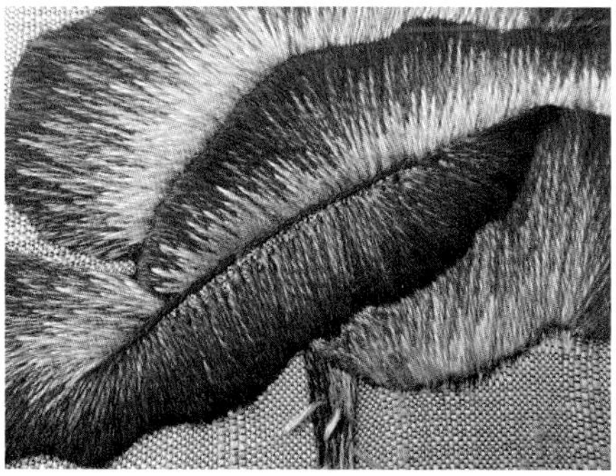

26. Stitch the second row of this petal in your medium shades. Finish the last row of stitching in your lightest shades, making sure to get the stitches as neat as possible where they go over the split stitch.

Shading Birds and Animals

Stitching birds and animals in thread painting truly shows off the beauty of embroidery. They are natural subjects for long and short stitch, due to the almost feathery quality of the stitch itself and the amazing effects that can be achieved with shading to create fur and muscle tone, for example. A clear picture is essential to work from for embroidering birds and animals, it gives you the chance to study the direction and layers of the feathers, fur, scales and so on, and the subtle or contrasting colours needed to give a natural effect. If you have a big shadow across your picture or a part cropped off and you make up what you think should be there, it can ruin your embroidery. Be happy with your picture in the first instance.

A clear stitch plan is essential; you can then work out which area to start on and if you are taking a section of your subject or a full-size picture. A close-up section means you can stitch individual feathers or subtle movements in fur. Obviously, the size of your embroidery may determine the amount of detail you can put in. Do not presume that smaller is easier. You are limited in the number of rows with a smaller embroidery. You may also not be able to turn the angles as smoothly as you like if the piece is too small; this is especially important for birds and animals to create a realistic effect. On your stitch plan you should also mark carefully the direction your stitches will take. Study the animal or bird closely, especially around the face. That is always the part that is looked at first. Sketch the stitch direction lines on your stitch plan – if you think that the design is too small for

This embroidery of Rosie the cat demonstrates how an accurate drawing and stitch plan is needed for a realistic picture. Every stripe on her fur was recorded on the stitch plan and then the fabric to give an accurate effect.

the number of rows and the amount of changes in direction then make it bigger. It is useful on your stitch plan to draw your direction lines in a similar length to the size that your stitches will be, therefore you have already had a run-through of your project.

If the feathers or fur lie smoothly then your stitches and directions should try and emulate this. Conversely, your fur or feathers may be messy and very textured so think about how you will achieve that with stitches, without your embroidery itself looking messy. You do need a bit of control!

If you are stitching an animal with short hair, such as a horse or short-haired dog, you will find that muscle tone is an important part of your embroidery. You will use split stitch and shading to create a three-dimensional effect. The order of your work is especially important to give the correct anatomical detail; you may have to stop and then start areas depending on overlapping parts of the animal.

The same rule applies in that the back/underneath parts of the animal or bird are worked first finishing with the elements that are forefront. Therefore, split stitch also needs to be carefully planned. Not all areas need split stitch, especially if the animal or bird is very textured. If you feel a split stitch is useful in that it will give you strong definition – for example in feathers on top of each other or a leg of an animal going over the belly – then use it to help give a smooth, neat edge and especially with animals, some perspective. You do not want a back leg looking like it is in front of a foreground leg.

To stitch an animal or bird in long and short stitch, the rule book can almost be thrown out! It is thinking about how to stitch creatively to achieve all the various textures that nature provides. Experiment

This deer photo and stitch direction plan show how the stitches will work with each other and the length of stitches that will be used in the embroidery. The photograph is a good example of a design that will work well as it shows very clearly the direction that the fur lies, it has no strong shadows across it and the colour is very true to life.

with different ways of working on the side of your frame before you start your main piece.

Fur

To create fur/hair and so on you must have contrasting colours within every area to create a three-dimensional effect. The length of stitch will also change in one embroidery piece depending on the effect needed. It is useful when stitching fur to take your needle down in the stitch; this somehow gives more of a fur effect than the smooth effect created by coming up in the stitch.

This close-up photograph of Rosie the cat shows the number of different colours needed in each row to create a realistic fur

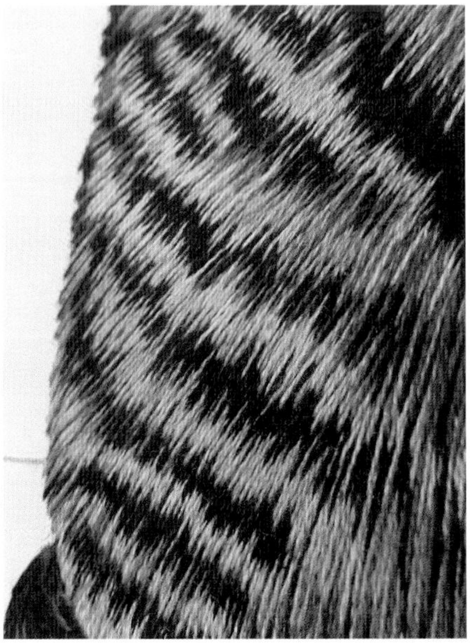

Detail from the embroidery of Rosie the cat illustrating how colours are used to create the impression of fur.

effect. The black stripe is not all black; it has occasional stitches worked in a dark grey and a green grey. These colours are not immediately obvious, but they prevent the black row looking flat, especially compared to other areas. It is also not a solid row of black – sometimes the black appears broken up by the other rows. The lighter stripes show that there are many colours needed to give a tabby fur effect; brown, light grey, pale orange-brown, yellow-brown and so on. Even in these lighter rows there are contrasting darker or lighter stitches occasionally to help give the look of fur. The direction of the rows also changes more dramatically than for something like a flower. They do not flow very smoothly into one another; there can be a jump in the direction of stitches. It is not messy, but it does have texture.

The textures in the following bullfinch project can be applied to animals that have fur, so the belly and shoulder areas would be how you would stitch fur with perhaps more contrasting dark and light colours.

This fat bullfinch is a common sight in many gardens in the spring where it will eat lots of apple tree buds.

Materials:

- Fabric with the design transferred, a backing if required and stab stitched if necessary.
- Frame and scissors.
- A range of stranded cottons or fine silks matched as closely as possible to the picture; black, white, a range of greys, a range of reds that blend into orange-peach and brown-green for the branch.
- Embroidery needle size 10–12.

Bullfinch

This is a good example of an embroidery that has many textures. Smooth tail feathers, small split stitched individual feathers, and a textured choppy underbelly. It also gives a chance for blending colours in rows such as orange and red together. The sample has been stitched in one strand of stranded cotton on a green cotton sateen.

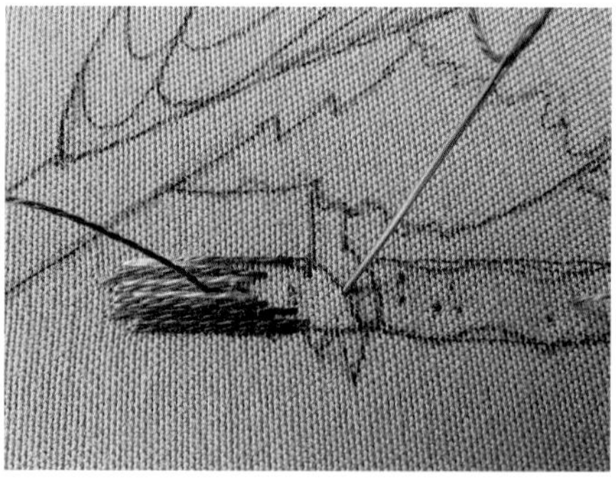

1. Start the long and short embroidery on the branch. Split stitch is not needed. Use a mixture of greens and browns. Use darker shades under the feet to create shadows. Use shorter stitches occasionally to give a more textured appearance. End neatly on the design line of the feet.

2. Use a range of greys for the feet. Split stitch around the shapes if you think it will help you get a better point and shape to them. A slightly lighter shade on the outside of the top claw as it goes over the branch will make it stand out. Add a single black stitch at the end of the claws to make a sharp point. Add some horizontal stitches over the long and short when you have finished for the little markings as shown in the photograph.

3. This shows the direction of the markings on the other claw. It is important to study your subject for tiny little marks like this and try and put them into your embroidery to make it look more natural. You may not always be able to long and short stitch everything, especially in a small space, so it is acceptable to be creative with some of your stitches.

4. Split stitch the small undermost area below the tail in a light grey. Stitch this area by taking the needle down over the split stitch as you would a flower petal, as this part of the bird is very smooth. Angle your needle as shown over the split stitch.

5. Fill *just* this section with long and short stitch. Make sure you work up to the line marked. Do not encroach onto any other part of the tail or you will get in the way of further stitching and it could cause a lumpy effect; you will also be covering your design lines.

6. The next part of the bird is the belly feathers. They are started at the bottom of the belly and will be stitched up to the shoulder area, which follows the premise that underneath parts are worked first. These feathers are more textured and less smooth, so a different approach is taken to stitch them. Start by bringing the needle up in the belly area and take the needle down into the area you have just stitched – you are encroaching a little bit on top of these previous stitches. Use a variety of greys; light medium and dark to create a textured look. You are also not trying to get a neat edge. There is no split stitch for this reason. Make sure that you do cover the design line, though. Some of your stitches will encroach a little bit beyond the line as shown in the photograph.

7. Work this 'messy' first row until you reach the right-hand claw. You can see the difference in textures between this row and the first little smooth section you worked.

8. The second row of the chest is worked by coming up in the fabric and taking the needle *back down* into the stitches of the previous row. The stitches are all of a similar length but vary in their placement. You are only going a little way into the previous row; you do not want to cover all your previous work. Make sure your stitches are not too small or you will get ridges and build up lumps if you are not careful. It should look textured due to colour and stitch placement, not because of lumpy stitching!

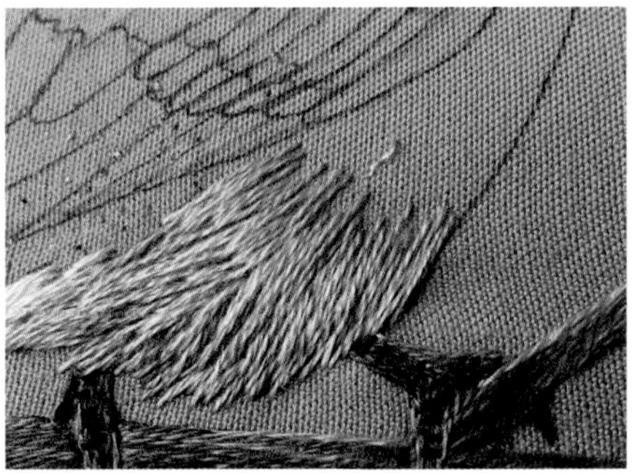

9. Continue up the belly to the chest in the same way row by row, start the light orange-peach range all at once rather than blending it in too much with the greys. This is because it is a marking and on the bird, it does start quite dramatically. There will be a little merge of grey and orange but do not spend time mixing rows of orange and grey together.

10. Continue up the chest getting redder and dropping out the orange and peach range. Stop about the shoulder area so you can start working on the tail and wings as they are under the shoulder and head.

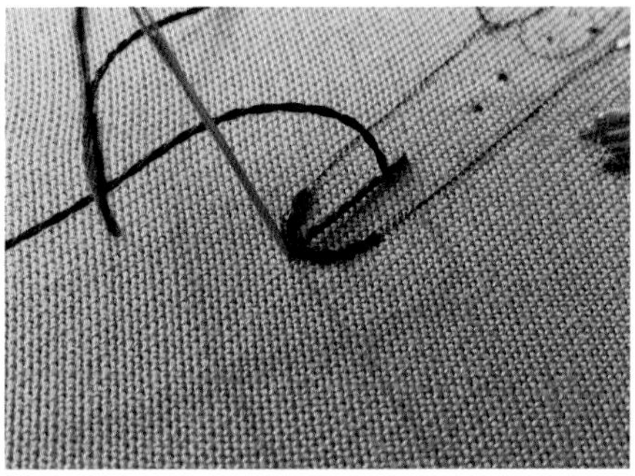

11. Start the undermost tail feather by just split stitching the curved end. You do not need split stitches for the rest of the tail as it will not help you get a smooth edge.

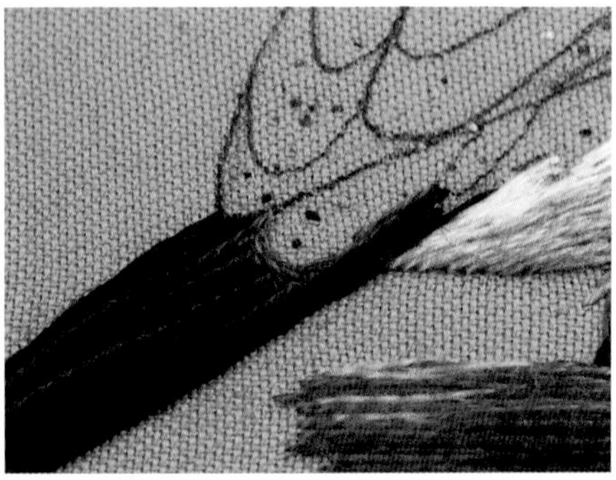

12. Work the undermost feathers very smoothly in black and grey by coming up in your stitch. They will look stripy but in this case, they are striped feathers, so this is the effect you want to achieve. Split stitch the next curve-ended feather that lies on top in a grey as shown in the photograph, as this will be next.

13. Work these feathers again smoothly and with little stripes.

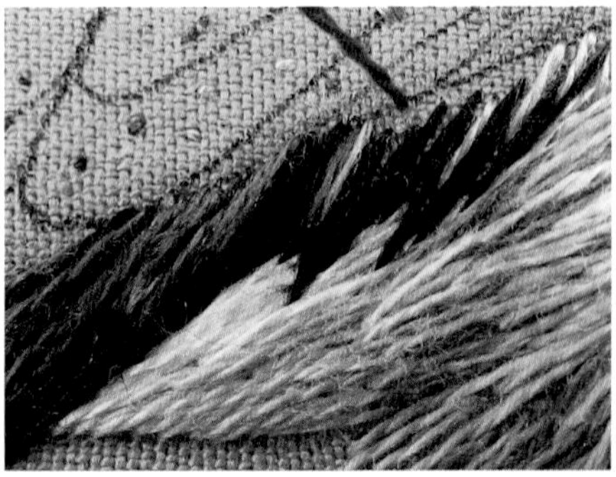

14. Just above and to the right of these smooth feathers is a small patch of textured feathers; work these without a split stitch and make an uneven edge by going down into your previous stitching as you did for the chest area. Notice that there are contrasting colours of black, medium and light grey in this area for a choppy effect.

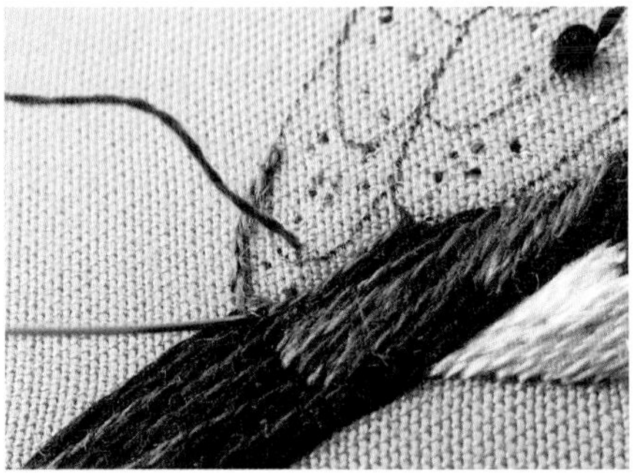

15. Now stitch the smooth feathers on the back of the bird; starting with the undermost feather, split stitch it in grey. If the area is very small, then it is perfectly acceptable to work a satin stitch. Angle your needle under the split stitch to get a sharp edge to these feathers as shown in the photograph.

16. Work your way up each feather on the left of the back doing rows of long and short where there is more space. Notice how the first row of long and short is grey and the second row is black. This will also help to separate the feathers as well as the split stitch. Notice how the needle goes down on the design line, not before it or over it.

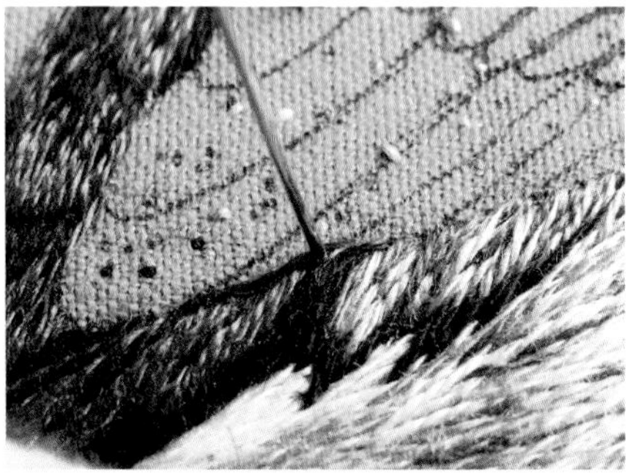

17. Next are the long, striped feathers on the right of the back. These are done in individual rows of long and short stitch. You could also look at it as doing long split stitch rows. Come up through your stitch and make sure these stitches sit right alongside your previous stitching. You do not want a gap. These feathers do not need split stitching first.

18. Fill this area in with long, smooth stitches. Change the colour with some of the rows so you get stripes.

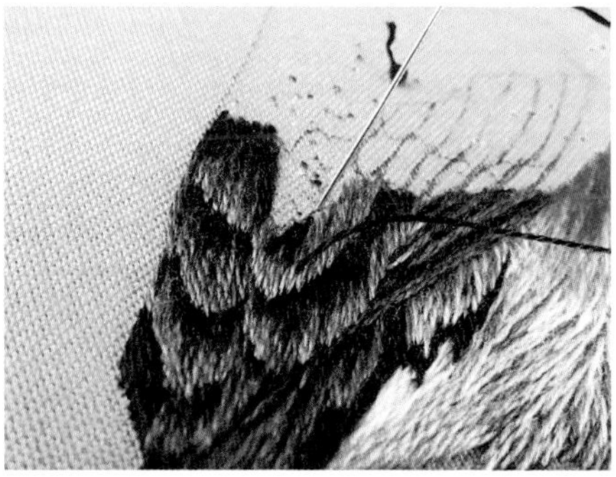

19. Next fill in the right-hand large feather area of the back in the same way as the left back.

20. Now the right-hand shoulder area; these are long, thin feathers that have distinct markings so look carefully at the pictures for correct placement. Even though they are thin they do need to have more than one row of long and short stitch each, so be careful with your angle on these feathers. Split stitch the undermost feather and starting at the bottom, work long and short stitches over the edge. Make long, angled stitches, leaving space for a second row. Draw your angle on the fabric if that helps you. Notice the angle of these white stitches is almost the same angle as the edge of the feather.

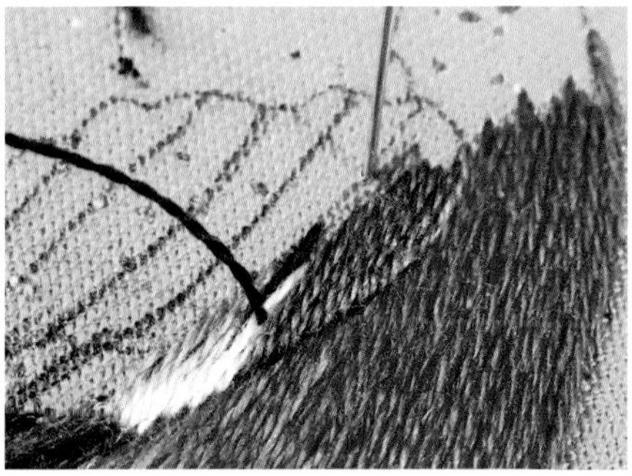

21. Stitch the second row, again using long stitches. The colours contrast a lot in this area so *do not* blend the colours together. They need to be separate for the markings. Notice the white, grey, and black stitches in the picture, very distinct bands of colour. The tips of these feathers are white with the other parts in grey and black stripes. Split stitch each feather individually to achieve the effect shown.

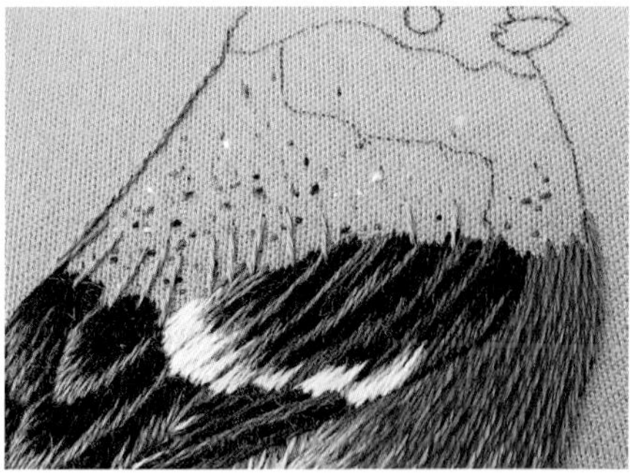

22. The top part of the shoulder is worked in the same way as the chest, with stitches going down into the previous row to get a ruffled effect. The left-hand outside edge of the shoulder, however, is smooth so make sure you split stitch this line up to the bottom of the head as shown in the photograph. Notice how the first row of stitches is spaced out rather than worked one next to another. This can help you achieve the right angle to your work, where there is a slightly messy effect needed with changing angles, especially if you have a larger area to fill. However, make sure you fill in *all* the spaces in this first row *before* you start the next row. This would be the technique you would use to create fur. You can also of course draw the angles of the stitch on to the fabric if this helps.

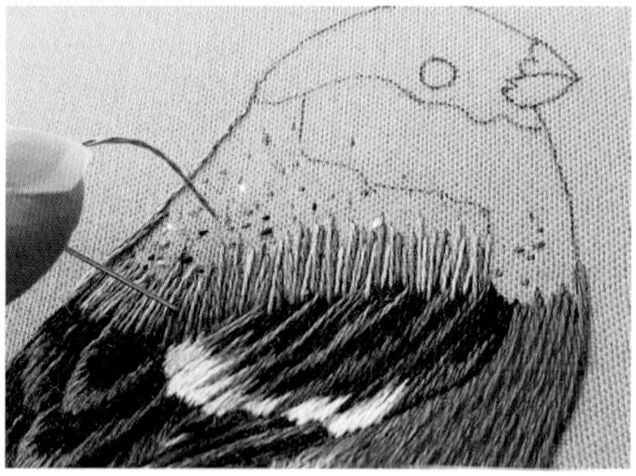

23. Once the first row is complete as shown, start the second row. Start around the middle coming up in the unworked area and encroaching a little in to the previous row. Notice the contrasting shades of grey in this section to give a slightly textured effect.

24. Stitch the shoulder up towards the head. Notice the direction of the grey stitches. Each row changes direction slightly. The contrast between the dark and light greys gives a textured look to this area; stop the grey colours as shown in the photograph. Next start the bottom of the head in a red colour that matches up to the one used in the chest area. These stitches will join the head and chest area together, so it can be worked as one row as shown. Notice the angle change in these stitches compared to the grey shoulder stitches. In some areas, there is quite a dramatic change. Space the stitches out as shown to set your angles, draw directions on if needed.

25. Before the main part of the head can be worked, the beak and eye needs to be stitched. Split stitch the outside edge of the beak and put a long black stitch in the middle, sticking out on its own to give the finch its distinctive sharp beak, as shown. Fill the rest of the beak in with grey satin stitch. Add a few additional stitches in lighter tones on the top to give a little highlight.

26. Next stitch the eye with a black vertical satin stitch without split stitch, as it will be outlined later. Then with a light grey colour, sew three little grey stitches horizontally towards the top of the eye. The needle position shows where to put the first stitch, which is the longest. This has a shorter stitch top and bottom to round out the highlight.

27. Now with a very light grey or white, add a vertical stitch over the end of the grey stitches to make the little eye shine.

28. Now fill in the red shoulder area, notice how the stitches are starting to angle towards the eye and beak. Add in a first outside edge row of long and short now for the head. Notice there are a couple of little grey stitches just towards the top of the head. Do not make your stitches too long, there is only a little space and the stitch angle must curve.

29. Now fill in the head, carefully changing the angle – this is vital for the correct flow of stitches. The angles are changing on every row but very smoothly; do not make your stitches too long.

30. Keep working towards the beak area as you fill in the space. Leave a tiny little gap around the eye.

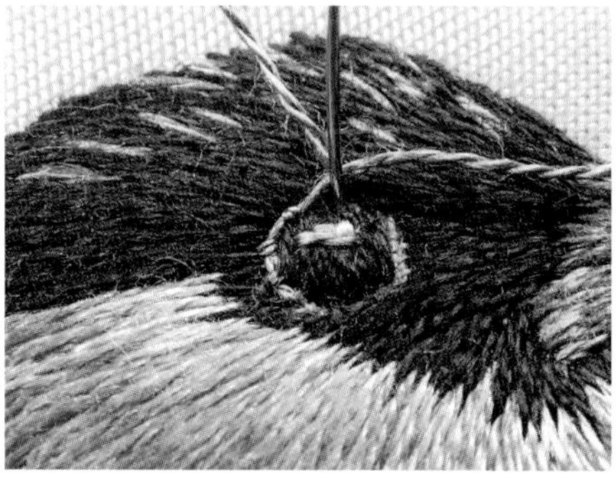

31. Work a tiny row of couching around the satin stitch eye in a single grey thread. Your stitches will need to be very close together to create the circular shape.

This green woodpecker has been worked in a similar way as the bullfinch project but as it is much smoother, it has all the stitches worked by coming up in the stitch.

Embroidering Circular Forms

Embroidering circular forms in long and short stitch needs careful working of the angles of the stitches. It is vital that the stitch direction is carefully planned before starting work. Very often circular objects can look flat if the stitch direction doesn't move around the object correctly and the highlights and shadows are missing, incorrectly placed, or not contrasting enough in colour.

Usually with natural shading in long and short stitch, you work towards the growing point. For example, you start stitching a petal on the outside edge and the stitches come row by row into the centre of the flower. With a circular shape it is much easier to start at the top of the shape and work down to the bottom, so if you are stitching an apple you would start where the stalk comes out from the apple. However, some people may find it easier to start at the bottom and work up to the top. Whichever way you choose to work it, the key to making it look good is smooth transitioning between rows, as you add and take away stitches and as you change the angle.

The placement of the first row of stitches is vital; you need to suggest the curving shape right from the very top. You must start in the centre and work round each side a similar distance. This will help you keep the correct angle. You can then make sure that each side of the circular shape has the same angle as it works down. You must increase stitches in the centre of the shape and decrease as you get to the bottom. Increasing stitches into a row of long and short is a little harder than decreasing. You must make sure the rows are full of stitches as you have a larger space to fill before you start on your next row. You also need to make sure the angle is smooth – as you are adding extra stitches it can go off slightly. Drawing the angle on a circular embroidery is very important to help keep the angle smooth.

It is often the case that every row of stitches on a circular subject needs to change angle a little to help with the suggestion of a curving surface. This is especially important if your design is small as you have minimum rows to suggest the curvature.

The light direction is also important as any confusion in placement will create odd highlights and shadows, which will not look natural. Really study your subject and make sure there is a definite highlight and shadow area.

This early twentieth-century fire screen, although stitched in what looks like rows of stem stitch, shows how the stitch direction can really enhance circular shapes. The shading has been stylized to give even greater emphasis. The glass bowl has only been partially stitched to give the impression of transparency. (Private collection)

A close-up photograph of the pomegranate showing the beautiful flow of the stitch direction that accentuates the curves.

This sample of a tomato illustrates the curved effect that can be created in embroidery.

Cherry Tomato

This little tomato has an obvious highlight and the placement of it is important, so you may want to mark this on your fabric before you start.

The sample has been worked in one strand of stranded cotton on a linen cotton blend.

Materials:

- Fabric with the design transferred, a backing if required and stab stitched if necessary.
- Frame and scissors.
- A range of stranded cottons; range of dark reds and browns, a range of medium reds and three or four colours for just the highlight area – the sample uses white and coral-pink for the highlights. The reds and brown all blend well together the highlight colours are quite contrasting. A range of four or five greens from light to dark.
- Embroidery needle size 10–12.

1. Mark the approximate centre line of the tomato before you start stitching with a dotted line. Split stitch around just the tomato from one side to another in a dark to medium shade. Make sure the split stitch is very smooth, so your long and short stitch edge will keep its shape. You do not split stitch any part of the leaf yet, just the outside edge of the tomato.

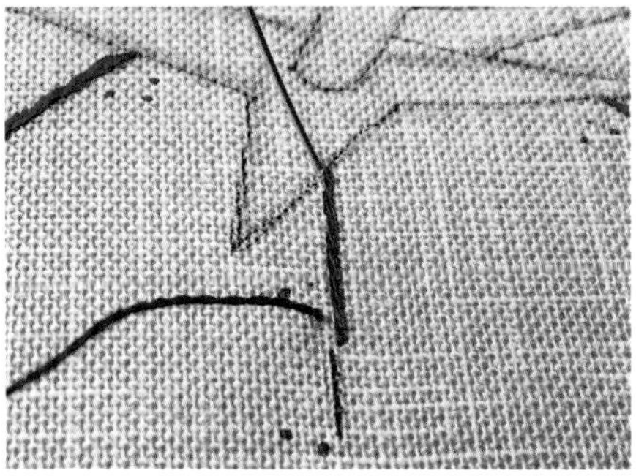

2. Using your darkest red or brown shade, place your first stitch on the centre line you have drawn. Then using a different dark shade, bring your needle up a little distance away from the first stitch at the bottom; there will be a small gap. Then take your needle down at the top *very* close to the first stitch under the leaf as shown.

3. Continuing with your dark shades, work a row of long and short stitch, each stitch coming up at the bottom a small distance away from the last and then tucking in very close at the top under the leaf. Notice how the angle needs to start turning from the second stitch that you work. It is a good idea for this project to draw all the angles on your fabric as shown, as they will be constantly changing, row by row.

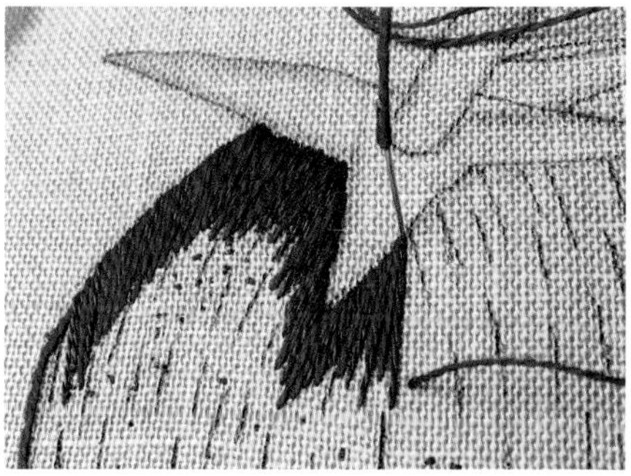

4. Work your first row of long and short stitch around to the left-hand 'shoulder' of the tomato and then stop. You can see the shades are very dark under the leaf and then as the stitches start to work down the outside edge, the darkest shade is not used as much. Notice that the angle changes quite quickly as it moves to the outside edge. Come back to the first stitch that you worked in the centre and start working towards the right-hand 'shoulder' of the tomato, changing the angle of the stitch in the same way.

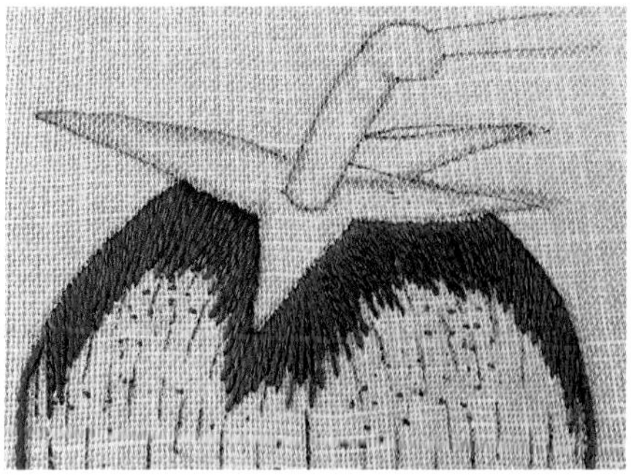

5. This shows the first row of long and short stitch completed. Again, the right-hand side has darker shades under the leaf area and the dark shades are used less as the stitches get to the outside edge.

6. Start the second row from the centre again, the very first stitch is completely vertical and follows that centre line you drew on at the very start. Bring in some medium colours in this row and drop your darkest colour completely. This row is at a slightly different angle to the first row, so follow your drawn-on lines and the photograph carefully. Stop stitching just before the end of your first row.

7. Once you have finished your second row to the tomato 'shoulders', you can add in your highlight colours. They are very contrasting and do not blend in at all. They are going to be added all at the same time in a block so that they are positioned correctly. Start with a medium shade from your highlight (in the sample it is a light pink) and work about twelve stitches in a block in the area shown in the photograph.

8. Next, using the lightest colour (in the sample it is white), add a slightly smaller row of colour in a block. Surround this block with the first highlight colour as shown in the photograph. Remember to turn the angle as you work the highlight.

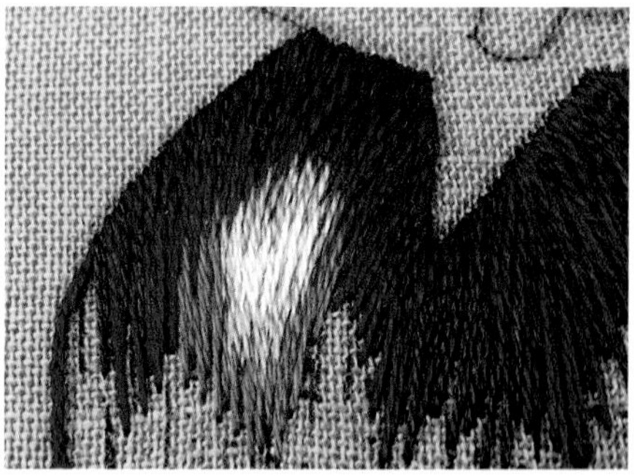

9. Now surround the second colour of your highlight with the darkest colour you have chosen (in the sample it is a dark salmon colour).

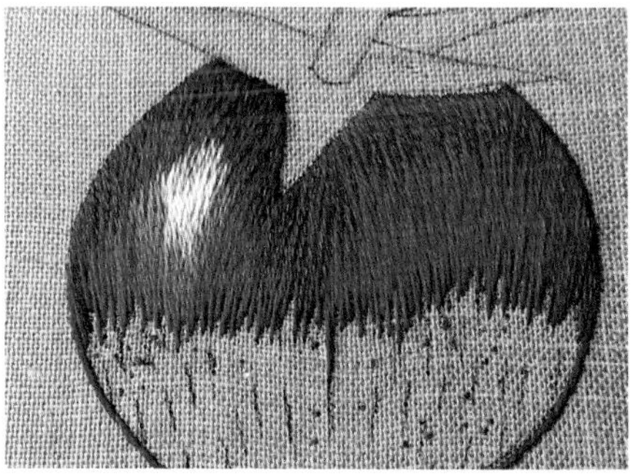

10. Now go back to the outside edge on the right- and left-hand sides and work a few stitches over the split stitch so you reach halfway down to the 'belly' of the tomato, curving the stitches in as you work. Then come back to the centre and fill in with your long and short rows so half of the tomato is worked. It is important that the edge is worked first before you start filling in the middle. This part of the tomato is worked in your medium colours.

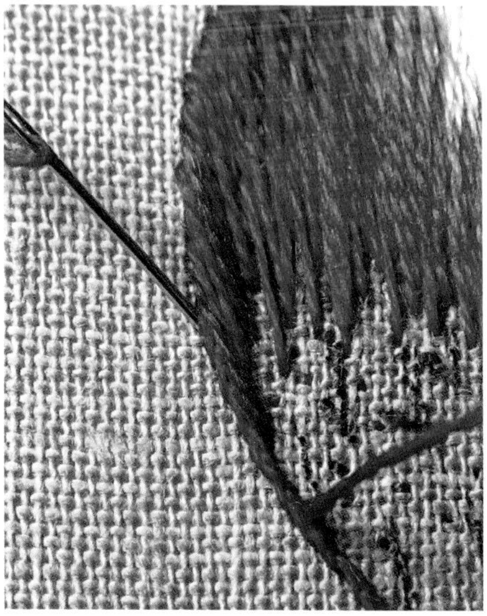

11. At some point towards the bottom edge of the tomato, you will find that your outside row of long and short is the same angle as the split stitch, as shown in the photograph. When you reach this point, bring your needle *up* in the split stitch row and down over the split stitch edge as shown, for one or two stitches each side. This is to get the exact angle needed.

12. OPTION: sometimes it is necessary to add a stitch that is just placed on the outside only, as shown in the photograph. This can help to round off the edge. It *must* be really close to the embroidery; bring your needle up really close to the split stitch edge on the *outside* of the split stitch and then tuck the needle in really close under the split stitch at the top as shown. If you do put a stitch on the outside edge and it sticks out or does not look part of the main embroidery, then take it out and omit this step.

13. This photograph shows one stitch on the outside and how it has helped to curve the edge of the tomato.

14. From now on the edge is covered by coming up in your embroidered rows and going *down* over the split stitch. Notice how the needle really tucks in under the edge. Make sure you repeat this on the other side. Then go to the centre and fill in the middle of the tomato as before.

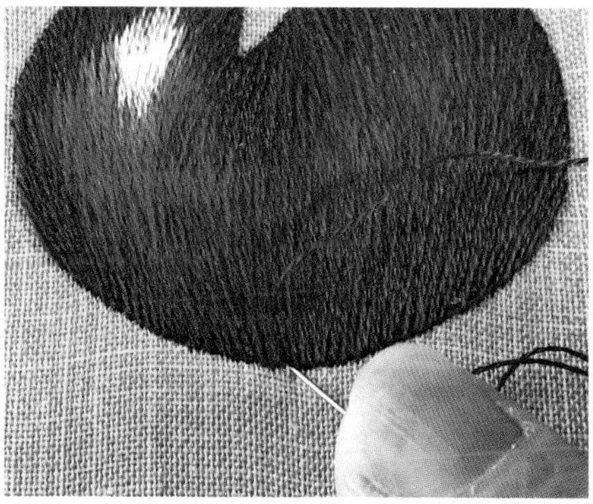

15. As you reach the bottom of the tomato make sure you do not make the stitches longer to reach the edge, they should all be a similar size; in the same way try not to have a bottom row of short stitches. The whole fruit should flow evenly to the bottom. Notice how the very last row uses just the darkest tones.

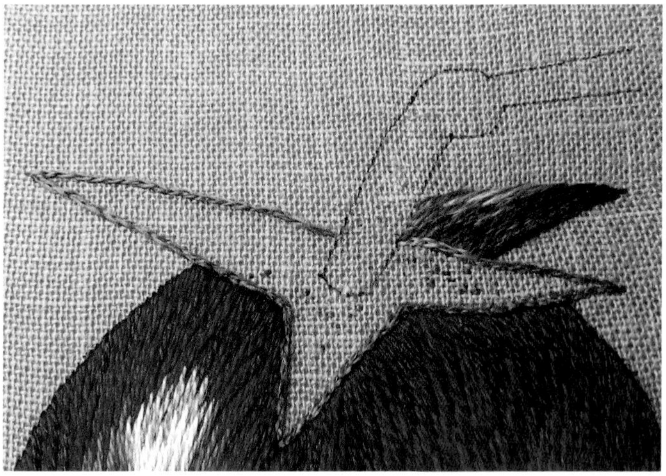

16. The leaves and stem are worked in three stages. Firstly, split stitch and fill in just the very back leaf. It is mostly stitched using the darker greens to create a shadow. Then split stitch the rest of the leaves as shown in the photograph. Make sure the split stitch sits right alongside your tomato stitching.

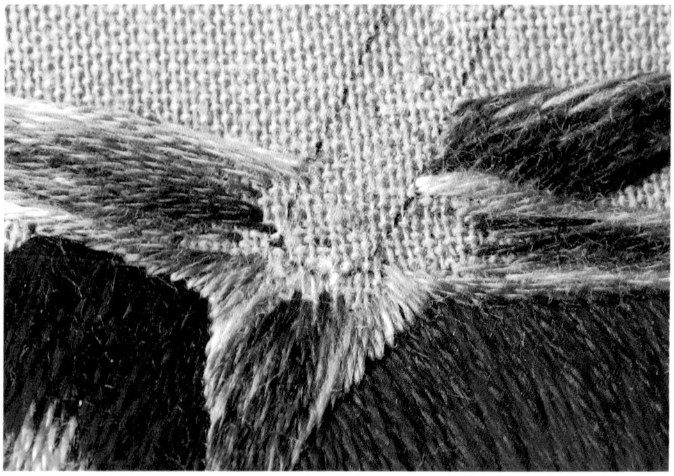

17. Work the leaves by starting at the points and stitching towards the stem. Notice how the stitches get much shorter as the leaves join each other at the centre. The angles change very rapidly.

18. The last row of the leaves has been worked in a light green colour. Try and fill in the last row in one go all the way round, so that the leaves seem to meet flawlessly. You can then split stitch just the very end of the stem in a darker green as shown. Work the stem in rows of long split stitch or long and short following the shading in the main photograph.

Shading In White

Embroidering a white subject is often avoided. If you look at a white flower you may think that all you can see is white. How can you stitch that? If it's all white and there is no other colour, then everything blends together. Wrong! If you really look at a white object there is always a lot more than just white going on.

> **Hints and tips**
>
> If you have a photograph of a flower that is white, then putting it under the photocopier to make it a grey scale picture can help you see where the darkest and lightest areas are.

Again, it is seeing what other colours are present. You will have to bring other colours into your embroidery for a white object. There are usually very few white shades in thread ranges so there is no other option. The pale greys, greens, blues, lilacs and browns can always be brought in to go from white to darker shades. You would usually pick just one or two options. You do not want a multi-coloured white subject. So, your subject could go from white to pale blue to grey for example. It is vital that you use darker tones to give your embroidery a three-dimensional effect. It is no different from using another colour once you have realized what is in your picture.

> **Hints and tips**
>
> When stitching in white or very pale colours, generally make sure your stitching fully covers the background fabric especially if you choose a dark colour. The background fabric will show though any gaps in your embroidery, which will spoil the overall effect.

Shading in white is a challenge, but an interesting one. You need to make sure that your subject stays looking white even though you have other colours in it. You do not want it looking dirty! A white embroidery is a good practice exercise in the use of colour and can look very beautiful.

(left) This sample of an embroidered white tulip has an interesting way of making the highlight and therefore the white stand out by using a different thread. The lightest part has been stitched in a pure white untwisted silk floss which naturally catches the light while the rest of the tulip has been stitched with greens and a thin twisted silk. It is a clever way of using the natural sheen of the thread to do all the hard work of embroidering the shading. (Royal School of Needlework, RSN841)

This range of stranded cottons shows some of the colours chosen for the crocus sample. The transition is very smooth from white through to grey, by picking a very bright, light grey next to the white, then a grey-green to make a smooth jump from grey to green.

The finished crocus illustrates how colour is used to separate each section in a white subject.

Crocus

This crocus is a good example of how other colours must be included in a white subject to show the separation of each section. There is also a small turnover in this flower, so the direction of the stitch is important to leave enough room for two rows to create enough shading top and bottom of the turn.

This sample is worked in one strand of stranded cotton on a textured antique kimono silk.

Materials:

- Fabric with the design transferred, a backing if required, stab stitched if necessary.
- Frame and scissors.
- A range of stranded cottons matched as closely as possible to the picture. The brightest shades are white and then another white or cream and a very light, bright grey – these blend together very smoothly. There is then a mid-tone grey. The two other darker greys have a tinge of green to them to stop the flower looking too 'dirty'. There is also a dull mustard colour, which is used with the greys again to break up any area that is too grey. If you find you have quite a few whites in your stash, then use all of them to help the flower look more natural. Use the brightest whites for the last top petals and any duller white for the background petals. You will also need a range of greens for the stalk and stems, the lighter shades can be used in the base of the petals too as they join into the stem if they blend smoothly.
- Embroidery needle size 10–12.

1. Start on the far-left petal. After split stitching, start at the point with your second lightest white, it may be a cream or a duller white. Work a few stitches down the outside edge and then switch to your very brightest white for quite a few stitches on the outside edge. Notice the angle of the stitches as you work your way down; they are very straight. The needle comes up in the petal and then stretches quite a long way back over the outside edge. Do not do short stitches, do not turn your angle. Stop doing the first row about halfway down your petal as shown.

2. Start your second row. You now use some of your darker tones. Do not use your bright white or cream in this row. You want to give the impression that this part of the petal is in shadow. Notice that this row does curve in slightly. There is a mix of darker tones, lighter near the top bringing in slightly darker ones towards the middle. Notice the differing length of the stitches to stop a hard line forming.

3. Once half the petal has been stitched, go back and continue working your first row over the outside edge. Drop out the bright white now and use slightly darker tones. Then work the inner part of the petal, again using darker tones, and bringing in a little yellow or green towards the bottom. This part of the petal is very narrow. Make sure you split the stitches in the first row when you are stitching the second row. It is very easy to leave this stage out due to the shape of the petal and just fill in the narrow space; really try and split as many outside stitches as you can, otherwise you will have a narrow ridge forming on the edge of the petal.

4. The next petal is the one lying just on top of the first one you stitched. Split stitch carefully, trying to get a smooth edge. Start at the top again with your long and short stitch, using your brightest whites. Notice the angle of the needle as it goes over the edge, also notice the angle of the stitch – it is very straight. Just work the first row halfway down.

5. Work your second row just at the top, with darker tones. The angles are straight in the middle and slightly curved toward the outside on the left. Then finish the outside edge, first row using your brighter white, so it stands out against your previous first petal, as shown in the photograph. If you made this edge darker it would blend in with the first petal as the angles are very similar. Notice the angle changing as it moves down the petal. Continue to make the stitches alternatively long and short, even though they may look as though they are the same length at times.

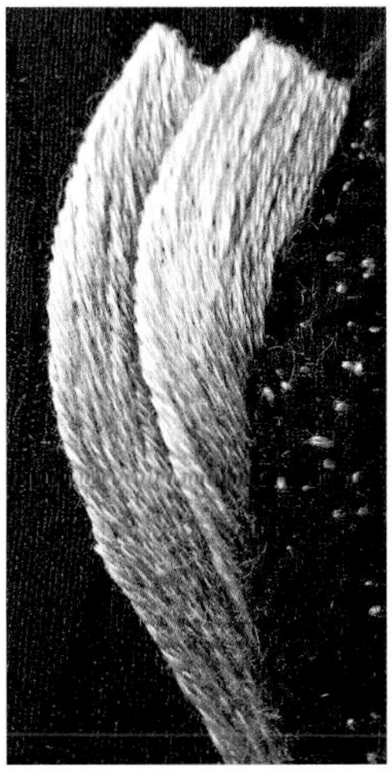

6. Finish the inner part of the petal with your darkest tones, curving the rows of stitches as you work down.

7. The next petal is the one on the right, which has a turnover and another petal sitting on top of it. So, *all* this petal must be in the darker tones. Do not use any brighter whites on this petal. Notice how the first and second rows on this petal have stitches curving in towards the middle. This part of the petal has no split stitch on either side, as other areas surround it.

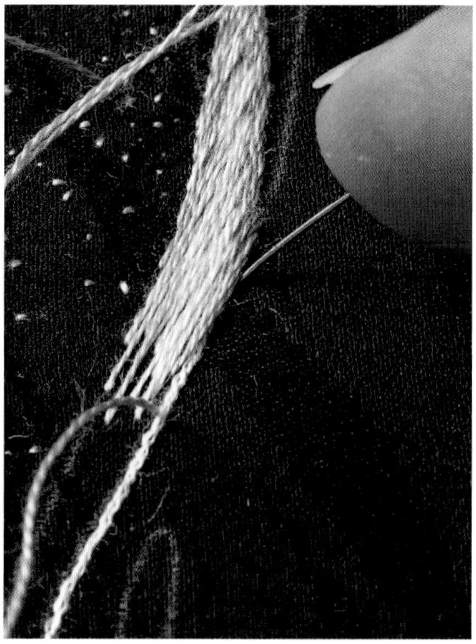

8. As you work down the petal you will have to stop and add a split stitch to the outside edge where it emerges from under the turnover. Notice the angle of the needle as it covers the split stitch and the length of the stitches. The needle comes up very close to the split stitch to get the correct angle. As you work the stitches just below the turnover over the outside split stitch edge, they do not have to be as dark – use slightly lighter shades. This way it will look like the turnover has created a shadow on the upper part of the petal. Finish any remaining space on the second row of this petal in darker shades.

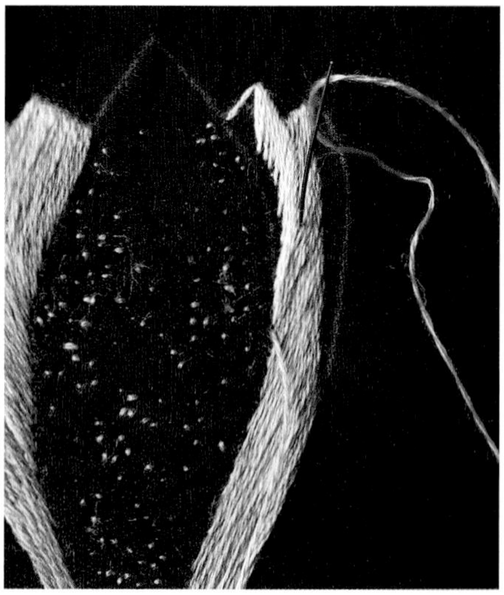

9 Work the next petal on top, split stitch first, then work your first row of stitches in your brightest whites so it stands out from the petal below, as shown. The stitches start straight at the top and then curve as they move down the petal. The second row will be in your darker tones.

10. Next is the turnover. Split stitch completely round this. Start on the left-hand side with long and short stitch in your brightest whites. This is a very narrow part, so almost come to the other side with your stitches.

11. Now do the right-hand side of the turnover with darker shades. Notice how the angle of the stitches gets straighter as they go down the turnover; they are almost vertical at the bottom. Notice the angle of the needle as it fills in the right-hand side of the turnover, it really tucks in against the split stitch. Using darker shades on the right side of the turnover will give the impression it is turning away behind the crocus.

12. Work the centre petal now after split stitching all the way round in a lighter colour; the stitches can be longer as there is more space. Notice how the first row of stitches is in the brightest whites, this will make it stand out against all the other petals. Bring in slightly darker shades towards the centre of the petal, as shown in the main sample photograph at the start.

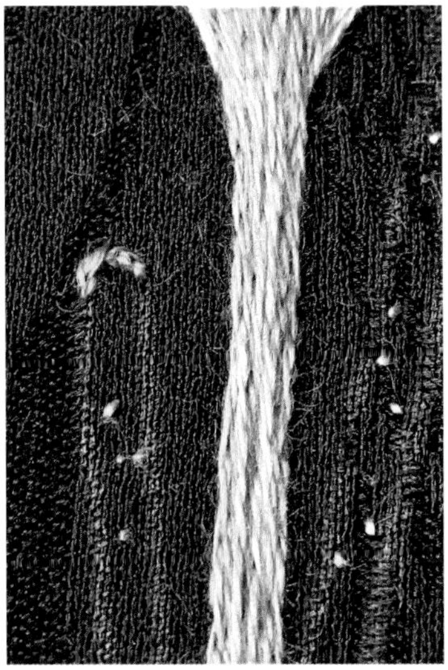

13. Embroider a tiny curved row of split stitch at the top of the leaves to create a neat end. Notice the long, smooth split stitch rows of the stem, no tiny outside split stitch edge needed for leaves or stem.

This embroidery shows how just using white long and short and satin stitch, you can create shadows within your stitching. The stitching has stopped and started in very definite places to create ribs and muscle tone on Saint George and the horse. The direction of all the stitches has been very carefully thought out to accentuate the feeling of movement in the embroidery. (Royal School of Needlework, RSN1812)

LIBERTY
& Co LTD
BY APPOINTMENT
HONI SOIT QUI MAL Y PENSE
INVENTORS AND
MAKERS OF ARTISTIC
WARES & FABRICS
REGENT ST.
LONDON W.1 AND PARIS

CHAPTER 8

HISTORICAL AND CULTURAL STYLES OF THREAD PAINTING

Looking to antique embroideries and other cultures for inspiration is a great way of bringing new ideas to your work. We should not presume there is nothing new to learn from these embroideries. Museums can be a huge resource for sparking different approaches to thread painting and embroidery in general. Even if you do not have access to a museum, many of them offer fantastic photographs online to be able to study their collections in detail.

It can be a very satisfying challenge to try and reproduce a historical piece of embroidery. Researching materials and threads, matching colours and working out the techniques used are very rewarding. Sampling is very important for reproducing antique styles – we may not have access to some of the materials that were once used, so experimenting to try and reproduce an accurate effect is crucial.

Using an antique embroidery as inspiration and trying to bring it up to date, perhaps with a new colourway or more contemporary materials, is also a great way to spark new ideas in your work. Design styles, colour ideas and unusual embroidery techniques that have been forgotten can all be discovered with a close look.

Cultures all over the world have differing styles of thread painting, all of them equally inspiring. This chapter looks at only a small amount of them, picking out just a few details. They all have much more in the way of history and technique than can be included in this book.

OPPOSITE: A pin cushion embroidered on Liberty of London™ fabric in the Leek embroidery style.

CHINESE SILK EMBROIDERY

Many consider Chinese silk thread painting to be the most highly skilled and earliest of all the thread painting styles. Its history goes back many thousands of years and can be traced back as far as c.1600–1027BC; the Shang Dynasty. There are many styles in Chinese embroidery, with differing areas of China developing their own distinct techniques.

Historically Chinese embroidery is known for its large use of symbolism within its designs. Birds, animals, and flowers embroidered into the designs were all associated with religious or mythological beliefs.

Peacocks are known to represent great beauty and dignity. The colours on this just shine out like a real peacock due to the silks used. This peacock embroidery shows the scale carving stitch technique used to reproduce feathers and scales on fish and dragons, for example. (Private collection)

This peony shows the distinctive way in which tiny little spaces are left between the petals, almost giving an outlined effect. Again, the shine on the silk threads is beautiful. Peonies represent wealth and distinction. (Private collection)

Chinese silk thread can be divided up so many times that it almost becomes invisible and is the width of one quarter of a human hair. The colour ranges can contain up to 1,000 colours, which results in the photo realistic effects sometimes produced.

Another amazing technique that has arisen in Chinese embroidery is the two-sided technique, where an embroiderer stitches a design on each side of the fabric at the same time, sometimes having a different colourway or even another design on the reverse. The embroiderer would however work on one side of the fabric only and just keep in mind the design that needs to be stitched on the reverse. When the same colour is needed back and front, one needle is used; when the colour is different back and front, two needles are used. All loose threads and the starting and finishing of threads are completely hidden.

Chinese silk embroidery is still being produced and taught today with traditional designs for small embroideries or huge wall hangings, all exquisitely made. Even French Impressionist paintings are reproduced in silk embroidery.

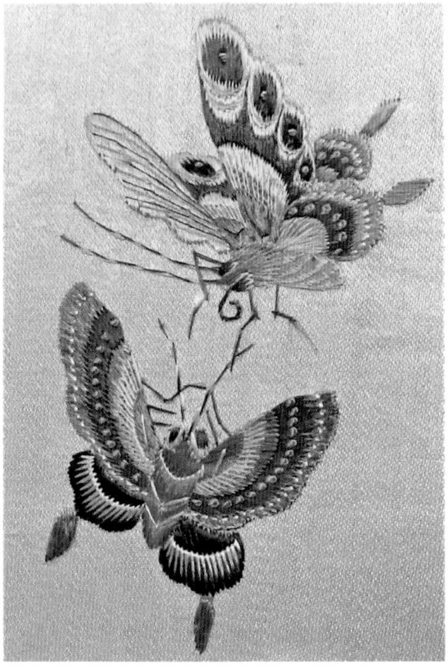

These two fantastically coloured butterflies represent a meeting between two people, a very romantic notion and a common symbol on Chinese embroideries. (Private collection)

These simple embroidered flowers are often seen on Chinese embroideries with leaves surrounding them. They show how just a simple split stitch in two colours can produce stunning results, as flower petals and a centre of knots on a bed of satin stitch finishes it off. (Private collection)

Chinese style flowers

The sample is worked with four strands of very fine silk floss on a flat silk backing. There is no template at the back of the book for this design.

This sample has been embroidered without leaves and is using the flowers in an almost abstract pattern. The background in the photograph is a paper Chinese thread packet.

Materials:

- Silk floss or stranded cotton in three contrasting colours.
- Silk fabric or fabric of your choice in a frame; it would be better to use just one layer of fabric for this design.
- Needle appropriate to how many strands of thread you are using; sometimes a larger-eyed needle will help silk threads glide through the fabric much more easily.
- Scissors.
- Air-disappearing ink pen (if you do not have access to an air-disappearing pen then you will have to transfer the circles using the tacking method).
- Round stencil or template.

1. Using a template or stencil, draw two circles on your fabric with the ink disappearing pen (or tissue tacking method).

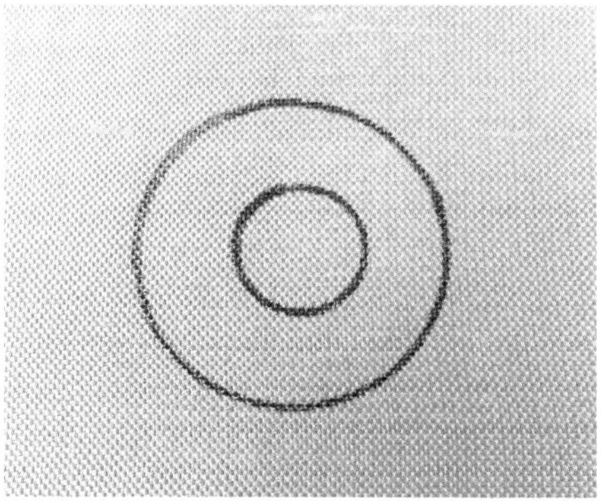

2. The circles need to be one inside the other. The sample circles are 8mm diameter for the smaller inside circle and 18mm diameter for the outer circle. You can make the circles any size you wish. Two differently sized coins for example could be used for your template.
   Try and get the smaller circle placed centrally inside the larger circle as much as you can.

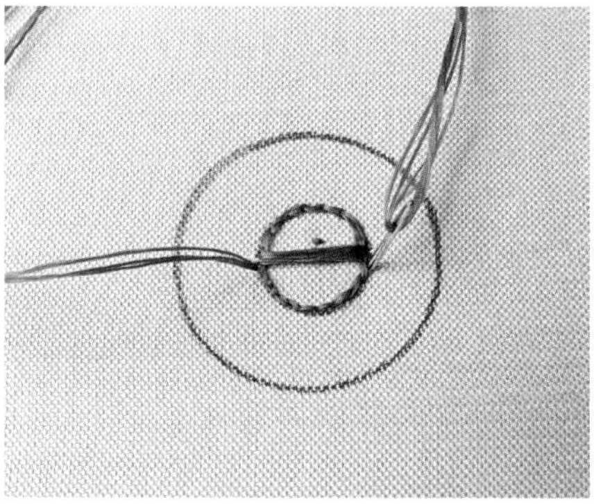

3. Decide on how many strands of thread you are going to use for your stitching. It is better to have a few strands in your needle if you are using fine silk or stranded cotton so that the colours show when the outside petals are stitched. Work a row of small split stitch around the inner circle if you wish (as we are partially covering the outside edge later you could just work satin stitch straight on to the fabric without an outline, this is traditionally how it is stitched) and then stitch satin stitch over the top. The satin stitch can be in any direction you like.

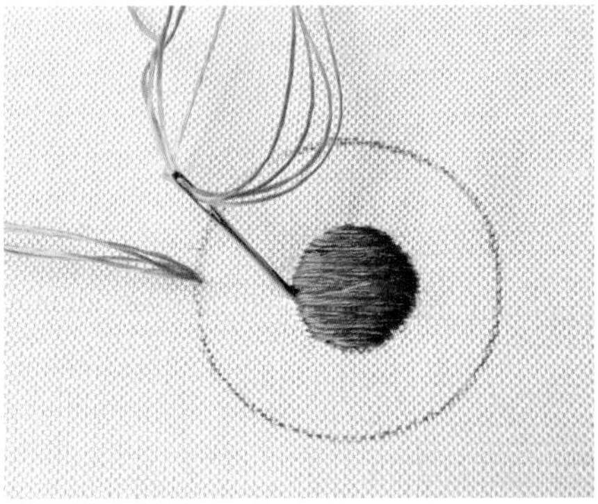

4. It is easier to start your threads for this project now on the reverse of the embroidery, so weave a new colour in from the back and bring your needle up on the outer circle line. Take your needle down on the outside edge of the satin stitch. You can see in the photograph that the needle is sharing the hole with the satin stitch.

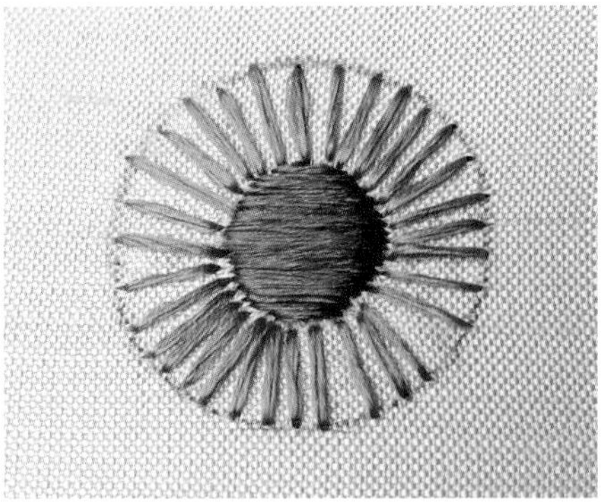

5. Work as many spokes around the circle as you wish; they do not need to be evenly spaced.

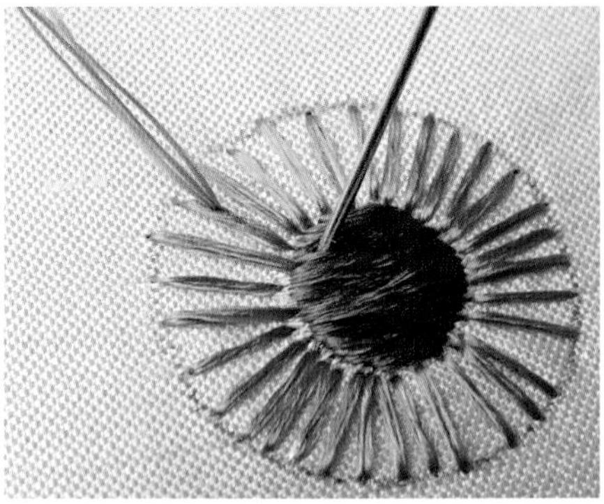

6. Now with your third colour in the needle, come up in one of the spokes splitting the stitch. Where you split them is up to you, for example you could split them halfway, so an even amount of colour is seen or as in the sample, the needle is coming quite a long way up that first stitch so less of the first colour is seen. Take the needle down a little way into the satin stitch.

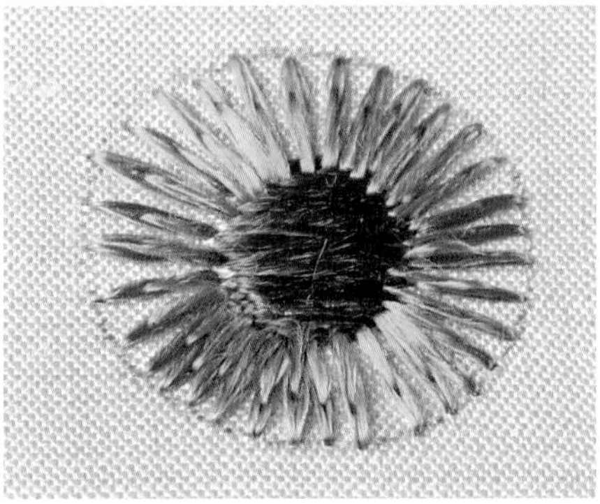

7. This picture shows the dominance of the blue colour as it is covering a lot of the orange.

8. Now add some French knots to the centre of the shape with one of your spoke colours. Be careful you are not disturbing your satin stitch too much.

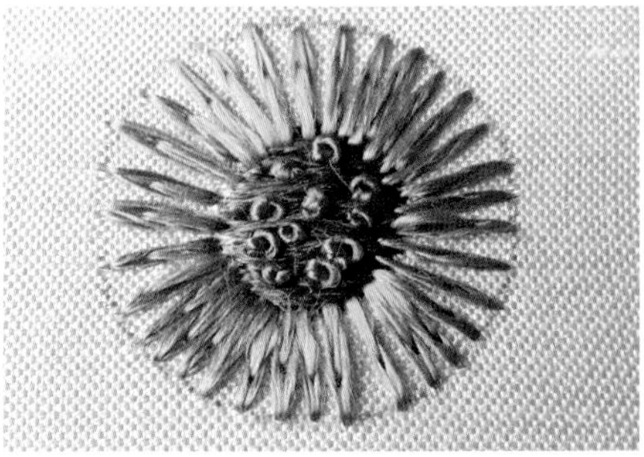

9. Make sure you still have some of the satin stitch colour showing by placing the knots evenly on the satin stitch and not stitching them too close together.

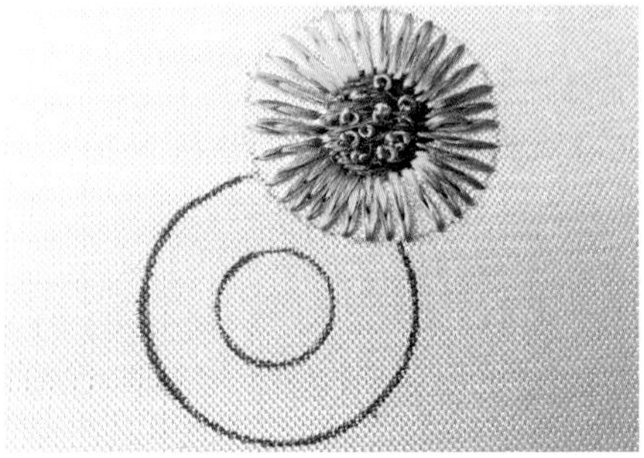

10. Now draw another pair of circles near your first; it can be slightly hidden by the first embroidery or spaced further away. Embroider this circle in the same way – no need to overlap the embroidery, just stitch alongside the first circle.

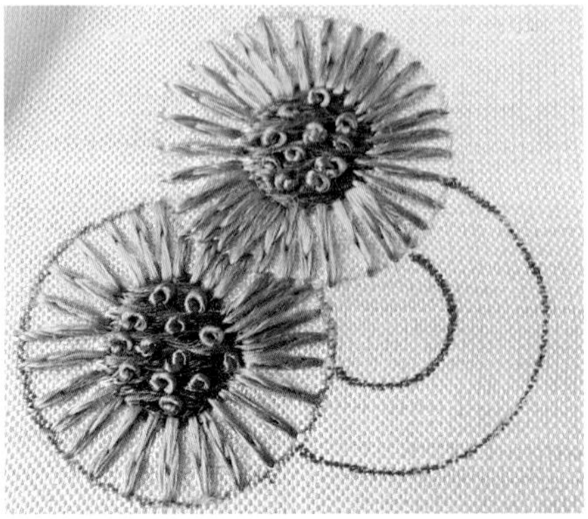

11. Continue in the same way, adding as many circles as you wish to the design.

English Thirteenth- to Fourteenth-Century Opus Anglicanum

Opus Anglicanum is translated as English work. In medieval Europe, it was considered the height of wealth and luxury to possess embroideries made from silk and gold threads in this technique. Many of the surviving pieces are church vestments but originally, they would also be made for royal ceremonies and for the wealthy to adorn their homes. The *Opus Anglicanum* technique is worked on a tiny scale to produce these exquisite embroideries. It would have taken huge teams of professional embroiderers months to produce a piece.

One of the characteristic motifs of *Opus Anglicanum* is the embroidered figures that adorn the embroideries in great quantity. Very often saints with gold halos, they are mostly embroidered in split stitch. The split stitch is tiny and follows the shapes of facial features and folds in their clothes. They have cheeks which spiral round in impossibly small-sized split stitch creating hollows, which themselves create shadows and highlights using just one colour of silk. Some do have remnants of pink in a cheek, but many just rely on one colour.

Surrounding the silk stitching would be gold embroidery, very often covering the background in intricate patterns; this mix of gold and silk embroidery being one of the most beautiful embroidery techniques ever produced.

This angel's face is worked in split stitch in just one colour. The contours that the stitching produces make all the highlights and shadows themselves, so no other colours are needed. The collar of the angel is white silk thread, which has been couched in a diamond pattern in a metallic thread. All the embroidery is original apart from the heavy black outline and the gold twist halo. They have been added later. (Private collection)

A side view of the angel showing just how sculpted the split stitch faces are. The cheek here can really be seen to dip down and the nose can be seen to be padded with parchment or linen thread. (Private collection)

The shading of the figure's clothing is often very limited in its colour palette; however, it relies on the light reflecting from the silk stitches for its suggestion of drapery and movement.

This embroidery shows the very simple colouring used for hair and clothes. The background of the embroidery is fully covered in a couched gold thread in a red diaper pattern. No background fabric is visible; this is a very common feature of *Opus Anglicanum* embroidery. The black outlines, gold twist outlines and star sequin are later additions, but you can just see under the gold twist embroidery on the head of baby Jesus the original embroiderer has used very fine gold thread and curled it into spirals to suggest hair. (Private collection)

Saint Margaret of Antioch

This design of Saint Margaret is adapted from the Pienza Cope, which dates from c.1330–1340. Saint Margaret was an early fourth-century martyr and parts of the Cope show stories from her life. This cope is one of the best-preserved examples of *Opus Anglicanum* and is now in the Diocesan Museum in Pienza, Italy. This sample has been stitched with two strands of fine silk floss on a tightly woven linen.

Materials:

- Very closely woven linen fabric; if you feel that your linen is not closely woven then a thin layer of silk may be placed over the top and you can work through two layers. This is also a traditional way of working *Opus Anglicanum*. The design should be transferred to the fabric and if you are using two layers, stab stitches should be made to secure them.
- Frame and scissors. Fabric needs to be very tight in the frame due to the tight tension in this project.
- Very fine silk floss thread. You will be pulling your stitches really tight in this project so you need to sample your silk first to see how many threads you will need in the needle without it snapping. It is preferable to have the least number of threads possible. You may also use stranded cotton if silk is not available. One flesh colour, one hair colour, eye colour, light peach lip colour, two or three drapery colours – traditionally they are from one colour family and are quite contrasting, black and darkest brown for outlining.
- A metallic thread, hand, or machine.
- Size 10 embroidery/crewel needle.

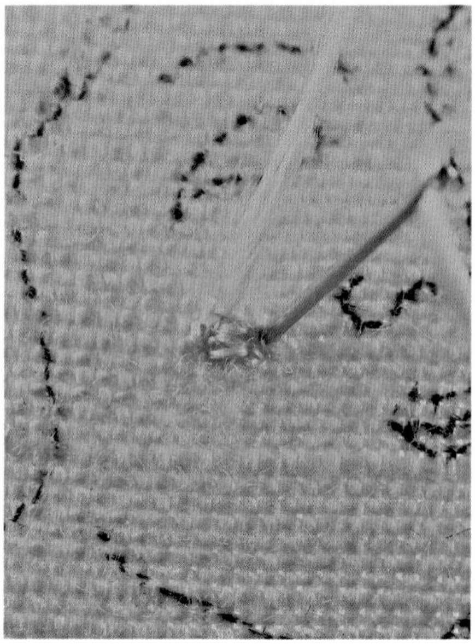

1. The starting point for this embroidery is the middle of the left cheek. If you wish you can make a pin mark in the fabric so you know where to start. The cheek stitches are *very small and tight*. This is vital to achieve the hollowed-out effect. In the sample, the left cheek has been pulled the tightest, the right cheek less so and the chin even less. You can choose how deep you would like the hollows. These tiny stitches are almost impossible to unpick. It would therefore be prudent to practise these spirals on a spare piece of fabric; this will help you get an even circle and see how tight you need to pull your silk thread to get the best effect. The very first stitches are the smallest split stitches you can possibly make. Make a small, tight stab stitch in the middle of the left cheek then come up in this stitch and take the needle down very close beside it, then circle round these stitches with really tiny and tight split stitches. *Pull very tightly.*

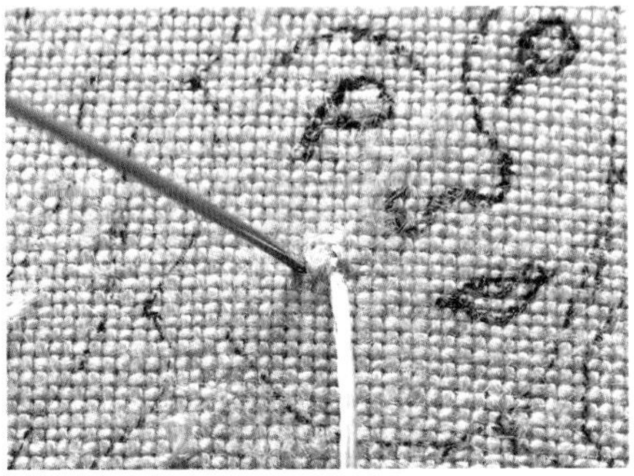

2. Continue circling round with split stitch. It would seem as if there is no hollow forming but do not worry – if the stitches are very tight and small it will appear. Do not be tempted to make your stitches larger as the circle grows. Notice in the picture the cheek is circular, not oval, and there is not a hollowed effect yet.

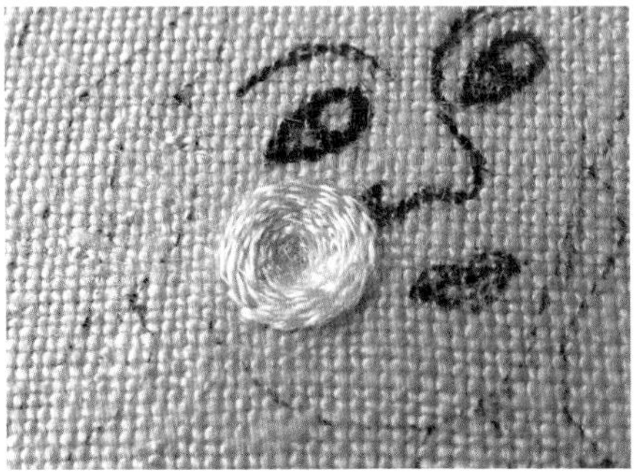

3. As you continue circling round, the first stitches that you embroidered will appear to dip in to the fabric to make a little hollow. This is correct; once you see this happening you can lessen your stitch tension slightly and you can make the stitches a little bit longer. This will be towards the outside of the circle. Stop working the circle when you reach the edge of the nose design line. If your cheek is slightly oval then you may hit the edge of the eye first, this is fine. Regardless, stop when you reach a design line.

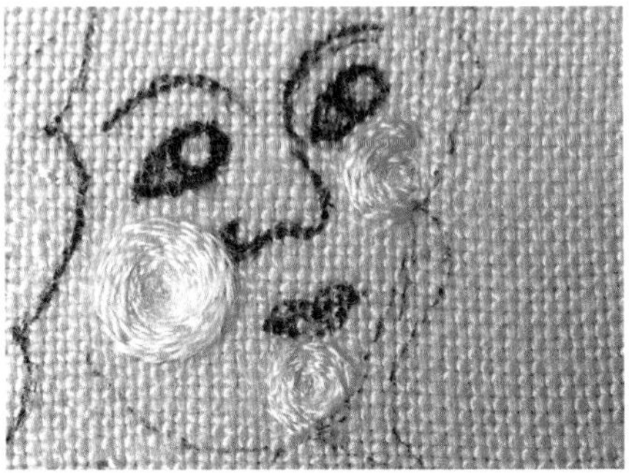

4. Work the right-hand cheek next, as before starting a little to the right of the cheek rather than in the centre. As the cheek is slightly cut off on this side you will not be creating a complete circle; when you reach the far right design line on the edge of the cheek you will then just be stitching the left part of the cheek – it will look like a letter C. Continue working the C shape until you reach the edge of the eye or nose. Remember small, tight split stitches.

Work the chin next in the same way. When you reach the bottom of the chin, continue just to stitch the top part until you reach the lips.

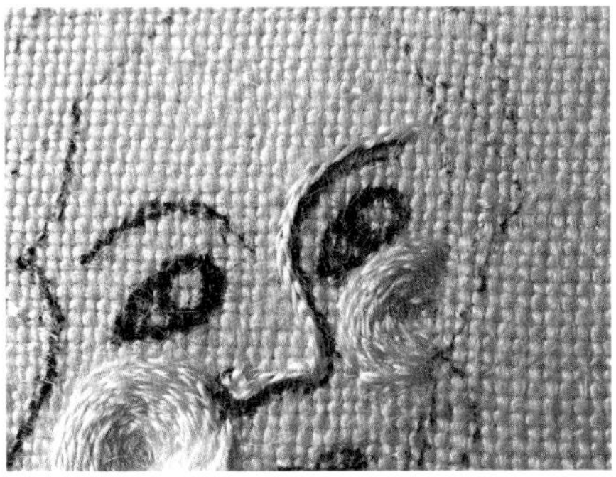

5. Next embroider a row of tiny split stitches from above the right eyebrow down the right side of the nose and curving around the nostrils just inside your drawn line. The stitches at the bottom of the nose will need to be tiny to get a good curved shape. *Do not* stitch over the design line; this line will be covered with a dark outline stitch later.

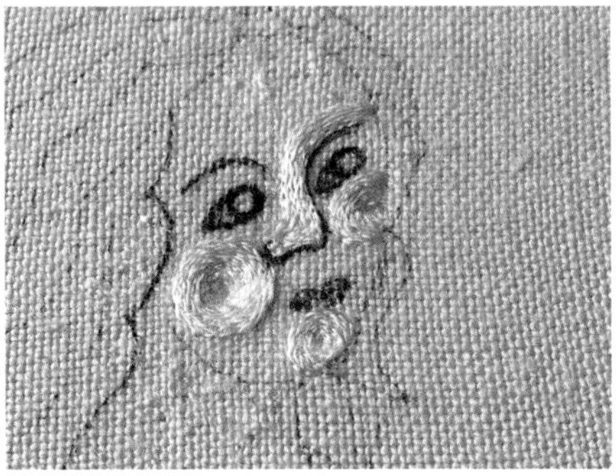

6. Continue to fill the nose in, trying to get tiny curved rows in the base of the nose. These stitches are an even tension; you are not trying to create any hollows in the nose area. Once these stitches have almost reached the other eyebrow, stop.

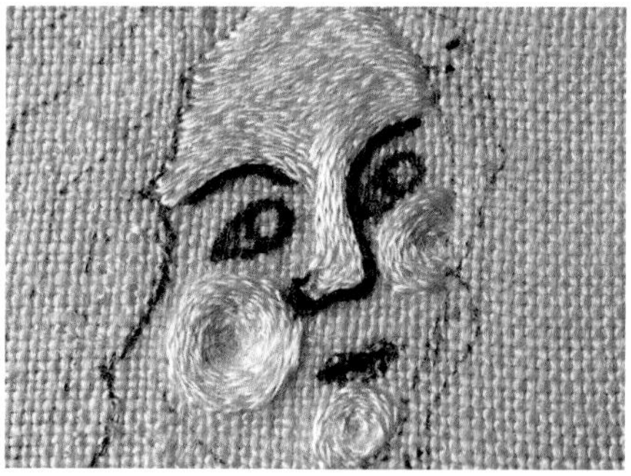

7. Start stitching from the left side now, across the left eyebrow to meet the nose. You will then be able to stitch across the forehead when the two sides are evened out. Keep these stitches an even tension so you get a smooth effect here too. Using your black outline colour, work one split stitch row on the left eyebrow, then the right eyebrow, continuing down the nose and around the nostrils and the centre of the mouth. Do not trail your dark thread over any area of unworked linen or these trailing stitches will come through to the front when you fill in the rest of the face. Secure them to the back of your stitches on the reverse.

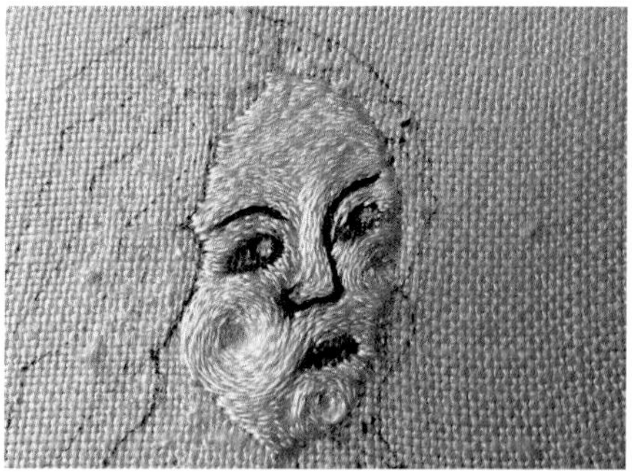

8. Now fill in all the shapes that are left voided in the face. Work directly under the eyebrow first, then fill in towards the eye. Fill in the spaces around the cheeks, working in a circular direction. Then stitch some lines under one cheek going towards the nose and then under the other cheek. Fill in the segment between the cheek and nose and any other spaces that need to be filled. All these stitches can be an even tension to accentuate where the cheeks and chin hollow in. Follow the stitches in the photograph for direction guidance.

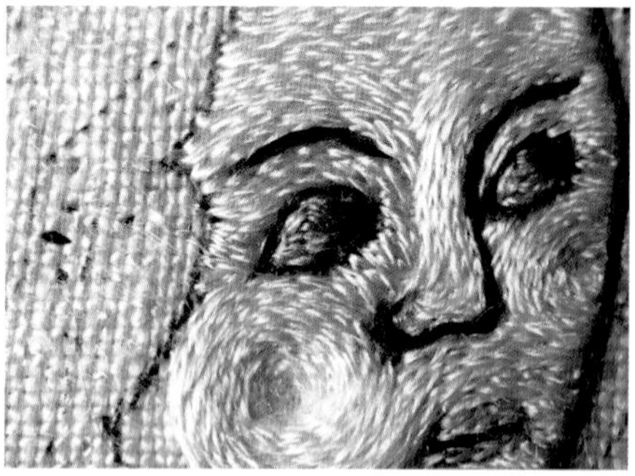

9. To work the eyes, make a row of tiny black satin stitches horizontally for the pupil on the right side of each eye, followed by a row of colour for the iris in the centre of the eye, then a row of white to the left of the eye. Add a row of black split stitch around the eye to create a neat shape. For the lips, stitch one row of split stitch for the bottom lip and two for the top lip in a light peach colour.

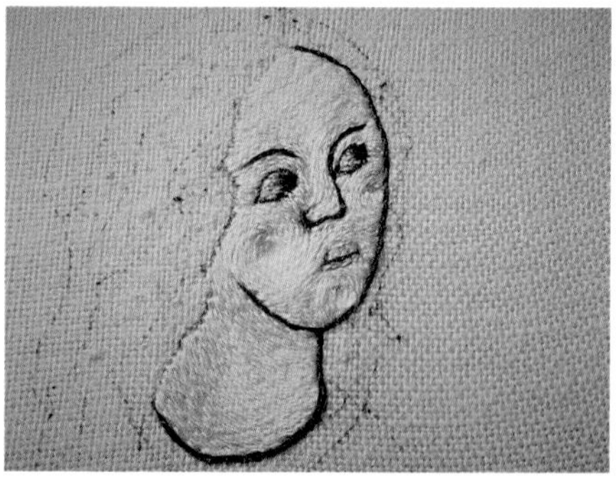

10. Stitch a black split stitch outline around the hairline of the face on the right, around the chin and up toward the cheek, stop just before the hairline on the left side. Now stitch the neck area starting from the top, working down. When you reach the centre of the neck you can pull your stitches a little tighter again to achieve a slight hollow in the neck area. Then outline the neck on the bottom and right side with black.

11. Using the darkest brown or black, outline all the segments of hair with tiny split stitch.

12. Fill the segments of hair with tiny split stitches, following the shapes of the segments to create movement. You can spiral round and round or just work rows up and down. These stitches are all an even tension.

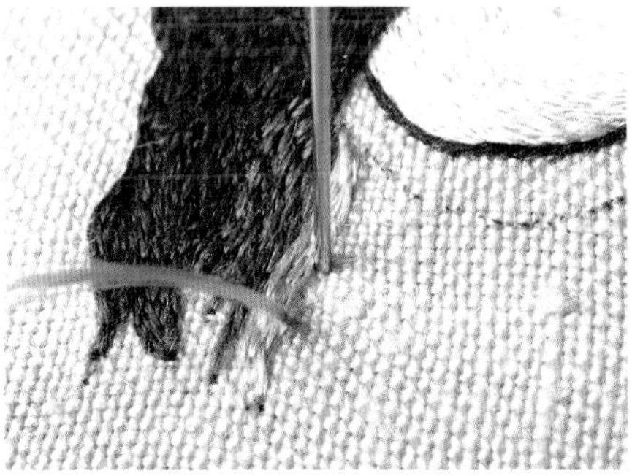

13. Work vertical rows of split stitch in your chosen drapery colours. Draw some lines on the linen if you need to get some direction guidance. Some of the drapery parts can be pulled a little bit tighter to create small dips.

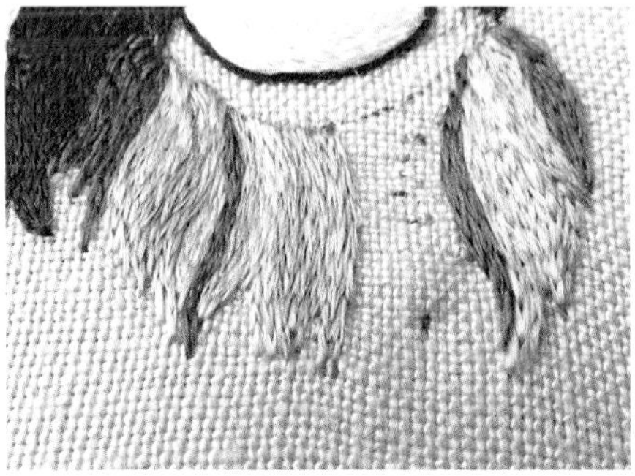

14. Make the width of the rows different; this will give the effect of clothing. There is no order to the colours and they should all be quite contrasting.

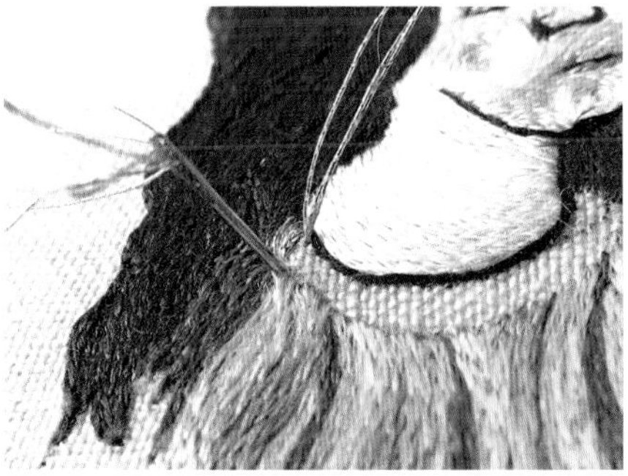

15. Using some metallic thread, work a narrow band of satin stitch around the neckline. This can then have some French knots in a contrasting colour to decorate it on top if you wish. You may have to use a larger needle, such as a number 5 or 7, for the metallic thread if you are having trouble pulling it through the linen. You can then add a dark row of split stitch to the bottom of this collar.

Japanese Silk Embroidery

Embroidery developed in Japan after being brought there from China. Some consider that there is a very formal set of rules to follow in order to acquire the true technique of Japanese embroidery, taught by masters to apprentices. It is thought that Japanese embroidery developed its style as a way of decorating clothing. Since the sixteenth century, Japanese embroidery has commonly been used to decorate silk kimonos.

As with Chinese embroideries, there are many symbolic motifs used in Japanese embroidery. The crane for example, one of the most popular bird motifs, represents longevity.

Japanese embroiderers have specific tools for enabling the silk threads to lie in certain ways. One of these is called a 'stroking needle', which allows complete control over the silk threads while being stitched so they lie flat and smooth.

The silk thread used in Japanese embroidery can be used flat as it is, or can be twisted together to create further thread types. These twisted silks are stronger than the untwisted variety and can create beautiful effects as the light hits the various twists in the silk.

This section of a large panel shows some of the wonderful effects of the Japanese silk as it is embroidered using differing techniques. The bird bodies are embroidered with beautiful shading and have additional outlining on the curved feathers. Some of the longer individual feathers on the front bird have been padded. The brown colouring on the background is where the top surface (cream silk) has worn away. (Royal School of Needlework, RSN1568)

This close-up of the panel shows the raised surface of the flower petals, which are stitched in flat silk floss contrasting and catching the light with the stamens of the petals stitched in a twisted floss. The rust-coloured leaves are also stitched with a twisted floss. (Royal School of Needlework, RSN1568)

Japanese Blossom

The finished blossom displays an undulating effect that enhances the beautiful sheen of the silk floss.

This project is a chance to explore a padding technique called *hira-nikuire*. It gives a raised appearance to some parts of the embroidery and not others, so you can get an undulating effect that enhances the fantastic sheen and light play of the silk floss. To really recreate the true effect of Japanese embroidery, silk threads should be used if possible. Stranded cottons will not have the same effect; rayon floss is an alternative. For the padding it is not necessary to use silk as it will not be seen, so economically a stranded cotton or similar can be used.

This sample has been worked with two strands of thick Japanese silk floss on an antique kimono silk fabric. The padding has been stitched with six strands of stranded cotton.

Materials:

- Thick silk floss thread; if you only have thinner floss then you can increase the strands until you have the desired thickness (see the photographs for guidance on thickness of thread); dark pink, medium pink, light pink or white, yellow and green.
- Fabric with the design transferred. Traditionally this type of embroidery would not be backed with another fabric and would be drum-tight in a small frame. However if you need to, then add a backing fabric and stab stitch the design.
- Chenille needles number 24.
- Stranded cotton or similar for padding in a similar colour to the blossom petal colour.

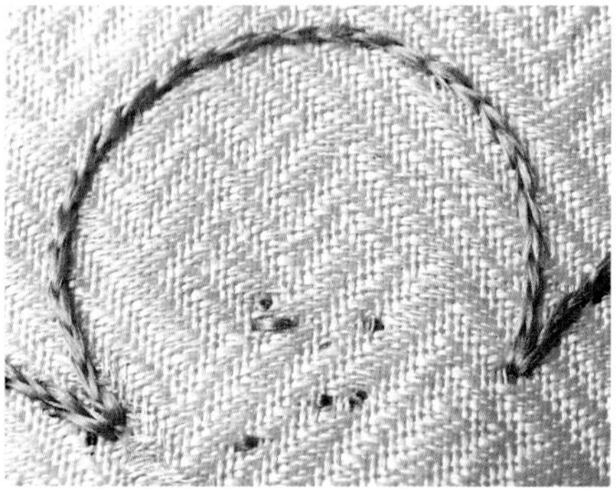

1. Option: Traditionally not all Japanese embroidery is outlined with split stitch. As there are lots of threads in the needle you may find that you can get a neat outline without it, so this step is optional. Split stitch the outside edge of the flower with the darker pink. As the flower is stitched without any indication of one petal on top of another you do not need to outline the individual petals, just all the way around the outside edge as shown, turning direction as the petals join.

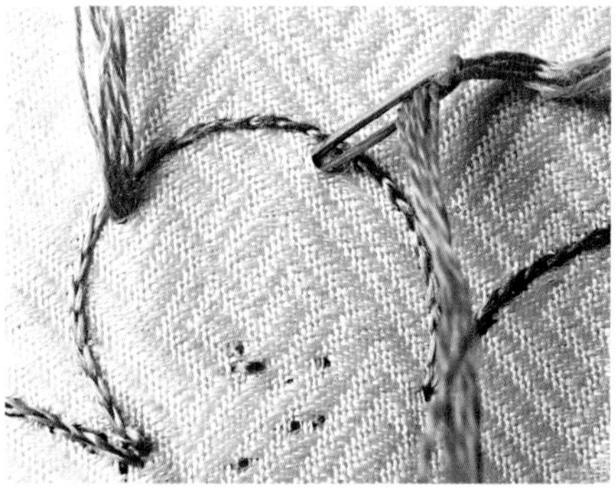

2. Embroider the stems of the blossom first in rows of green split stitch, with as many strands in the needle as you wish. To start the blossom, thread up your needle with six strands of stranded cotton that you have split up individually and then put back together. This will fluff out the threads and create a nicer padding base. Bring your needle up near the top edge of one of the petals as shown and make a stitch across to the other side of the petal. Leave a little space between this stitch and the split stitch/drawn outline. Do not work all the way to the edge. You could add more strands of cotton to the padding for a higher padding effect if you wish.

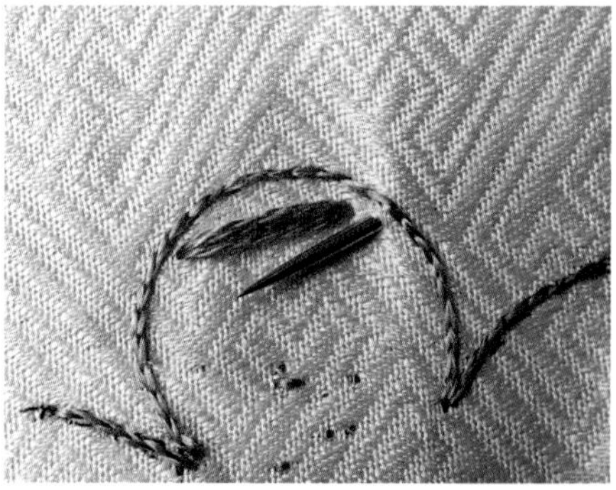

3. Now bring your needle up under the stitch you have just made, slightly to the right of where your needle went down into the fabric, do not cross over to the other side as you would with satin stitch. This means that you use less thread but more importantly you are not padding the back of your work. This technique can be used with any padded satin stitch that you embroider.

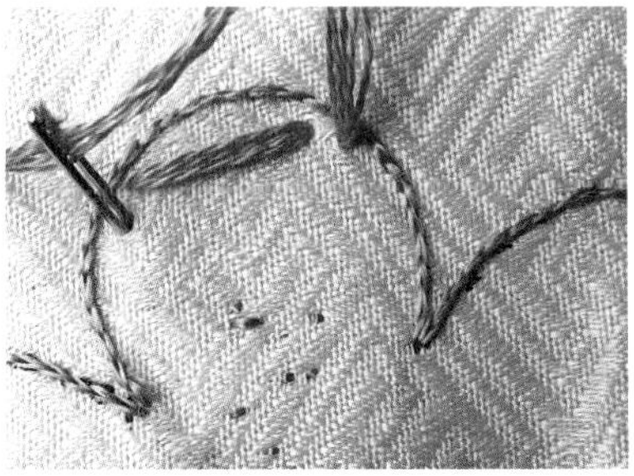

4. Take your needle down on the opposite side below and to the left of your first stitch.

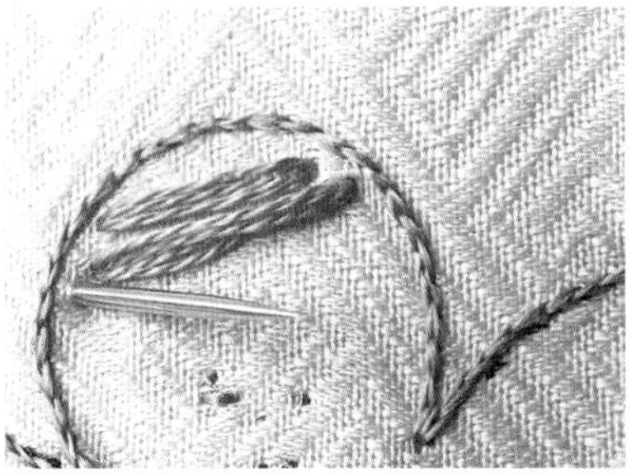

5. Bring your needle up below where you just took your needle down, continuing to pad the top but with no long stitches on the back.

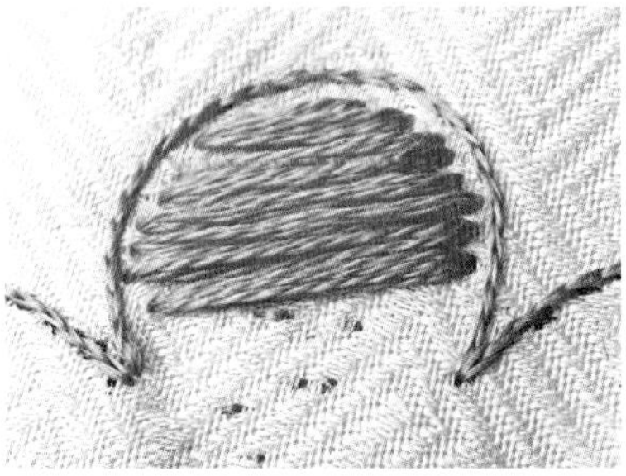

6. Fill the petal up about halfway. This way the padding will graduate from high at the edge, to no padding in the middle. Fill in padding on all the petals this way before you start any long and short stitch.

7. Thread up your chenille needle with your dark pink silk and starting in the centre of one of the petals, work a row of long and short stitch.

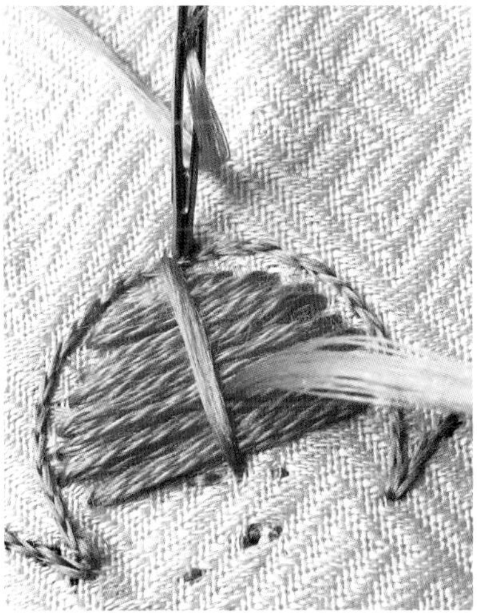

8. If you need to you can go into the padding to create your long and short stitch row, just pretend the padding is not there.

9. Stitch all around the flower as shown in one row of long and short stitch, using your darkest pink.

10. Now using your medium pink, stitch a second row of long and short as shown. Notice there is only a little space left for the third colour. The medium pink colour comes right back into the first row of stitching. Notice the variation of where the needle comes up through the first row.

11. (left) Add a third row of stitching to fill in the space with light pink or white.

Add yellow straight stitches over the top as stamens and place a horizontal stitch at the end; fill in the centre of the flower with a green French knot as shown in the photograph at the start. The little buds are half-padded as before and then stitched with tiny long and short stitches.

This Japanese embroidery sample is stitched on an antique patterned kimono fabric. Some of the motifs have been left unstitched to contrast with the embroidery. The green leaves have long stitches running across them, which are then caught down with a lighter coloured silk for the veins. (Photo and embroidery: Megumi Sorita)

English Seventeenth-Century Jacobean Crewel Work

This style of embroidery grew out of the new fabrics that were being imported into England in the early seventeenth century by the East India Trading Company. They featured exotic creatures and birds such as parrots amongst fantastic foliage, often much out of scale. The embroidery designs were influenced by these fabrics and were made into huge curtains and hangings to bring a taste of the tropical into your home. We are now used to seeing animals and birds from abroad but at the time it would have been the first time many people were aware of these creatures. These designs soon worked their way into domestic embroidery. This type of embroidery is not delicate but very big and bold, so perfect for large domestic furnishings. The designs are stylized and have simple shading, often worked in monochrome with a single, contrasting accent colour.

Tightly twisted wools called 'crewel' were the threads used for these embroideries. They were stitched onto a linen twill, which is a very thick, hardwearing fabric suitable for keeping the cold out of homes. Samuel Pepys documented his wife embroidering her furnishings for months on end for their home.

The colours of the wool were all naturally dyed but were still fantastically bright colours. We look back on some of these original pieces perhaps thinking that they were quite dull, but these natural dyes very often fade giving a muted look to some of the Jacobean crewel work we see today.

Oak Leaf

The oak leaf was a very common design motif, often seen on embroideries, not just crewel work.

The colour inspiration for this project comes from a crewel work leaf in the Royal School of Needlework collection. The darkest colour on the leaf is a very deep navy, which was a very common colour on crewel work of this period. This moves to a dark turquoise, soft green-aqua and finally a bright yellow. The photograph shows that the leaf colour has mostly faded but on the very right edge you can see the amazingly bright yellow and green wool in its original state, where it has been under a seam and therefore protected from the light. The original green wool has lost the yellow dye from it for the most part of the leaf and has faded to a soft blue. Therefore, many antique textiles that we see today have a blue tinge to them where originally there would have been a green colour.

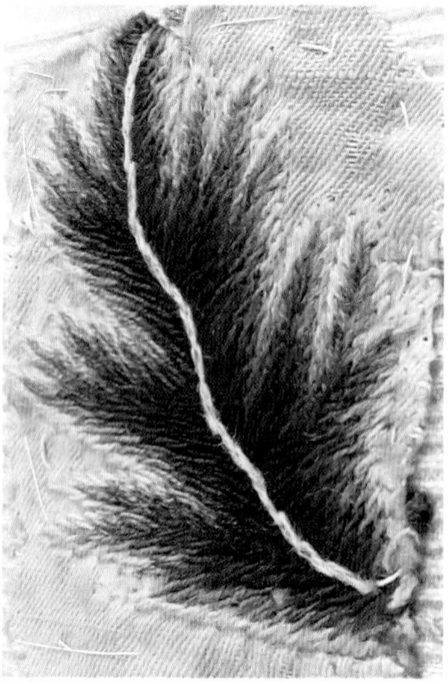

This embroidery is the colour inspiration behind the oak leaf project. Note the brighter colours at the edge where it has been under a seam, protected from exposure to the light. (Royal School of Needlework, Grove Book, page 40)

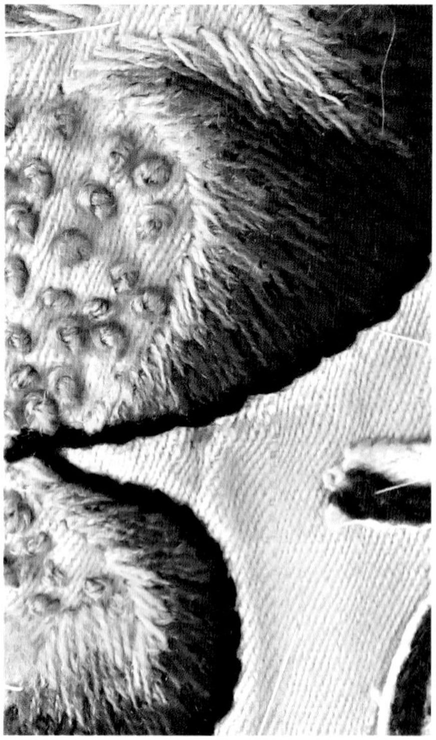

This leaf has the colours stitched in the reverse order and a heavy outline of navy blue. A cluster of huge French knots fills the centre of this leaf. (Royal School of Needlework, Grove Book, page 40)

The sample was worked on traditional diagonal weave linen twill using one strand of very thick wool; it tries to recreate the slightly naïve style worked in the domestic home of the seventeenth century.

Materials:

- Linen twill or other heavyweight fabric with the design transferred; there is no need to support this fabric. Draw the design on with the diagonal lines running bottom left to top right if you are using twill.
- Selection of wools, colours discussed above, for shading the leaf and one contrasting colour for the French knots.
- Frame and scissors.
- Chenille needles appropriate for your wools; it is helpful to use a chenille needle, which makes a large hole as it goes through the twill, to prevent the wool from being damaged as it is pulled through. If you are using fine wools you will want to have quite a few strands in the needle to recreate the chunky look of the original crewel work. Try a sample until you get the desired effect.

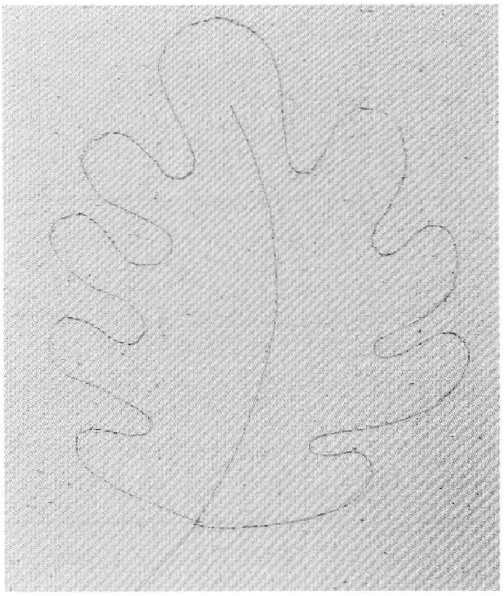

1. The design drawn on the fabric showing the diagonal weave of the linen twill running bottom left to top right.

2. If you wish you may outline your leaf with split stitch. Traditionally, it does not appear that split stitch was used under long and short stitch in crewel work at this time. As the wool is chunky you may find that it is easier to get a neat edge anyway. Start the long and short stitch at the top of the leaf in the darkest colour; if you have not used split stitch make sure your stitches cover your outline.

3. Work a row of long and short stitch down one side of your leaf with just the darkest colour. As there are veins in the leaf you do not need to worry about the stitches all flowing together down the leaf and joining up, they just need to flow together on each side. Mark direction lines on the fabric to help you create the direction you want for your stitches, mark the vein lines on the fabric too if this also helps. See the main picture as a guide.

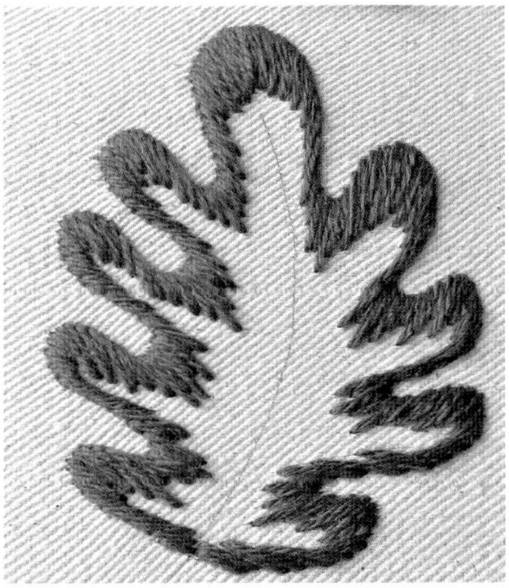

4. The first row of long and short covers the outside edge completely. Where there is space the stitches are longer, such as the tip of the leaf, and where there is a little less room the stitches shorten somewhat to allow space for your additional rows of colours.

5. Now fill in with your second row and second colour of long and short. Notice the stitches are angling towards the side veins of the leaf unless they are in the main section of leaf.

6. Now fill in the spaces left with the next colour and your third row of long and short. Where there is a vein to be stitched, leave a little space for the stem stitch to sit neatly on the fabric rather than sitting on top of your stitching. If you still have spaces after your third row, add a fourth row with either the same or another colour.

7. Notice that the third colour (soft green) only fills in the centre of the leaf, it does not extend down very much to the sides. It has only been stitched where there is room. Notice how the angle of the stitches flows towards a vein. Once the leaf is filled in, add the veins in your next colour using stem stitch. Leave a space for the veins, as it would be very difficult trying to get your needle through such chunky embroidery.

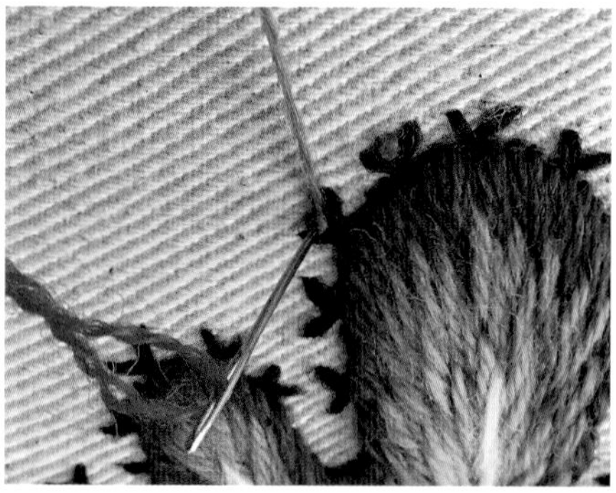

8. Around the outside of the leaf work little 'v's in another colour; they are just two straight stitches. One shade darker than your first row colour is effective. Then using your contrast colour, add a French knot to the centre of each 'v'.

A more contemporary crewel work leaf, this is embroidered in fine crewel work wool on a silk backing. The main stem is embroidered in Portuguese knotted stem stitch.

English Seventeenth-Century Silk Embroidery

Seventeenth-century English thread painting was often stitched by wealthy young ladies to cover wooden caskets, mirror frames, silk cushions and book covers.

It would have been the ultimate show of wealth to stitch with expensive threads such as silk and gold and to show their skill as needlewomen. They would have bought a kit in which the designs were already skilfully drawn on the silk fabric by draughtsmen. Engravings often inspired these designs, showing biblical scenes, classical stories, wild animals such as lions and leopards alongside classic English scenes and flora and fauna. Very often the same images appear on the embroideries, the only difference being the way they have been stitched. Looking at these differences is a wonderful exercise in the great variety of stitches that was used at the time. Your allegiance to the king (or not!) and your religious leanings were also often symbolized within these amazing embroideries.

Silk floss was used for much of the embroidery. Often alternative thread and additions were used; coral, mica, and pearls for example. Silks were mixed with metal thread to create twisted examples that shimmered in the light. Peacock feathers were used for insects to create beautiful shimmering effects. These lengths of feathers were most probably intertwined with other threads for stitching. Sadly, a lot of the peacock feathers used in these embroideries have now perished so we can only see small remains.

This wooden casket has silk embroidery on its outer panels which has sadly faded, but as you open the front doors it reveals beautiful drawers covered in silk floss embroidery showing the original colours as would have been seen in the seventeenth century. The motifs are all commonly seen on caskets of this type and are mostly stitched in long and short and satin stitch with French knot details. (Private collection)

This close-up photograph of a squirrel and hazel tree shows how the embroiderer has changed the direction of the long and short stitch. The squirrel body and hillock are stitched in tapestry shading, while his tail is embroidered in natural shading. The hazel tree has similar treatment. The ground to the right of the tree has been stitched in a knotted stitch to provide texture. (Private collection)

This little monkey on the lid of the casket (hence its faded colours) has extra threads added to its shoulder area. Silk thread has been over twisted into miniature cords and then couched down for texture. The spiral thread seen at the very bottom of the picture is a metal wire, which is wrapped with coloured silk threads and then made into a coil. (Private collection)

Embroidered Book Cover

The sample was stitched on slightly ribbed cream silk, using three strands of finest silk floss, gold coloured metal thread, peacock feathers, gold spangles and a silver colour twisted thread.

This design is an imagined spine from an embroidered book cover. All the motifs come from embroideries of this period. Strawberries were often used to denote love and passion, due to their heart shape and red colour. Cornflowers were symbolic of Christ and heaven; they were often embroidered on to Bibles. Butterflies were thought to represent joy and this motif comes from the embroidered casket above.

Materials:

- Fabric with the design transferred, a backing if required, stab stitched if necessary. You may wish to leave the outlines out or work the motifs horizontally. As the outlines are very straight you may wish to transfer those in the tacking method if you think you not be able to draw straight lines on your fabric.
- Frame and scissors.
- A range of silk floss. Red – three shades, green – four shades, blue – two or three shades, white and your choice of butterfly colours.
- Peacock feathers, or an alternative such as mixed colour metallic machine or hand-stitching thread.
- Gold and silver colour metallic thread; machine or hand-stitching thread are both suitable.
- Gold spangles or sequins.
- Polyester thread for couching to match peacock feathers and gold and silver threads.
- Embroidery needles; size 7–10–12 to be able to fit your silk floss in comfortably, or a fine chenille needle if you prefer.
- Larger needle for additional stitching of French knots and metallic threads.

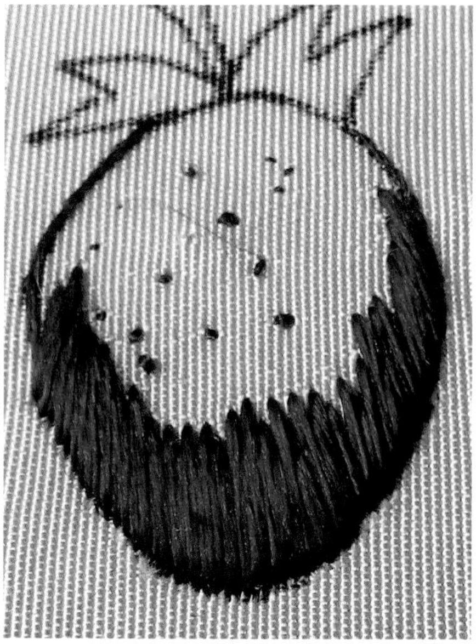

1. Stitch a split stitch around the strawberry in one strand of red. The strawberry is outlined in gold thread at the end but a split stitch will help you get a neat edge allowing you to just have a very fine gold outline. The shading is very stylized on this project so the outside of the strawberry is all worked in a dark red. Start at the bottom and work towards the leaves. Remember the first row comes up in the strawberry and down over the split stitch. If you are using very fine silk floss, put a few strands together in the needle to make a thicker working thread.

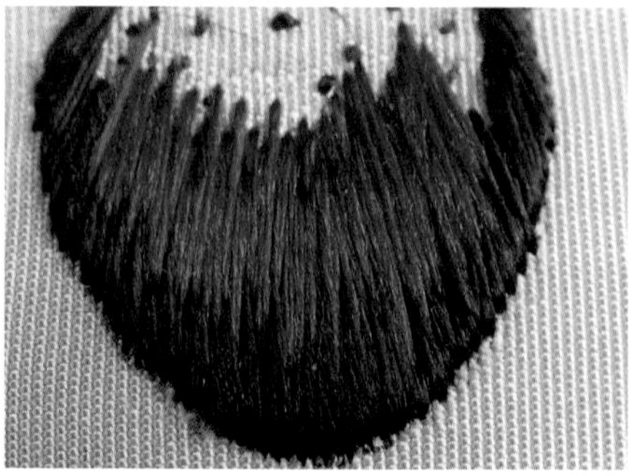

2. Continue to embroider long and short stitch as you work up the strawberry, getting lighter with each row towards the middle.

3. Add a really bright highlight near the top in a very pale red or white and add a darker red underneath the leaves to create a shadow. Embroider the leaves in green long and short stitch and add stem stitch in green for the stem.

6. All of the cornflower is outlined in gold thread. The other motifs have part outlines. You may wish to outline everything, or just parts. The outline is designed to highlight so try to use a fine gold if you can, rather than something heavy and thick. The sample has a gold thread couched down with a polyester thread. The gold thread sits on the silk fabric not on the embroidery, so as not to damage any of the previous stitching. Bring your polyester couching thread up in the silk fabric and down towards your embroidery as shown, so that the gold sits really close to your stitched motif. You will need to work your couching stitches close together around some of the smaller details, such as the curved outlines of the cornflower and butterfly. To start and finish your metallic thread it needs to be attached on the reverse of the work securely by weaving it through some of your previous embroidery.

4. To embroider the pips, you will need to use a gold metallic thread. A larger needle is useful here so the metal does not get snagged as it goes through the silk embroidery. Use as many strands of thread as you think you need for the pips to show. If the thread is very fine it will fall through the stitches and not show. Come up in the embroidery with a straight vertical angle with the needle, so as not to damage the embroidery or thread. When you take the needle down again try to take it at a slightly different angle to the red stitching as shown. This will help the gold to sit on top and not disappear through your previous embroidery.

7. Embroider the wings of your butterfly in your chosen colours leaving the circles voided (no need for split stitch around voids). Work from the outside of the wings towards the body. No split stitch is needed.

5. Embroider the cornflower from dark blue outside edges to medium to light blue or white in the third row. Embroider a cluster of French knots in the centre of the flower. Using a larger needle will give you large French knots. Remember, just once around the needle. Add the base of the flower in green long and short stitch and a stem in split stitch, or stem stitch if you prefer.

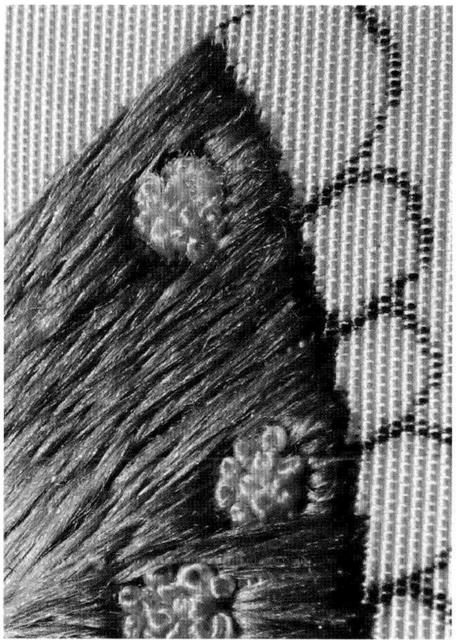

8. Fill the voided circles with French knots in a contrasting colour. Fill the body with long and short stitch, and the head with satin stitch.

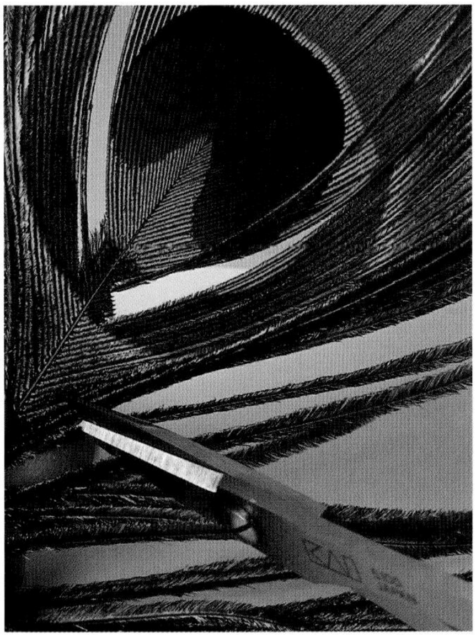

9. If you are using real peacock feathers you will need to cut lengths of 'thread' from them. Use a sharp pair of small scissors and try and cut long lengths from the eye of the feather. You may prefer to get bluer or more copper colour in your embroidery, so be strategic in your cutting. The longer the thread, the less joining you will have to do on your embroidery.

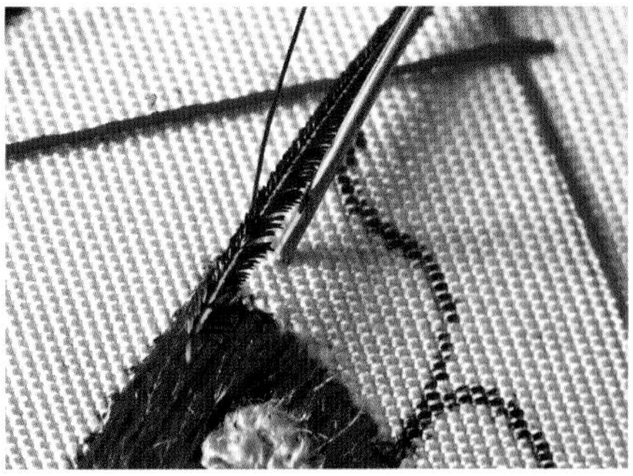

10. Lay a piece of feather on your butterfly wing and couch over it with a matching polyester thread from the embroidered side towards the outside edge. Try and get the shiny side to sit uppermost; it may try and twist the opposite way to how you want it to sit. The stitches need to be small and tight otherwise the feather will move. If you are using metallic thread you can stitch it in the same way or use satin stitch for a similar effect.

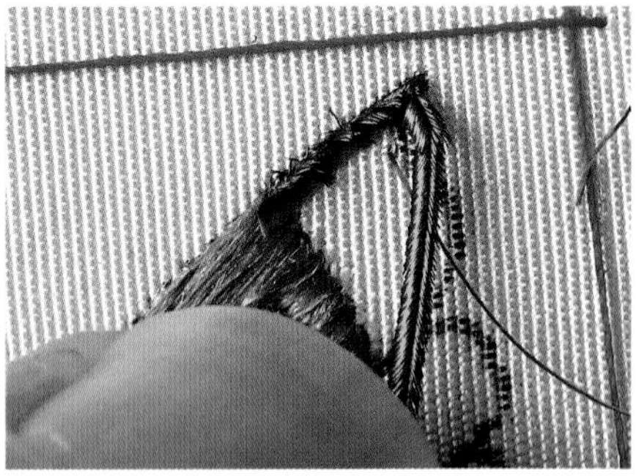

11. When you reach the edge of the wing you will need to bend the feather round. Make sure you have a couching stitch on the outline and hold the thread tightly with one hand. With the other hand, bend the feather so it now faces the opposite way and continue couching back and forth. The rows need to be very close together.

12. When you are reaching the end of the feather length, you can just cut it to fit the shape and start a new piece.

13. The antennae on the head have just one area of stitching securing the feather to the fabric so that the ends are 'free'. You may wish to stitch a few stitches on top of one another so it is secure. Cut the feather to the desired length. Be careful of this part of your embroidery, as it will be very delicate.

14. To finish, stitch gold thread around any parts of the silk embroidery you wish to highlight. Embroider gold spangles or sequins over the background with two stitches to secure them and outline the three motifs in silver couching if wished.

Embroidered Silk Costume of the Eighteenth- and Early Nineteenth-Century France and England

Formal clothing of the eighteenth century shows the most fantastic elaborate embroidery – and it is not just reserved for the ladies. Men's coats and waistcoats were stitched in sumptuous silk threads with spangle decoration. The fabrics were often silk and sometimes velvet. Thread painting on velvet creates its own problems due to the delicate silk embroidery being lost in the pile of the velvet; this was overcome by placing a layer of silk gauze on top of the velvet in which the design had been transferred and so stitching through two layers of fabric. This gauze was then cut away after the stitching had been completed. The embroidery was therefore slightly in relief and did not get lost in the pile of the velvet.

The designs on these costumes were almost always floral. The flowers were seen to almost grow up the body of the wearer. The garden was truly an inspiration.

These elaborate clothes, reserved for royalty and the very rich, were made in professional embroidery workshops. Thus, the highest quality stitching would be guaranteed and the logistics of embroidering such large pieces of fabric (which needed to be tight on the frames) was solved.

This panel of fabric is a remarkable survivor from the late eighteenth- or early nineteenth-century. It shows silk floss embroidery stitched on silk satin fabric for a waistcoat before it has been cut out and assembled into a garment. The stand-up collar parts and pocket flaps are also stitched, and the little green stars dotted around would have been made into buttons. (Royal School of Needlework, RSN174)

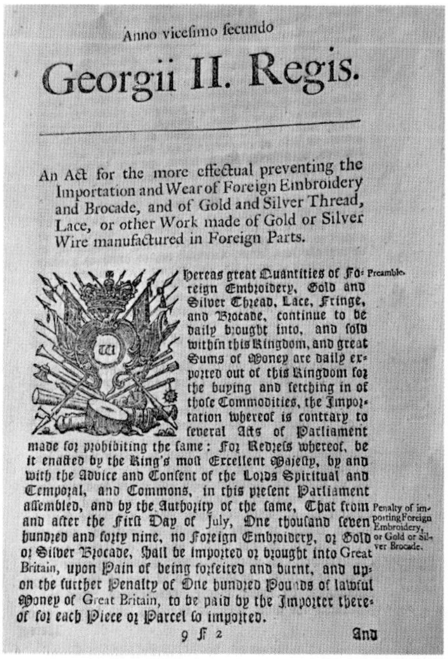

Anno vicesimo secundo

Georgii II. Regis.

An Act for the more effectual preventing the Importation and Wear of Foreign Embroidery and Brocade, and of Gold and Silver Thread, Lace, or other Work made of Gold or Silver Wire manufactured in Foreign Parts.

Whereas great Quantities of Foreign Embroidery, Gold and Silver Thread, Lace, Fringe, and Brocade, continue to be daily brought into, and sold within this Kingdom, and great Sums of Money are daily exported out of this Kingdom for the buying and fetching in of those Commodities, the Importation whereof is contrary to several Acts of Parliament made for prohibiting the same: For Redress whereof, be it enacted by the King's most Excellent Majesty, by and with the Advice and Consent of the Lords Spiritual and Temporal, and Commons, in this present Parliament assembled, and by the Authority of the same, That from and after the First Day of July, One thousand seven hundred and forty nine, no Foreign Embroidery, or Gold or Silver Brocade, shall be imported or brought into Great Britain, upon Pain of being forfeited and burnt, and upon the further Penalty of One hundred Pounds of lawful Money of Great Britain, to be paid by the Importer thereof for each Piece or Parcel so imported. — Preamble. — Penalty of importing Foreign Embroidery, or Gold or Silver Brocade.

9 F 2 And

This Act of Parliament dated 1749 details the consequences of importing these types of fashionable embroideries, brocades, threads and so on into Great Britain as it was seen that too much money was being spent abroad and not enough been spent in British workshops. Anyone caught would have their embroideries surrendered, burnt and be given a fine of £100! (Private collection)

This photograph from another waistcoat shows the detailed patterns that were often used in addition to the floral embroideries. There is a satin stitched band on the very edge of the garment and then a series of embroidered circles with a French knot between them. An embroidered button with colours tying in to the main waistcoat finishes off this elaborate piece of costume. (Royal School of Needlework, RSN529)

Embroidered Dandelion with Sequin Relief

The original on which this sample was based was possibly intended for a waistcoat or men's coat.

This embroidered dandelion head is adapted from a silk embroidery in a sample book from the Metropolitan Museum of Art in New York, possibly originally intended for a waistcoat or men's coat. It was originally stitched on velvet but for ease, the sample has been worked on silk.

The sample has been stitched on flat silk fabric with four stands of fine silk floss. The large central sequin is 8mm, the smaller sequins are 4mm.

There is no template for this design in this book as it is just a circle, with a line for a stem.

Materials:

- Fabric with the design transferred, backing if required and stab stitched if needed.
- Frame and scissors.
- Silk threads or stranded cottons in white and green.
- Sequins in sizes of your choice, two different sizes if possible. Try and match your sequin colour to a similar colour of your thread. Sequins with a matt surface rather than shiny are preferable.
- Chenille or embroidery needle to fit your silk threads. You may want a chenille needle if you are using silk.

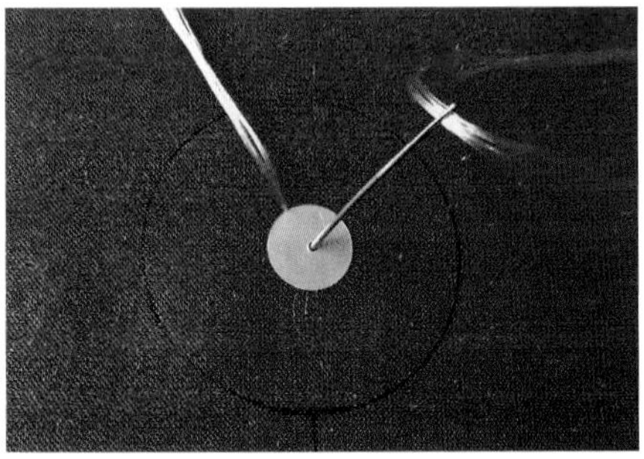

1. If you have two sizes of sequins, stitch a large one in the centre of your circle. Use just four stitches to secure. It needs to be firmly attached but you need to be able to angle your needle under the sequin later so allow a little movement if possible.

2. Now stitch smaller sequins randomly around the central sequin. Use only two stitches to secure the sequins and follow the approximate angle of fastening stitch as shown in the photograph. These fastening stitches will then not be in the way of the long and short stitch later. Do not crowd too many sequins into your dandelion. If they are placed very close together, the stitches between them will be very short and messy.

3. Using your white silk thread, bring your needle up a little way outside of your design line and push it under a sequin as shown. It does not matter where you start around the circle. The stitch direction is like the markings on a clock so if you want to mark lines on your fabric, do so with this in mind to help you.

4. For your next stitch come a little way out from where your first stitch started as shown and again push the needle under the sequin. Continue in this way all around the circle.

5. This shows the first row completed all the way around the circle. If there is no sequin placed as you bring your needle into the dandelion flower, then extend your stitch further into the circle as shown. Make sure you extend the stitches away from the outside design line randomly to give a spiky dandelion effect. Make sure there are no spaces between the stitches.

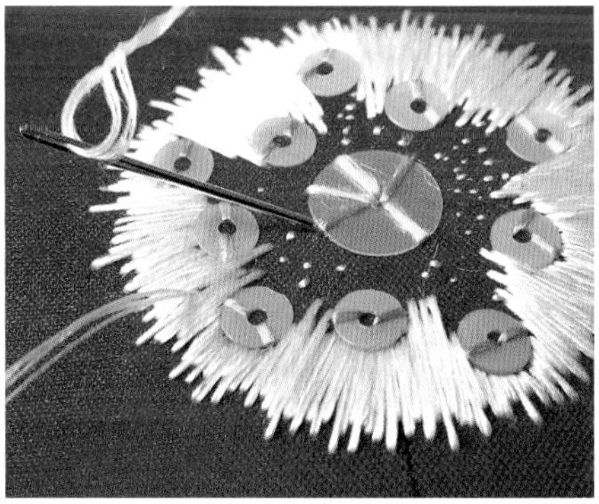

6. Start the second row of long and short stitch by coming up in the first row and taking your needle under the central circle as shown.

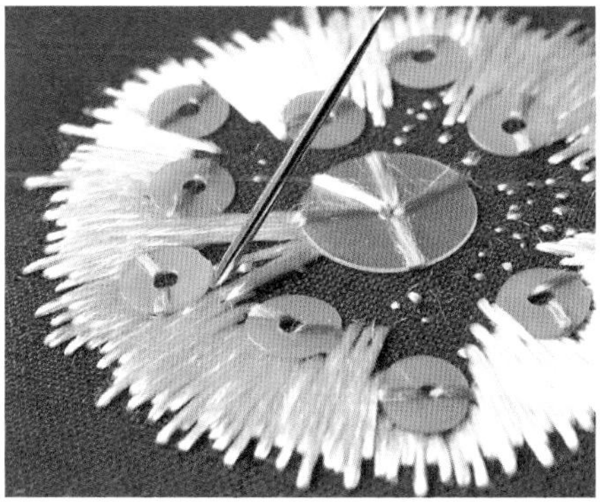

7. To fill in the space between an outside sequin and the central sequin, bring your needle up at an angle from an outside sequin as shown.

8. Then angle the needle underneath the central sequin as before.

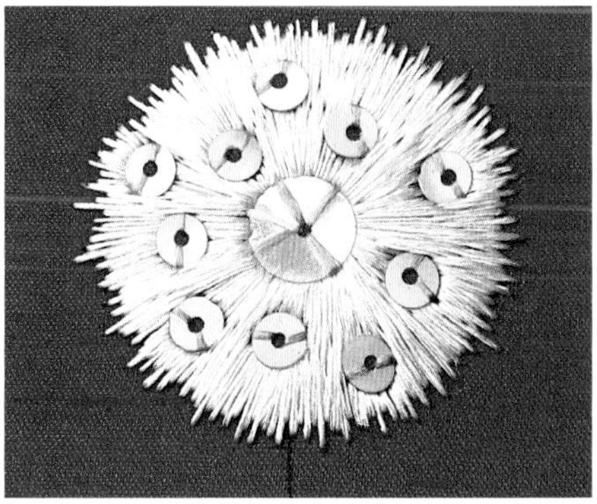

9. This shows the second row fully completed. You want to try and make sure that as little background fabric as possible shows around the sequins.

10. Now bring your needle up on the outer edge of a sequin, angling the needle as shown.

11. (left) Take the needle down over the sequin following the same stitch direction as the long and short stitch and angling it under the sequin. Continue covering all the sequins in this way.

Embroider the stems in two shades of green stem stitch and add clusters of green straight stitches in varying lengths for the leaves, as shown in the sample photograph. The sample has added handmade buttons and edging to give an idea to what it may have looked like as a stitched garment.

LEEK EMBROIDERY, LATE NINETEENTH-CENTURY ENGLAND

Leek embroidery is named after the town of Leek in Staffordshire. Thomas Wardle, a resident of Leek, was an importer of silk from India, which he then dyed and printed. Together with William Morris, he discovered how to dye these imported silks with vegetable and mineral pigments to great success. He could produce skeins of silk thread for embroidery in beautiful colours that were a welcome relief from the harshly coloured chemically dyed wools that were being used for domestic needlework at the time.

Thomas's wife Elizabeth, already a very talented embroiderer, founded the Leek Embroidery Society along with her husband. They produced embroideries using Thomas's silk fabrics and threads exclusively.

Very often a design was printed on to the silk and then 'coloured in' with long and short stitches; parts of the design were then outlined with stem stitch or metal thread. The silk thread was twisted and gave a beautiful textured appearance to the embroidery.

The society produced kits with which you could stitch these designs yourself or you could buy finished items in fancy London department stores such as Liberty™.

This angel's face was embroidered by the Leek Embroidery society on to a stole. The fabric is completely covered in embroidery so there is no backing fabric to be seen. This detail shows the very subtle colours of silk thread that were used in the face embroidery. The beauty of these silk threads is shown here as the face is almost glowing. (Stole, All Saints Church, Leek; photo: Victoria Jervis)

Richard Norman Shaw designed this beautiful altar frontal for All Saints Church in Leek in 1887. He was also the architect for the church itself. The backing fabrics are both plain and printed velvets. The silk and gold embroidery features olives, pomegranates, honeysuckle and sunflowers (sunflowers being a popular motif in art at this time). The Leek Embroidery Society stitched this frontal. (High Green Altar Frontal, All Saints Church, Leek; photo: Victoria Jervis)

POPPY DESIGN ON LIBERTY™ FABRIC

Choose your fabric according to what colour threads you want to use, to make sure that your embroidery shows up clearly against it.

The fabric chosen for this embroidery project is a grey monotone colour with a bold repeating pattern and strong outlines. This type of fabric gives the opportunity to have any colour range for the embroidery and to use the outlines to enhance the finished design. Any printed fabric can of course be stitched on but you want the embroidery to show up clearly. If you choose a fabric that has many colours printed on it already, then your embroidery may disappear into the background. Think about the colour ranges you want

Using a fabric with bold outlines such as this enables you to incorporate the pattern into your design.

to use in your stitching and how they will enhance the colours already printed on the fabric.

You may decide you want to leave parts of the design on the fabric unstitched. Traditionally the foremost parts of the design were filled in fully and then other parts less so. Using differing amounts of thread in the needle is also a very subtle way to enhance this. Leaving the very background of the printed patterns unstitched gives a great contrast to the slightly raised effect of the embroidery.

Beads, metal threads and other stitches can also be added to create interest. Plan your project first before stitching; this way you can think about how much or how little of the print you want to cover.

The sample was stitched using a cotton Liberty™ lawn fabric as shown, two-ply twisted silk floss and a silver metallic thread. One and two strands of silk were used in the needle.

Materials:

- A patterned fabric, suggestions for style discussed above, backed and stab stitched if necessary. Use the ideas in the project below for your chosen fabric.
- A selection of threads in colours to enhance your fabric, traditionally twisted silks were used but cotton perlé or a twisted rayon could be used if you wish to have a traditional effect, otherwise any thread can be used.
- Frame and scissors.
- Needles suitable for your chosen threads.

1. It is useful for this project to stitch the areas that you want to mostly cover with embroidery first. For the sample that means the main poppy flower and its corresponding leaves. You may wish to use split stitch if you would like a smooth edge for any parts of the design but in this case the sample has been given spiky leaves even though the outline is rounded. As the leaves are in the foreground of the design, two strands have been used in the needle. The outline of the leaf has been used as a guide to stitch one row of long and short stitch in an uneven line. Be careful when embroidering with a twisted thread as it can sometimes untwist while stitching. If it does untwist you do not have to start a new thread, just twist the thread up again in the right direction and continue working.

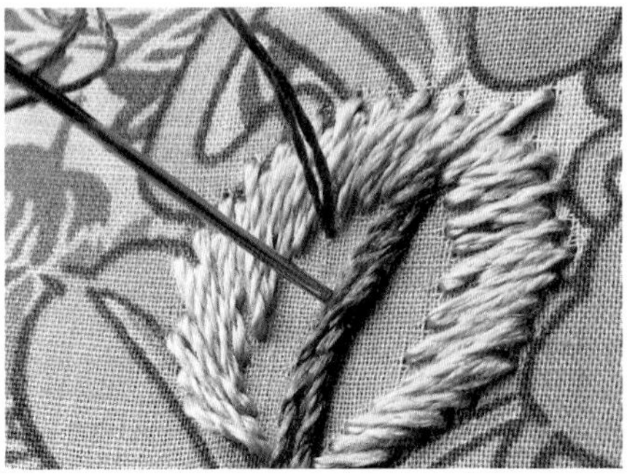

2. The centre veins have been embroidered using two rows of stem stitch. To add interest, the leaf has been given veins even though none are printed on the fabric. These are just simple straight stitches.

3. The poppy, being the foremost and central part of the design, is fully filled with embroidery. Using the outline as a guide, stitch the outside edge of each petal with a row of long and short stitch; add a split stitch edge if you need it to obtain a neat edge.

4. The turnovers in the petals have been ignored and stitched over. Remember if there is something on the fabric you do not like or think it will be difficult to make work in your embroidery, you can of course stitch over it!!

5. A second row of long and short has been added to the petals in a contrasting colour. This is a thick silk perlé so only one strand has been used.

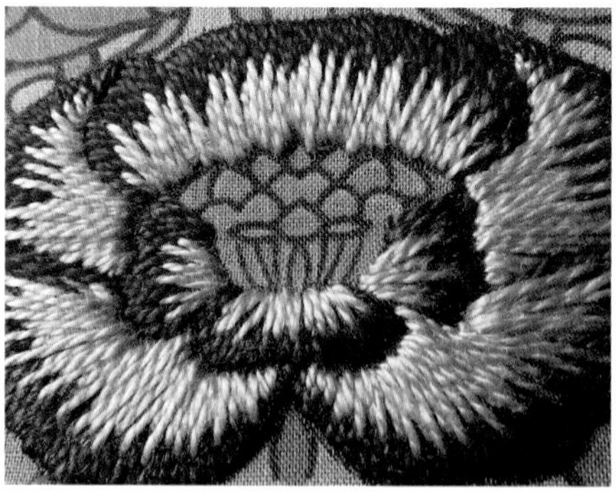

6. The poppy has no split stitch, so the petals are not overlapping in any way and have a tiny space between them. You can leave this little space as it is, or you can add outlines in stem stitch or couching.

7. The long leaves have been stitched with an outer row of long and short stitch in a darker green.

8. The inner part of the leaf is worked in a lighter colour with a row of stem stitch for the centre vein.

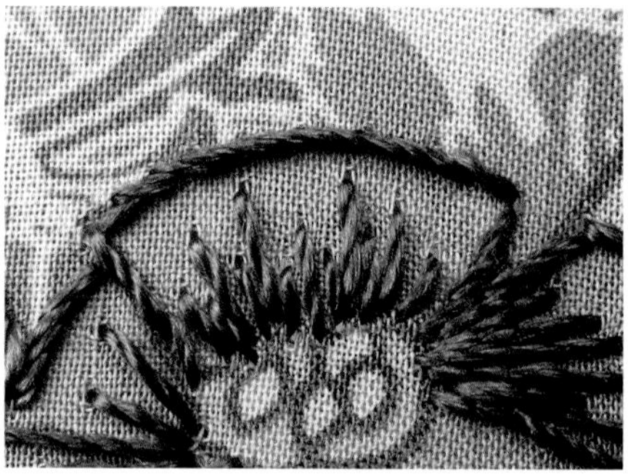

9. The blue poppies are worked in one strand of thread, so they are not as raised as the red poppy. They are outlined in stem stitch and then have one row of very spaced-apart long and short stitch. This will make them merge a little into the background, as they have quite a lot of the grey colour showing through them.

10. To bring the main poppy element forward, it has been outlined with two strands of couched silver thread once the embroidery had been completed on it.

11. (left) The centre of the poppy has a cluster of French knots to add texture.

Other elements of the background of the design have been outlined in stem stitch with additional French knots added to fill in areas if they look too empty.

The Morris legacy

William Morris was a huge influence on textiles in the nineteenth century. His interest in embroidery was fuelled by his apprenticeship with G.E. Street who was an expert on medieval embroidered textiles. Morris taught himself to embroider and one of his favourite stitches was long and short stitch, which featured heavily in many of his embroideries. The fact that Morris himself could embroider gave him a great insight into what worked as an embroidery design. Some of these designs were worked professionally but he also designed embroideries as bespoke commissions for people to stitch themselves to be made into hangings and soft furnishings. Morris was determined to bring embroidery, considered a craft at the time, into being considered a more artistic practice, referred to as 'art needlework'.

His daughter May was also a talented embroidery designer and stitcher, and was manager of the embroidery department at Morris and Co. She contributed to various publications and was a highly regarded teacher of embroidery.

Strawberry Thief, one of William Morris's most popular designs, has had the Leek Embroidery Society treatment with the addition of metallic thread embroidery.

This retro fabric has got space-dyed threads to give it a new lease of life with the addition of straight stitches, French knots and stem stitch.

CHAPTER 9

FURTHER TECHNIQUES

Using other embroidery techniques with thread painting can produce some very exciting results. Embroidering onto unusual surfaces or with alternative threads will give your stitching a contemporary twist.

It will help with these projects if you are confident with your long and short stitch to achieve the best results.

STITCHING ON ALTERNATIVE SURFACES

If you can put a needle and thread through it, then technically you can thread paint it. So, use your imagination to think of inventive ways to thread paint.

OPPOSITE: A stone angel from Highgate Cemetery stitched with straight stitches allowing the background fabric to show through for a mossy effect. Eight colours of stranded cotton were used.

This pendant is made of a heavy-weight plastic, it has pre-drilled holes so you can only stitch through it in certain places. It has a base layer of cotton perlé, then a layer of stranded cotton with a final layer of fine metallic machine thread.

Park benches, tennis racquets and kitchen utensils have all been given the embroidery treatment to create contemporary art. The threads and needles you use may need extra consideration but it is fun to broaden your ideas to create an exciting embroidery.

This contemporary tie has the addition of Swarovski™ crystals to bring it up to date.

Embroidered Beads

The sample has been made with 1.25cms felt balls and one strand of space-dyed stranded cotton.

Materials:

- Felt balls in the size of your choice.
- Thread of your choice – anything too weak may break as it goes through the ball so make sure it is strong enough.
- Needle suitable for your thread, a slightly larger one than you usually use for the thread will make it easier for your thread to pass through the ball.
- Scissors.
- Large needle with a sharp point to make a big hole for stringing the beads later.
- Jewellery components of your choice for making items.

Felt beads are an easy way to create unique embroidered jewellery. Felt balls are readily available to buy in many sizes and colours. They can also be used for garlands or other home decorations. The embroidery can be added to with beads, ribbons and sequins to create fantastic effects. Let your imagination run wild.

1. Thread up your needle with one strand of thread and a knot; make sure you have a long thread, so you do not have to start and finish your thread (unless you want to change colour), put the needle through the ball anywhere and come out on the opposite side.

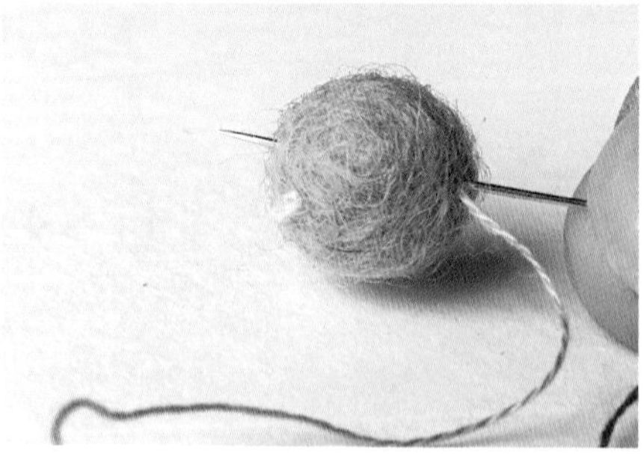

2. Now put the needle through the ball very close to where it came out to make a tiny stitch, as the needle pushes through to the other side wiggle it about so that it gets caught on the felt on the inside. Repeat this process once more and then cut your knot off.

3. The position of where your thread has emerged from the ball is going to be the centre point of your star pattern. Now take the needle through the ball as shown in the photograph.

4. Your ball should now look like this.

5. Take your needle through the ball going in to the centre point and coming out on the outside of the ball. The stitches do not have to be the same size.

6. Repeat again, going into the centre and coming out on the outside.

7. Repeat this process and you will see the star shape starting to form.

8. Fill in the star until you have the desired amount of stitching. Notice how the stitches are all different lengths.

9. To finish your thread securely, take it to the back of the ball and repeat the starting procedure by taking a tiny stitch and wiggling the thread through the felt ball to secure. Cut the excess.

10. To make a hole through the ball for stringing, take an extra-large needle and push through the centre of the ball. It is helpful to go through at the same point several times to make the hole large enough. Increase the size of the needle if necessary.

11. Small eye-hooks can be screwed into the beads to allow for attaching to other jewellery components. Make sure the thread on the screw is long enough to grip the felt.

Padding with Felt

Although you can create a three-dimensional effect with long and short stitch by shading, making your embroidery three-dimensional by using padding can give a whole different look to your work.

This is not a new idea. In the seventeenth century wool padding was used to make high relief embroidery; this is known as stumpwork.

Stitching through lots of layers of padding can make it hard to follow the design that is drawn on the fabric as often your needle will come out in a different place to where you want it. So too many layers can make it impossible for a complex design. Keep it simple. If you did want to pad a complex design, then either have less padding or pad it up at the end when it is finished.

This little beetle has layers of felt padding to create high relief. These are then covered with a layer of fabric which has the design drawn on and you work your embroidery through all the layers. You need to use a good quality felt. If your felt is too hairy, the fibres will come through to the front of your stitching and give your work a hairy effect. Useful perhaps if you are working a shaggy dog but not when you are after a smooth, shiny beetle!

Pink and Black Beetle

The sample has been worked on one layer of fine white linen with one strand of stranded cotton. The shading is very simple on this sample, so the technique can be learnt easily. Follow the main photograph for colour placement.

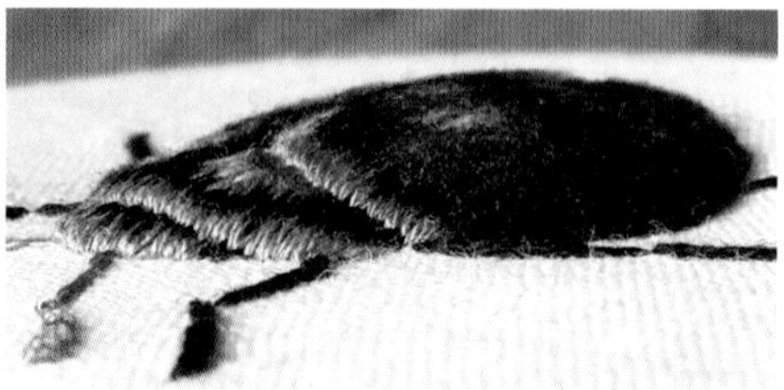

This photograph shows the graduated layers of the beetle and how the segments are clearly defined.

Materials:

- Fabric with just the outline of the beetle and legs transferred, stab stitched if necessary.
- Fabric to cover the felt layers, closely woven if possible, for example linen.
- Frame and scissors.
- Good quality felt – a lighter colour is useful so you can draw on it.
- Stranded cottons in black, greys, white and a contrasting colour such as bright pink in three shades; light, medium and dark.
- Needles size 10–12.
- Fabric glue and paintbrush or glue pen.
- Pins.
- Marker pen or pencil that can be seen on the felt.
- Thin paper or tracing paper.
- Sewing cotton, or polyester, such as machine thread for basting and applying.

1. Make a paper pattern of the body of the beetle by tracing the template to paper and cutting it out on or just outside the line. Pin or hold this on to the felt and draw around the shape. As you are drawing around the paper, you are in fact making the felt outline a fraction bigger.

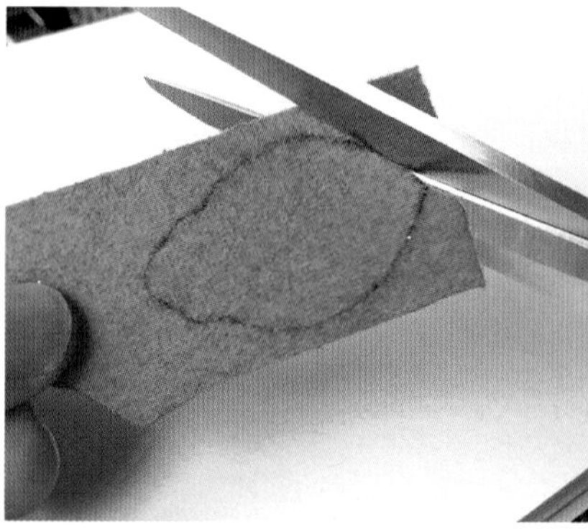

2. Cut the felt shape out on or just outside the drawn line.

3. Make four more felt shapes. Each one is cut smaller than the one before, but still following the approximate shape of the beetle until you get to the smallest shape, which will be a little oval.

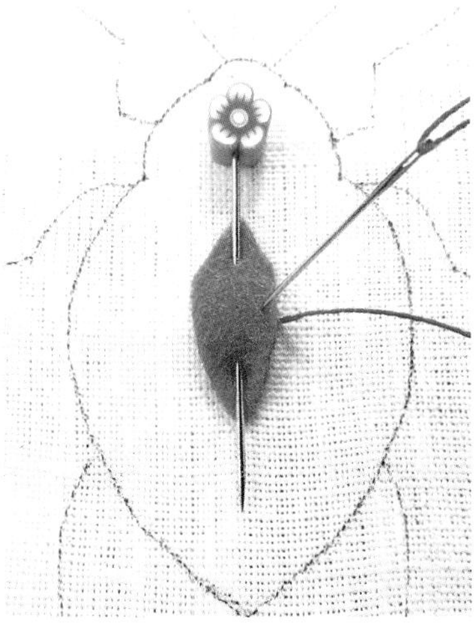

4. Pin the smallest felt shape in place in the approximate middle of the beetle's body. Using one strand of your machine thread, stitch the felt template down. It is important that the needle comes up in the background and down into the felt padding as shown in the photograph. This will help the felt stay smooth. Use small, neat stitches.

5. As you have a few layers going on top of the first piece of felt you do not have to do lots of stitches. It just needs to be smooth and secure. As you progress, add more stitches to each layer. You do not need to make the stitches longer.

6. The final layer of felt, although it was cut slightly larger than the body of the beetle, sits on the inside edge of the design line. This is because it is going over padding and therefore shrinks in. It is important that the design line is showing. If when you get to the final layer of felt and it covers the design line or is a long way in from the line, either cut it down or make a new piece.

7. Transfer the design of the beetle body and its markings to the fabric you are using to cover the felt. Do not use felt for this layer; a closely woven fabric is used to try and prevent the fibres from the felt coming through to your embroidery. Using a fabric glue or glue pen suitable for fabric, draw around the outside of the beetle design line. This line extends for a good few millimetres from your drawn line. It does not need to go on top of your drawn line.

8. When the glue has dried, cut around the beetle on the outside of the glue line. The glue is there to prevent this layer of fabric from fraying when it is applied on top of the felt.

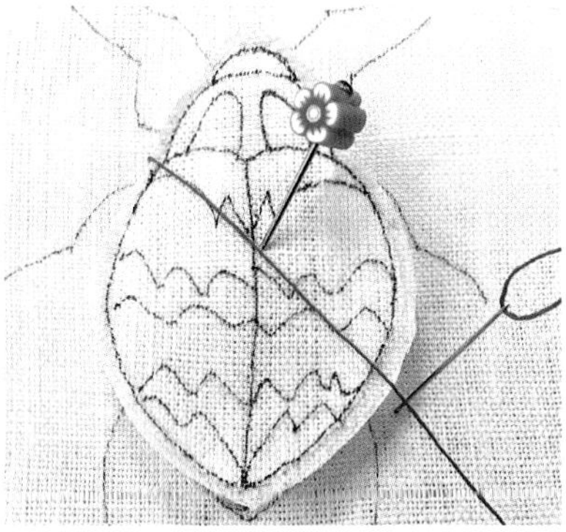

9. Put a pin straight down through the glued layer of fabric to temporarily hold it in place on top of your felt padding. Using your machine thread, stitch large basting stitches across the beetle, coming up and going down in your background fabric just outside the body of the beetle. Do not stitch through the beetle at all. These stitches will be removed later and they allow the beetle body to be adjusted as needed in the next stage.

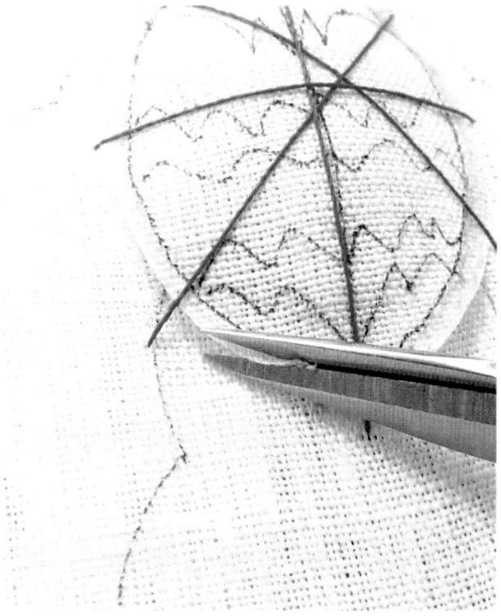

10. With a small pair of scissors trim the glued edge down if you think it comes too far outside of the design line. When this glued layer is attached you need to see your original drawing on the background fabric. You may not need to trim this layer at all. It needs to cover all the felt.

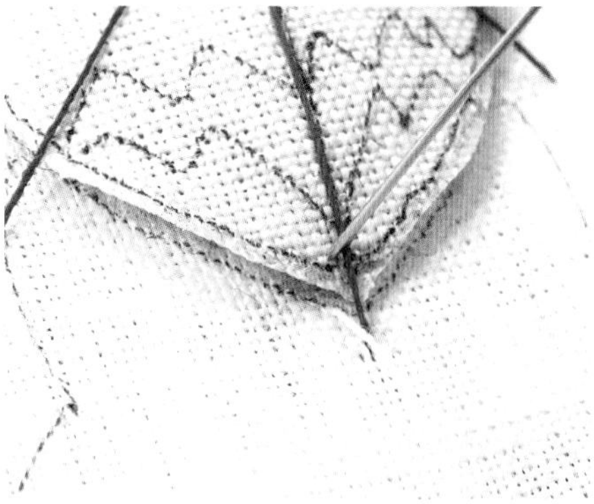

11. Using a machine thread, you will need to attach the glued layer to the backing fabric. You can match the colour of your thread either to your fabric or to the colour of your beetle. These stitches will not show at the end but do make sure they are small and neat. Bring your needle up in the background fabric just outside the design line of the beetle body and take it down into the glued layer.

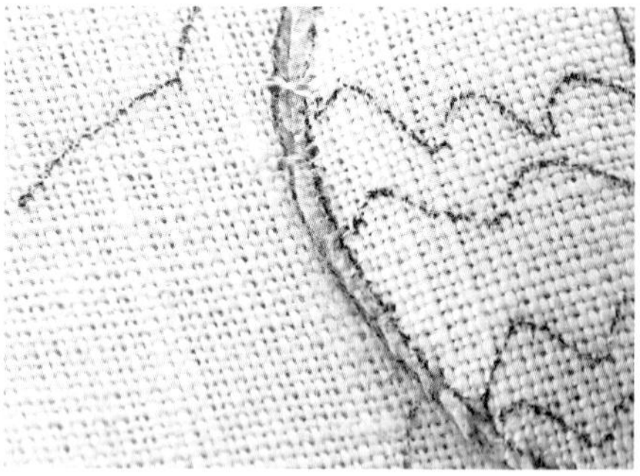

12. Continue working around the beetle, removing the basting stitches as you need to. The beetle is now ready to start embroidering.

13. Split stitch in grey on the outside edge of the very top of the beetle. The split stitch only goes through the background fabric, not through any of the other layers. Work long and short stitch as usual following the sample picture for colour placement.

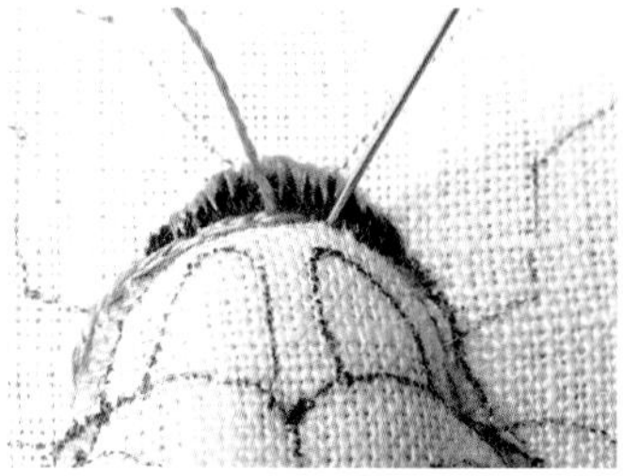

14. Split stitch the head by starting in the background fabric on the outside edge and then through the felt layers and back to the background fabric on the other side. Small, tight stitches to create a smooth curve. It is a little harder to stitch this line as you are going through layers of felt but it is vital to create a crisp edge. Long and short stitch the head using the photograph for colour placement.

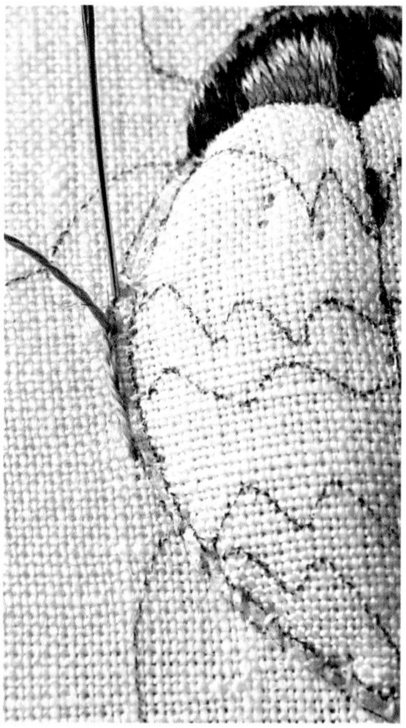

15. For the body, split stitch in the same way; the split stitch goes just through the background fabric except where the head meets the body. Again, do try and get a neat line where the body and head meet.

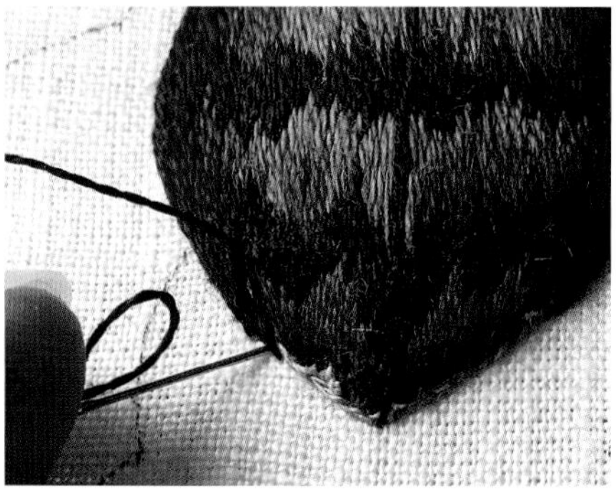

16. (left) Fill the body in with long and short stitch. You can stitch the black line down the centre first and work the two sides separately if you wish. They are not symmetrical. Notice the needle really tucking under the split stitch to get a smooth edge at the bottom. Stitch rows of stem stitch and French knots for the legs and antennae.

Incorporating Background Fabric into Embroidery

One way of giving your thread painting a different feel is to use your background fabric as part of your design area by leaving spaces within your stitching. The easiest way to do this is not to do traditional long and short stitch but to make single straight stitches throughout your design.

The choice of colour of your backing fabric is important for this style of stitching as it is going to be part of the embroidery rather than just in the background. Look at your design and decide what overall colour you would like the embroidery to have. If you are doing an embroidery with lots of trees and fields for example, perhaps a green would be good to have throughout to suggest foliage.

This type of embroidery does not have to be stitched in any particular order as none of the stitches interlock and are therefore not overlapping. You can easily fill in stitches very sparsely and then add increasingly more until you have the density you want, remembering that different densities will have differing amounts of background showing through. This embroidery style can also have a sketched appearance to it and is not so structured as traditional long and short stitch.

This detail of the Highgate angel shows tiny, closely-packed stitches in the face to create the detail and much more fabric showing through on the wings to give a mossy effect.

Winter in Venice

The sample has a grey-blue silk to suggest a winter sky and cold water in the canal. The sky has been left completely unstitched but could have had clouds added. The buildings have various amounts of silk showing to suggest peeling paint. The canal has lots of silk showing, as it is appropriate for the water rather than stitching a blue in. This embroidery also uses the direction of the stitch to give the impressions of texture; buildings are all vertical stitches and the water horizontal to create the ripples and reflections. Length of stitch has also been used here to suggest perspective – longer stitches generally in the foreground and smaller stitches in the distance. This is especially important in the water stitching.

The sample was worked with one strand of stranded cotton on a blue-grey flat silk.

Materials:

- Fabric with the design transferred *except* the reflections in the water (see instructions below), stab stitched if necessary.
- Frame and scissors.
- Stranded cottons to match the picture; if you are choosing your own colours for the buildings then be aware the reflections are a slightly duller version of the building colours.
- Needles size 10–12.
- Sewing cotton or polyester, such as machine thread, for tacking reflections.
- Tissue paper for tacking reflections.

This sample uses the colour of the silk background and the direction and size of the stitches to create different effects.

1. After you have transferred the main design on to your fabric you need to transfer the reflections by tacking them with machine thread. This is because you do not want a strong design line on the water as the embroidery stitches are quite sparse in this area. Use a polyester cotton to mark on the lines. As the stitches will be removed it does not matter what colour you use.

2. Start with the buildings in the very back of the picture. It may be helpful to fill the windows in first then fill in the areas around them. Some of the windows are just a single stitch; others are blocks of stitches. Do not worry about making the windows perfectly neat or all the same size. The roofs on the furthest buildings are in a slightly diagonal direction. Remember to stitch the little part of the building that appears under the bridge.

3. Fill in the yellow building with longer stitches than the back buildings. This helps with the perspective of the embroidery; the smaller stitches are furthest away to help with the idea of distance with not much detail. More detail and colour shading as you move forward in the embroidery.

4. Next is the white and grey building. Fill in the windows first as before as well as the lamp post, all in the same dark colour. Then using both white and grey fill in around the windows; the stitches are longer than in the previous buildings. There is more white and light grey than the dark grey. Stitch this roof in long, horizontal stitches. Notice the areas of background that are showing in this building, it adds to the peeling paint effect.

5. Add some detail to the window frames with small, horizontal, white straight stitches.

6. Add some horizontal dark grey stitches for the small part of pavement showing under the white building. Make these long stitches. Fill the windows of the front building in as before with a dark colour. When you are filling in the walls of this building make the stitches longer than you have worked elsewhere. This is because it is in the foreground, again to give a sense of perspective. The front of the building is lighter than the side facing us.

7. Notice the strong definition in colour between the front and side of the building. Notice the amount of background showing through. Outline the windows in the same way as before. Try and keep the stitches all as vertical as possible.

8. Work some long white stitches to the edge of the canal side. Three or four stitches at the front, two immediately behind the boat, one just before the bridge. This gives the impression again of distance. Stitch the bridge in tiny horizontal grey and white stitches. Embroider the small wall going into the water with a mixture of dark grey and green. Notice the stitches are longer at the front and smaller as they go towards the bridge.

9. Embroider the front wall on the left-hand side with much smaller stitches, with little amounts of the background showing throughout. This is to give the impression of brickwork. You do not have to line up the bricks in any way, just little stitches will give the impression successfully. Stitch a line of grey, then green and grey for the parts of the wall as they go into the water.

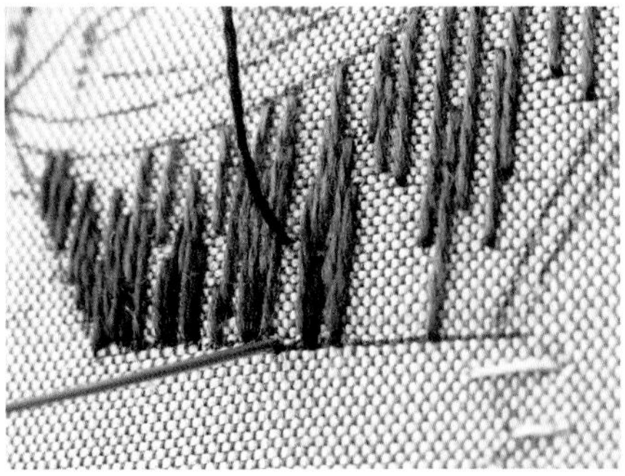

10. Embroider the boat with longer vertical stitches for the main part. The bottom of the boat as it hits into the water should be darker.

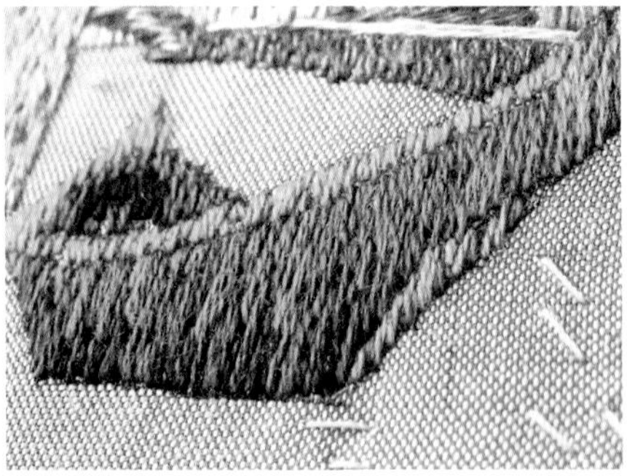

11. The boat is almost fully filled in with no background showing.

12. A line of dark stem stitch is worked just under the top edge of the boat to add to the detailing. French knots are worked in clusters of green thread against the red building. You can work differing sizes of knots if you wish. Three or four greens are sufficient to shade this area.

13. Work horizontal stitches onto the canal area for reflections. Try to get them as straight as possible with each other, any stitches that are slightly wonky will show up in this area. As there are less stitches, mistakes will be more noticeable. Longer stitches to the front of the embroidery, shorter ones at the back. The colours of the reflections are duller than the buildings so try not to use the same colours as you have used previously.

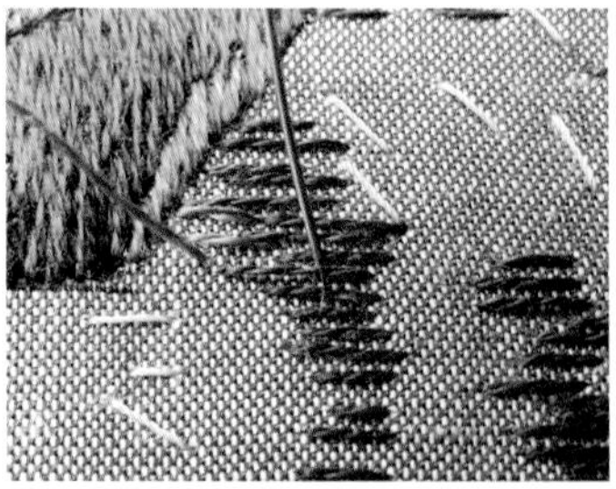

14. Use the tacking lines for placement of windows in the reflections and change of colours. Take the tacking stitches out as you go so you are not stitching over them.

15. Add definition to the boat with a dark colour and partial outlines.

This dramatic embroidery has been enhanced by using a silver lurex and silk mix fabric for the water. The clouds have been fully stitched in horizontal long and short stitch and the water has just horizontal stitches spaced apart so the silver fabric shines through.

Three-Dimensional Embroidery with Wire Edges

Thinking about the fabric you are going to stitch on is important when you are cutting out the embroidery to make it three-dimensional. Any fabric that has fluffy threads in the weave will give a fluffy edge when it is cut out, even when you put glue around it. Another consideration is the colour you use; choosing a colour of fabric that blends in with your embroidery is useful in case there are some threads showing after you have cut out. Fine fabrics such as organza and habotai silks are useful as they cut very easily. You can always stitch through two layers if one is not enough support.

Incorporating wire into your embroidery means that it can be free of any fabric around the outside of the stitching area and it can be manipulated into shapes to then be used for sculptural pieces or perhaps jewellery.

Many wires are available that can be used. Florist and beading wire, for example, comes in many widths including very fine, which would be suitable if you need just a small amount of strength. The very fine wire can also be stitched down throughout your fabric rather than just on the edge to give more options for manipulation. Be careful to use wire that shows no signs of rust and has not been stored in damp conditions… like a florist's shop!

Electrical wire comes in many colours and is often sold by embroidery thread suppliers; this could be an option if you wish your wire to be part of the embroidery itself and have the wire showing as part of the design.

This project uses cake-decorating wire. This comes in many widths and has the advantage of being covered with paper. The white paper wires can be painted or coloured so that they blend into the embroidery and are a good choice for the beginner. If you are using fine threads in your embroidery use thin wire; for thicker threads such as tapestry wool in your embroidery use thicker wire.

Variegated and space-dyed threads

Using threads in your thread painting projects that have many colours in one skein can be an easy way to get shaded effects without you having to think about the shading yourself. Some skeins will have the colours distributed randomly. These are very often hand dyed and are known as space or overdyed threads. With these you have no control of colour placement, the shading and colour changes just happen before your eyes.

Machine-dyed and commercially manufactured skeins, sometimes called variegated, have threads with an exact amount of colour before it changes to another shade. This can be useful for some projects but be careful, as some ranges can give a very striped regimental effect when used in long and short stitch.

HYDRANGEA

Hydrangeas are the perfect subject for using space-dyed threads as they bloom in many colours all on one branch. Adding rusty nails or copper sulphate powder to the soil they are grown in can turn the hydrangea many different shades of red or blue.

The template for this is in the back of the book. It is very small. You may wish to stitch a larger petal shape but be careful you use a heavy enough wire if you change the size of the template. You may also need to add more rows of long and short stitch.

The sample is stitched with one strand of four different dyed stranded cotton thread on two layers of synthetic organza, with number 28 white-covered cake wire.

Materials:

- Fine fabric as discussed previously.
- Frame; if you are using two layers of fabric then using a small frame is important to keep the layers the same tension and stop movement between them. You could use a dressmaker's lightweight fusible web to keep the layers together. Follow packet instructions and do a test piece first. You do not have to work all the petals on the same frame. A small ring frame is sufficient; you can stitch four or eight petals at a time.
- Paper-covered wire.
- Air-disappearing ink pen.
- Fine space-dyed or variegated threads; you can choose similar toned skeins or just choose one skein if you like the colour range it contains. There is no real control over the colours that appear in the stitching so perhaps work a sample of long and short stitch to see if you like the effect a particular skein gives.
- Thick green thread for wrapping the stem.
- Needles 10–12 embroidery/crewel and chenille size 22–24.
- Scissors, two pairs; one to be small and sharp for stitching and cutting your finished embroideries out and another that can be used for cutting wire. *Do not* use your embroidery scissors for cutting wire; fine clean pliers are an alternative.
- Fabric glue and paintbrush or a glue pen.
- Artificial flower centres (optional).
- Fine flat tweezers.

This hydrangea branch can be used as a little sprig in a bottle, its petals will never fade or droop, it can have a pin attached to the back and be used as a brooch.

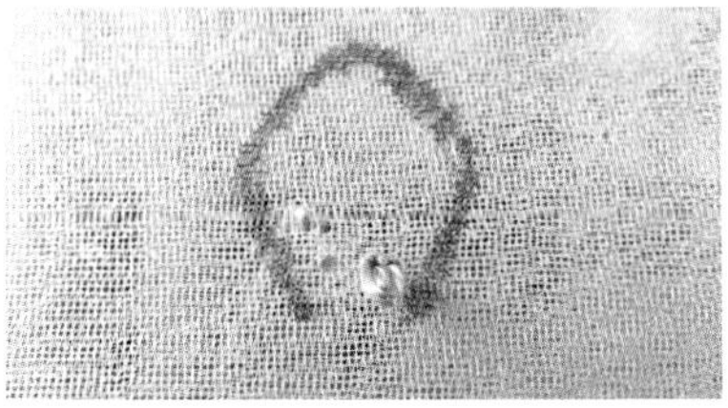

1. Place your fabric in your frame tightly. If you are using more than one layer make sure they are both the same tight tension and there is no movement. Draw a petal shape on the fabric with the air-disappearing pen. This is used so when we cut out later there is no harsh outline in case the wire doesn't cover it fully. Start one of your threads off in the usual way and trim your knot. We are using the thread we are going to embroider with to couch down the wire so it does not show.

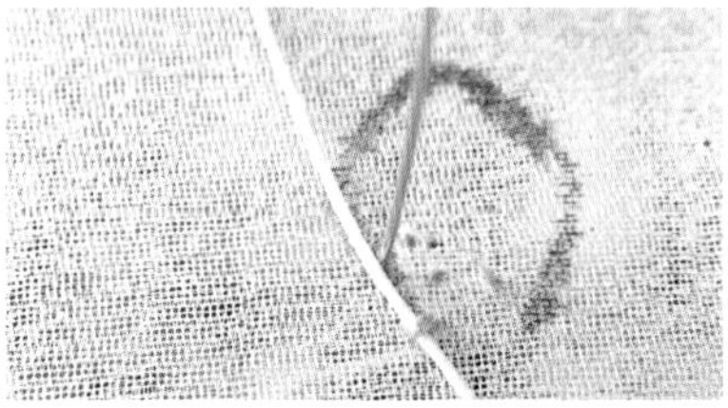

2. Cut a piece of wire long enough to go around the petal and with excess of about 3cms each end. Hold the wire in place so there are about 3cms of wire before you start stitching. Couch the wire in place coming up on the *inside* of the petal and down on the outside; this is so there are no trailing threads near the outside of the petal. Try and come up and go down in the same hole in the fabric so the wire does not move about. The wire needs to be very secure. If you think it is too loose add more stitches, keeping them tiny and tight.

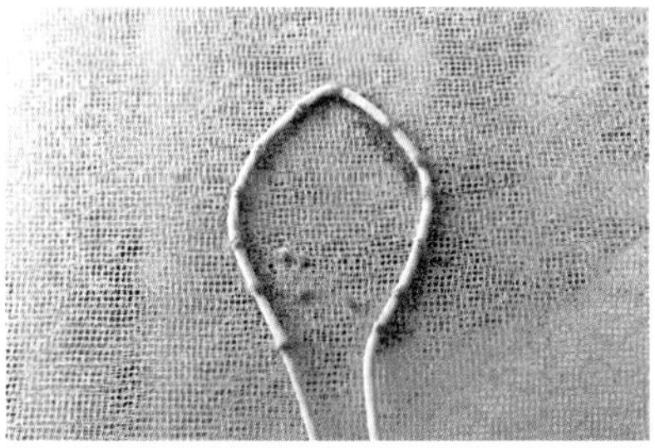

3. The finished wire in place should follow the shape of the lines you have drawn on the fabric. Finish your thread when you have finished inside the petal shape. Do not finish any of your threads outside the petal in your fabric, as these stitches will be removed when we cut out the petal and could cause loose stitches.

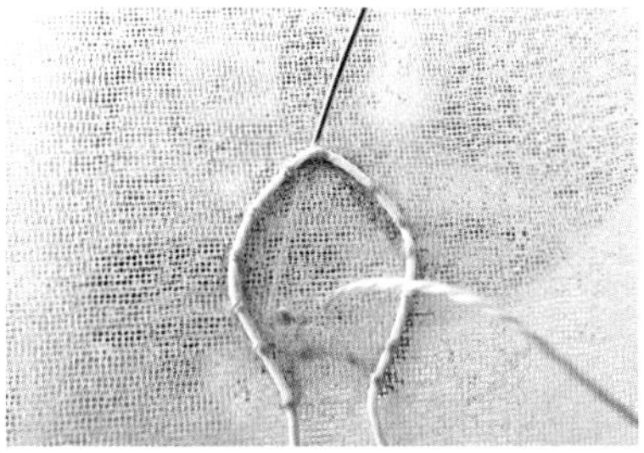

4. Start a new thread and begin working a row of long and short stitch from the middle of the petal. As this embroidery is going to be cut out, you need to be more aware of what the back of your work looks like as it may be seen. This means you cannot randomly add stitches in here and there if you have spaces. This would mean lots of crossing over so try and be controlled in the way you work. Make sure that the needle really goes down in the fabric against the wire; notice the angle in the picture.

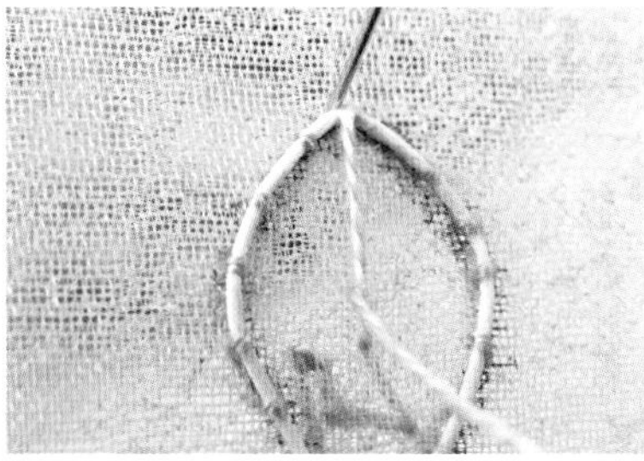

5. The stitches must be really close together as usual but you may find it difficult as the wire can be slippery, so make sure they are very tucked in at the top. Make sure that your stitches are a firm tension too; any loose stitches in this type of embroidery really spoil the effect when it is cut out.

6. Work your way down one side; you can use just one colour skein for the whole petal or you can change to another colour range. Notice in this picture there is an area where two of the skein colours are mixed. The choice is yours to produce the colour effect you like.

7. (left) The first row is complete all the way round. As the petal is so small the first row can be completed before starting on the second. The first row shows colours from three different skeins; two blue and one green.

8. Now work the second and final row of long and short stitch. Remember to fan the stitches out so you are not overcrowding the space. When you have finished your second row secure the thread on the back securely and as discreetly as possible by weaving it under your previous stitches. Repeat this whole process to complete as many petals as you need. The sample has ten small flowers, each with four petals, so forty separate petals in total.

9. Now using a glue pen or paintbrush carefully glue around the outside of your embroidery onto the fabric going right up to the edge of your stitching. Try not to get any glue on the top of your long and short embroidery in case the colours are not colourfast (many are not if they have been hand dyed). You need the glue to be a little bit thick if you have a very fine fabric as it may bleed into your embroidery.

10. Once the glue is dry cut the petals out carefully with some small scissors. It is easier to cut them out with some excess material around the edge and then trim them down when they are removed from the main fabric. Trim the hairy bits of fabric away from the stitching carefully.

11. Twist the two wires together at the base of each petal for 1.5cms unless you are using artificial flower centres – in this case see next step. Do not cut the excess wire yet.

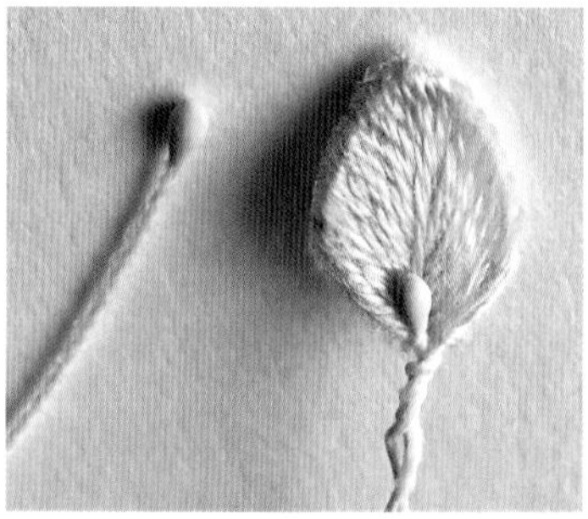

12. Artificial flower centres are usually on a small thread, if you are using these then twist them up with the wires for 1.5cms as above making sure they are secure and caught in the twists, or they will slip out. Do not cut the excess thread yet.

13. Gather four petals together in your hand and grip the wires at the base of the petals.

14. (left) With one hand, push the petals together so that all the wires are very close and in the same position, as shown in the photograph. With the other hand twist all the petal wires together. It is important that the wires are twisted from the base of the petals just under the embroidery otherwise you will have wires showing on the top surface. The bases of the four petals need to be very close.

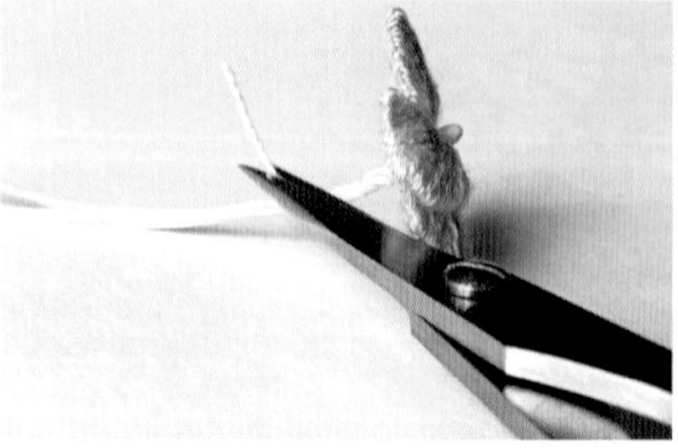

15. Pull the petals out flat now, you may wish to use tweezers to do this to prevent damaging your embroidery. If you have used artificial flower centres you can trim the excess now as shown.

16. Once you have repeated this process with all the flower buds arrange them into a pleasing display.

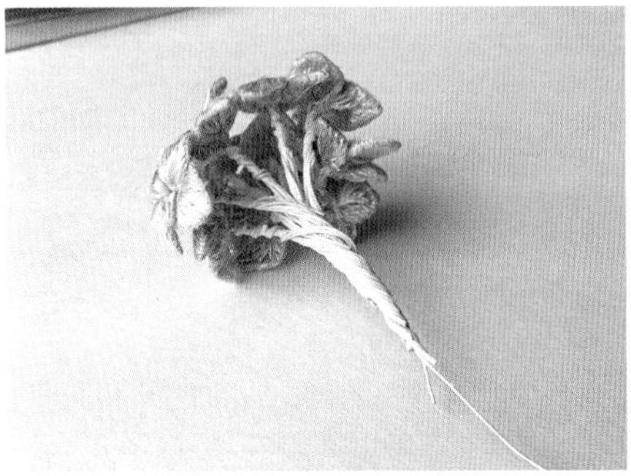

17. Now twist *all* the wires together as shown. Notice the twisting for this stage starts a little way down the main 'stem'. This allows you to move the individual buds easily into position later. If you do not like the arrangement of your branch at this stage, you can unwrap the wires and repeat until you are happy.

18. Once you are happy with the arrangement thread up a needle with a long (at least one metre) thick green thread to bind the stem with. Put a knot in the end of the thread and push the needle through the top part of the main stem.

19. Now bind the stem by wrapping the thread around the wires with the thread tightly covering where the knot is and working down the stem.

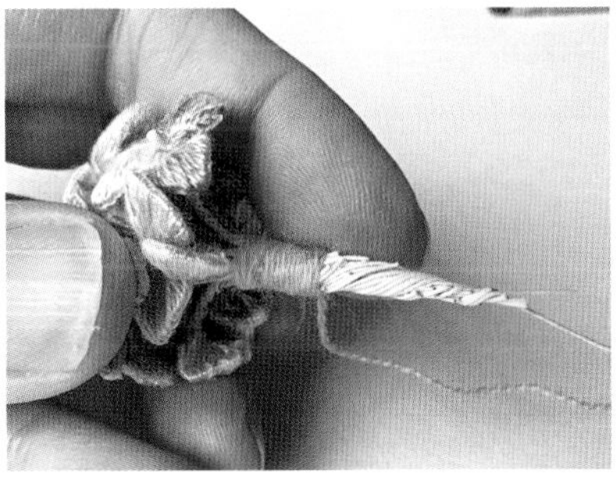

20. Continue working down the stem making it as smooth as possible. In areas where the wires are sticking out you can bind in the same place until they are fully covered.

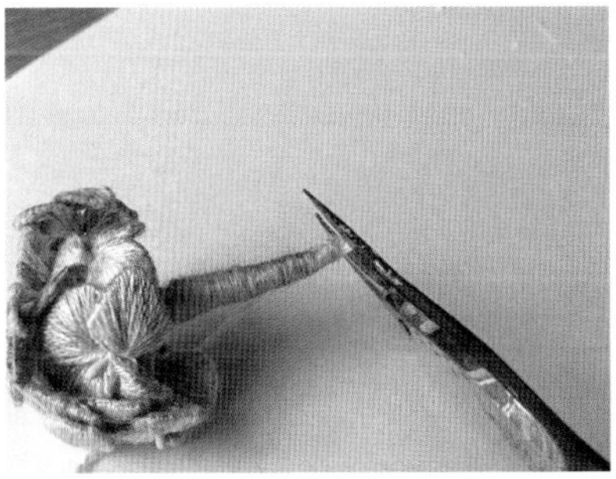

21. Stop before the end of the stem and cut the excess wires so they are a nice shape.

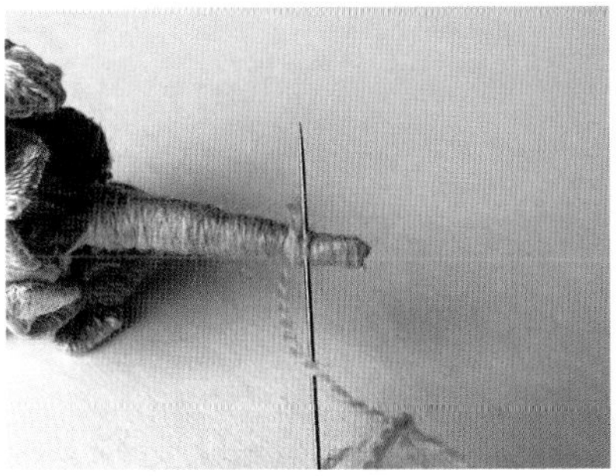

22. Bind down to the bottom of the stem; you do not want the wraps falling off the end. Then bind a little way up the stem and push the needle through the wraps a few times to secure.

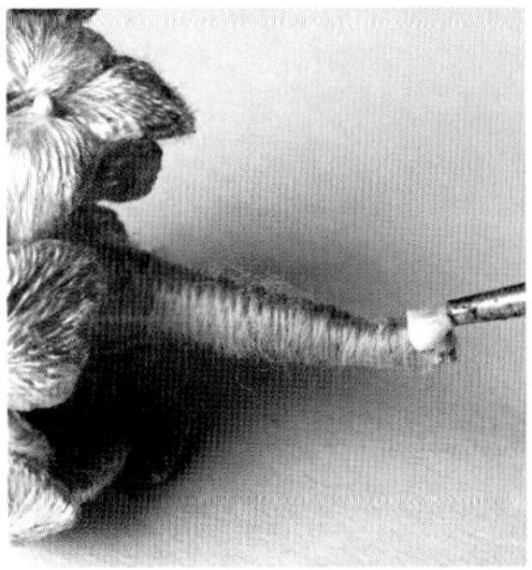

23. Glue the very end of the binding with a glue that dries clear to prevent the wraps falling away.

24. Using tweezers, bend and shape the flower petals gently into position to create a round 'ball' of petals.

CHAPTER 10

FINISHING YOUR WORK

So, you have stitched lots of embroideries, what to do with them? The most common way of displaying and finishing your embroidery is to mount them and put them in a frame on the wall. This is fine, but embroidery is a decorative art and therefore pictures are not the only way to show off your thread painting.

Traditionally embroidery was used to decorate homewares, clothing and soft furnishings as well as putting on the walls. Think of original ways to use your embroidered thread painting.

MOUNTING YOUR WORK IN PRE-MADE SETTINGS

Mounting your embroidery into a pre-made setting, such as a mirror compact or jewellery blank, is an exciting and original way to use your stitching.

OPPOSITE: A selection of mini embroideries in small wooden ring frames for jewellery.

This little embroidery is a perfect use of the simple shape of a pansy in a round necklace blank. The embroidery fills the frame of the necklace, which is important to make it look like a properly designed piece of jewellery rather than a spare piece of embroidery put into a blank. Always design your embroidery for the fitting it is going into.

Make sure that the settings you use are high quality, especially as you may have spent many hours stitching your embroidery. Lower quality blanks may warp or stain your fabric. Your design needs to be the right size for your setting; a good way to work this out is to use the supplied template form, draw round this onto paper and design inside this shape. This ensures you will know exactly how your finished item will look.

Be aware of how much fabric you do or do not need to enable mounting. Some settings allow only a small amount of excess fabric and you may only be able to put one layer of fabric in the setting, otherwise it may be too bulky.

As you make up your item be careful about over-handling your stitching. It is sometimes a good idea to pin or tack a piece of tissue paper over your stitching, so you are not touching your threads and causing damage unnecessarily.

You should never use glue directly on the back of your embroidery, *always* mount your stitching to a form which you can then glue into your setting. Although the glue you use may be safe for textiles and dries clear, over time it can yellow and cause damage to your embroidery.

Mirror Compact

This mirror compact already came with a form to mount the embroidery onto. For ease, try and buy settings that have a form already cut for you. If your setting does not have a pre-made form, then you will need a thick card or a strong plastic to make your own. Preferably use something that will withstand tight pulling of the fabric around it and will not warp.

Materials:

- Embroidered fabric.
- Ready-made setting with form to mount embroidery onto.
- Marking pen or pencil.
- Double-sided tape and craft felt, optional. This is only needed if you would like to pad out your embroidery slightly on the form. It can also help if you have small wrinkles on your fabric.
- Scissors; embroidery and fabric.
- Chenille needle 22–24.
- Extra strong thread such as buttonhole or carpet thread.
- Glue suitable for sticking fabric to the setting. Check the instructions on your glue pack to make sure that the glue is suitable for whatever material your setting is made of, for example metal, wood, plastic and so on.
- Soft grip pegs or clips. Soft grip will help to prevent damage to your material or stitching. If you only have normal pegs or metal clips, then protect your work with tissue paper or fabric before using.

1. Using the form, draw an outline around your embroidery in the desired position about 1cm from the edge of the form. This will be where the gathering stitch is worked; this is *not* the cutting line.

2. Cut the embroidery out about 1–1.5cms larger than the line you have just drawn. If your fabric is prone to fraying then cut even larger than this – you can always trim down after you have worked a gathering stitch. Thread up a needle with a very long length of strong thread, at least a metre. This is so the gathering stitch and lacing is done in one thread length, so the tension is kept as tight as possible. Put a knot in the thread and start stitching a running stitch on the line you have drawn previously.

3. Work around the line as shown pulling the long thread through.

4. When you get back to the knot, pull your thread so there is a little tension ready for placing over the form.

   If you do not wish to pad your form, miss out the next two steps.

5. Stick a large piece of double-sided tape to one side of your form and remove the paper to reveal the sticky other side.

6. Stick this form to a piece of felt and then cut around the form a little larger as shown, so the felt will just overhang the sides. The tape is there to stop the felt moving when you put your embroidery over the top. It does not need to overhang so that it goes onto the back of the form. Check that your setting has space for a layer of felt to be used.

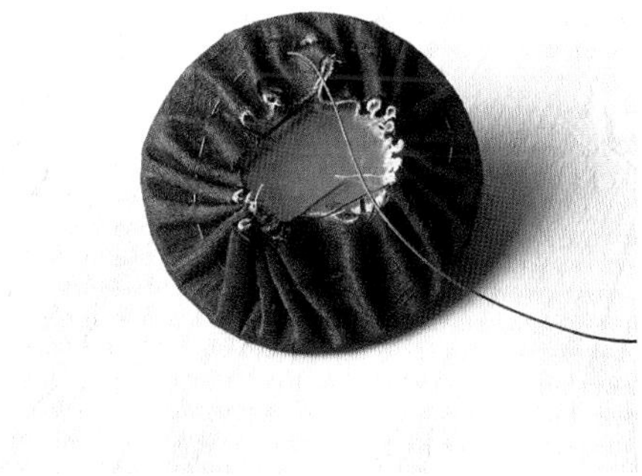

7. Place the embroidery over the form so that the felt (if used) is against the back of the embroidery. Gather up the thread a little as shown and check the embroidery placement on the front is correct. Once the placement is correct, pull the gathering thread as tight as you can.

8. Now take the thread to the opposite side of the circle and make a stitch horizontally as shown. Pull very tightly.

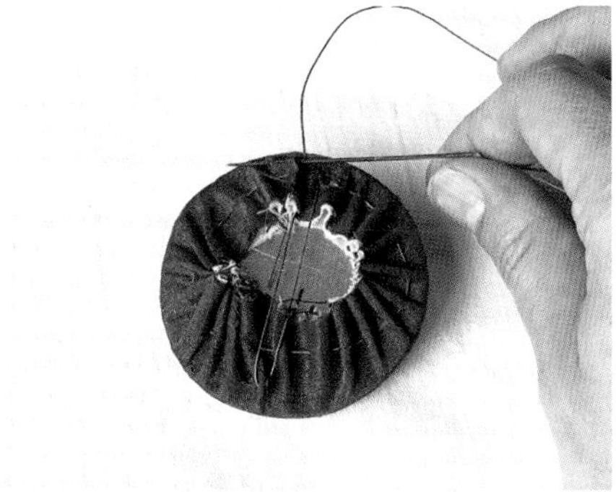

9. Now take the thread to the opposite side and take another stitch as shown. Pull tightly. Notice the tight gathering on the silk where the stitches are made. This is correct.

10. Continue working your way around the form until your embroidery is tight and there are no wrinkles on the front of your work. Fasten your thread off securely by working a few stitches into the backing.

11. Spread a suitable glue on the back of the form as shown. The glue needs to be near the edge but *not* right on the edge or it may spread out onto the front when attached. This will result in staining of your fabric. Make sure there is enough glue on the back of the form to allow the whole thing to be attached. If it dries and only part of the form is attached, it is extremely difficult to add extra glue afterwards.

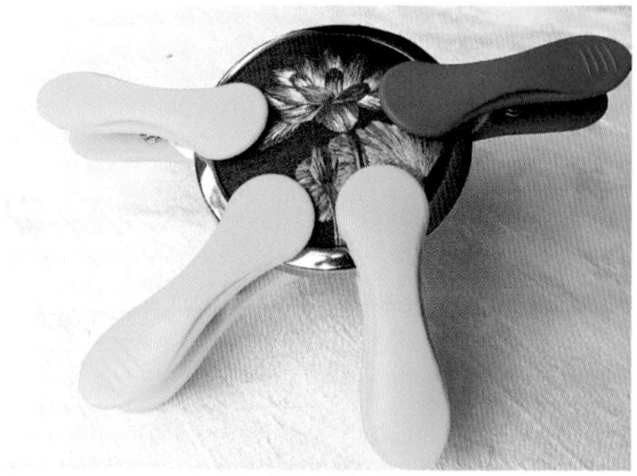

12. Push the form onto the setting and clip in place. Protect embroidery with tissue if needed. Check that glue is not seeping out from the edge. If you think there is not enough glue, pull the form off and add more *now*. Then reclip. Keep the pegs on for the recommended drying time of your glue. It is a mistake to remove them too early as you may think it is all dry, but the form can ping off if it's not. Try not to be too impatient!

Mounting Your Work for Framing

Displaying your thread painting in a frame for your home, as a gift or in a gallery is extremely satisfying. It is elevating your embroidery to art. However, professional framing can be very expensive, and you cannot guarantee that your work will be cared for or mounted without using glue near the embroidery, so knowing how to mount your work to a board is a very useful skill.

If you have spent hours creating your embroidery it is wise to use the best mounting materials you can afford. Acid-free mounting board is vital to prevent discolouration or damage to your fabric over the years. Making sure that your embroidered fabric is not glued but stitched to the board is also vital. Glue can discolour, and some glues will lose their hold after a few years which will create wrinkles in your work.

Putting glass in your frame is a personal choice. Glass will obviously protect your work from dust and dirt. Embroideries with no glass will allow people to touch – which is so very tempting but can be extremely damaging. Dust is damaging to fabrics over a long period of time and can be hard to remove for the amateur.

Glass will however take away some of the beauty and detail of your work purely because of its nature; it is highly reflective and may stop little details being seen.

Glass should not be pressed up against the embroidery. There needs to be a spacer between the fabric and glass. Box frames are useful for this problem, but be careful the glass is not too far away from the work. You want to be able to see the embroidery.

Today's technology has created glass that protects from light damage and there are non-reflective versions available, which although expensive, give an incredible effect as they are totally invisible, and allow you to see every detail. Use the best you can afford.

Mounting Embroidery to Board Using Herringbone Stitch

Mounting your embroidery by stitching it to a calico-covered board is a very secure and accurate way of making sure your embroidery is as tight as possible. The advantage of mounting this way is that it can be done in stages. Lacing your work (an alternative method described further on) means you must keep a tight tension constantly, which can be difficult to manage. Once the embroidery is mounted it can be inserted into a correct-sized frame or taken to a professional framer.

Materials:

- Finished embroidery, do not cut *any* fabric away from the embroidery before you start mounting. You will find measuring your embroidery is easier when it is still in the slate or ring frame as it is already stretched out, so you know what size to cut your card. You may want to mark with pins or a tacking stitch the centre points of your measurement to make placing on the board easier later.
- Calico or cotton for covering the mount board.
- White acid-free mounting board; this comes in various thicknesses, if it is thin board then you will need two sheets to prevent the board from bowing due to the tight tension applied.
- Cutting mat.
- Metal ruler that can also be used for cutting against; do not use plastic, if possible a thick ruler is better for safety.
- Set square.
- Sharp cutting knife or scalpel, suitable for cutting through the board easily.
- PVA glue; conservation grade glue is easily available.
- Old paintbrush or scrap piece of card.
- Strong pins that can be pushed into the board.
- White tissue paper.
- Strong linen or buttonhole thread.
- Curved needle.

1. Deciding what size to cut your board is important. If you are getting it framed remember that the frame will take up some of the board so add to your measurement accordingly. Add a half centimetre to each side to compensate if you are unsure. Draw your measurement onto your board using a set square to get a true 90-degree angle for all corners. If you are using two sheets of mount board you will need to cut them the same size. It is worth checking your measurements before you start cutting to be sure they are correct, and your angles are straight.

2. Place your board on your cutting mat and line your metal ruler up with one of your drawn lines. Let it extend beyond the mat. Using the knife, apply pressure to the board following your drawn line and resting up against the ruler. Do not attempt to go all the way through the board on your first go. Lift the knife, keep the ruler in place and repeat the cut as many times as necessary until the knife reaches the mat. You will feel the difference when it does. Repeat with the other sides of your board. Extend the cut beyond the drawn line when you cut corners; this is to ensure the corner is cut cleanly. If you have two sheets to cut, check they are the same size, then glue them together and allow to dry.

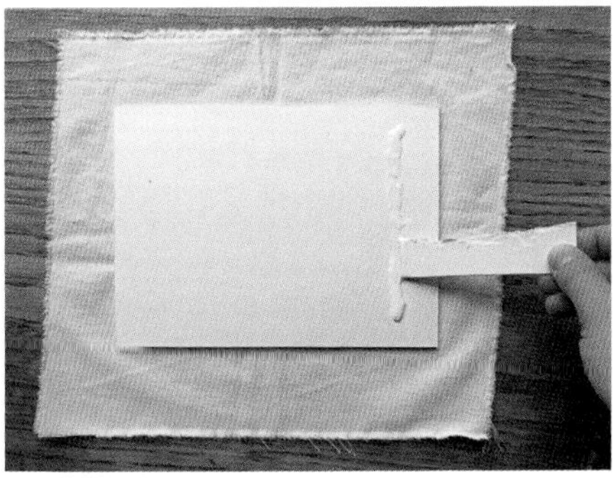

3. Cut your calico bigger than your board. If your board is 10cms square for example, then the calico should be 2.5–3cms bigger all round. If your board is bigger, adjust the measurement accordingly. Place your board centrally on top of the calico. Spread glue with an old paintbrush or piece of card along one side of the board as shown. Do not extend the glue into the corner and do not put any glue near the edge of the card. This is very important.

4. Pull the calico over the side of the board and press firmly so that it sticks. Push pins in it to hold it in place.

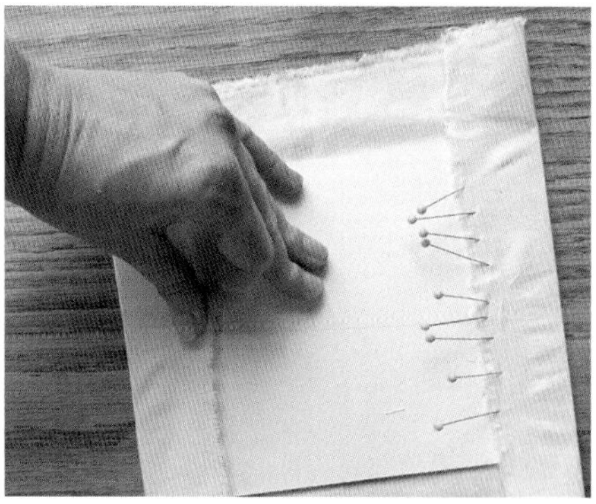

5. On the opposite side of the board, glue as before then pull *very* tightly and stick that edge of fabric to the board. Notice the way the fabric is being pulled as tightly as possible. There should be no loose fabric on the front of the board.

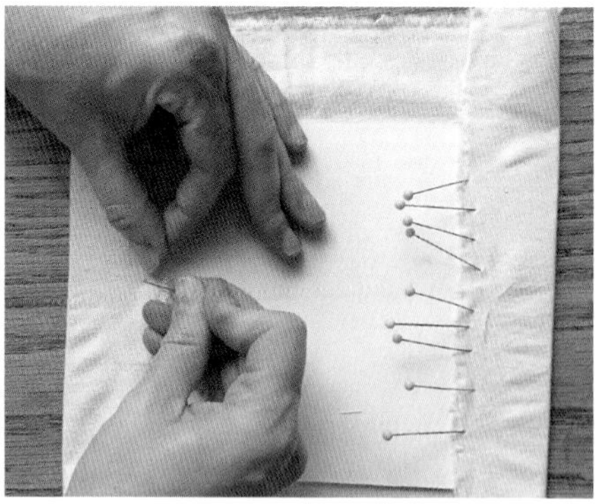

6. Add pins to this side too; notice the calico is still being pulled as the pins are being inserted.

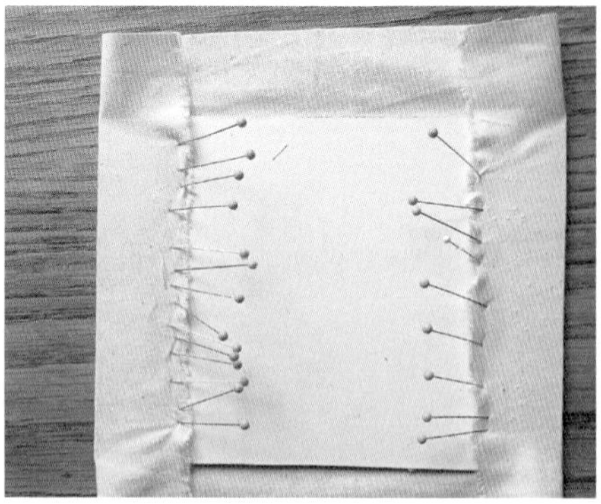

7. Notice how tight and smooth the calico looks on the board where the pins are. This is very important.

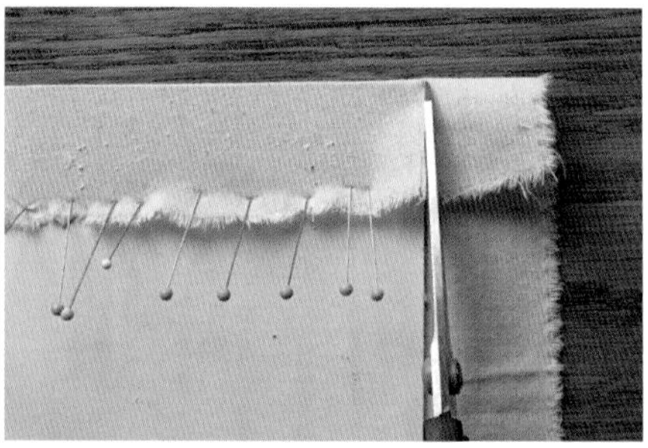

8. The excess is cut away from the corners to prevent bulk. Take your fabric scissors and cut the corner as shown towards the point.

9. Now cut the flap of fabric away on the diagonal.

10. This little flap can also be cut as shown.

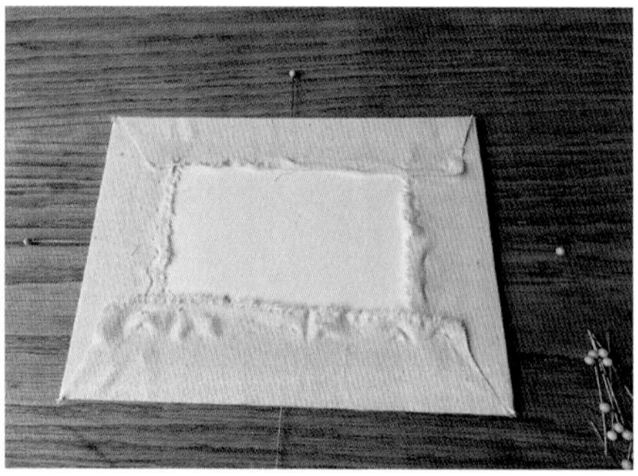

11. Repeat the gluing, sticking and trimming with the other two sides and let the glue dry completely before removing all the pins. Place a pin in the centre point of each side of your board if you have marked the centres of your embroidery for easy placement as shown.

12. Now place your embroidery over the board with the back of your embroidery against the calico, *not* the glued side of the board. If you have centre points marked match them up and push a pin through the fabric into the edge of the board where your centre pins are. Otherwise place the embroidery by eye and push a pin through your fabric in the centre of each side.

13. The centre points are all pinned first; check your measurements at this stage before adding more pins.

14. Continue to push pins through the fabric into the board around all sides. Pull the fabric tightly – if your hand doesn't ache, you are not pulling enough!! Try and get the fabric straight with the grain against the side of the board. There should be no wrinkles at all on your fabric. When you have finished pulling the fabric, leave it for a couple of days and then check it to see if it has relaxed; a few wrinkles may appear. Pull again until it is smooth.

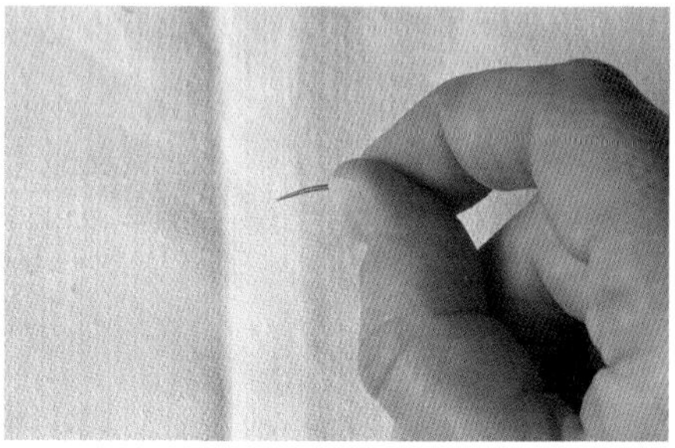

15. Now turn your embroidery over and place it on some tissue paper to protect your stitching. Thread up your curved needle with a longish length of strong thread and knot at the end. Practise holding your needle as shown, almost like a claw. It will take some getting used to but this stage in the process cannot be worked with a straight needle.

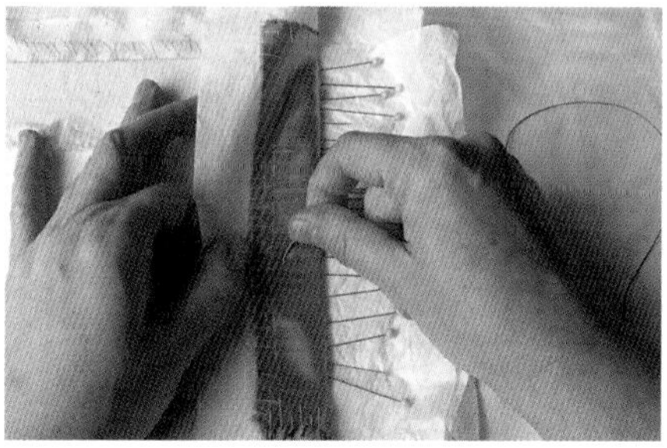

16. Pull your fabric tightly with one hand and start your thread by stitching through your embroidered fabric *and* the calico on your board in the middle of one side. Notice in the photo how the fabric is being pulled and creating a tight tension *before* the needle goes into the fabric. This is why we do not glue to the edge of the board. Notice how the needle point is coming towards you.

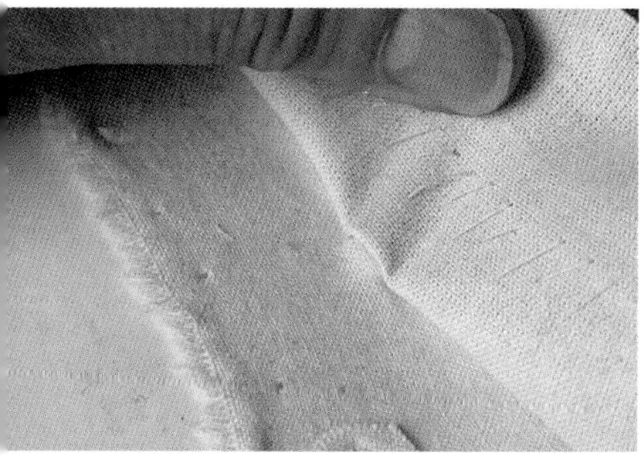

17. Check underneath the stitch you have just worked to make sure you have caught the calico that is attached to the board, not just the top and the backing fabric.

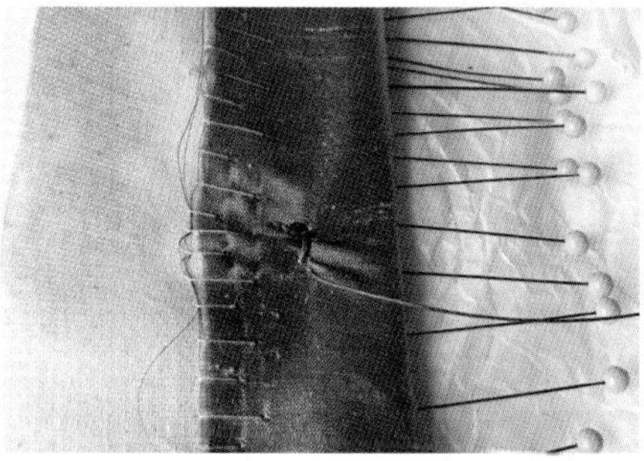

18. Do about three small stitches on top of each other. If you think your thread is secure cut your knot off, if you are unsure leave it. You finish your thread in the same way by working three or four little stitches on top of each other and cutting the excess away.

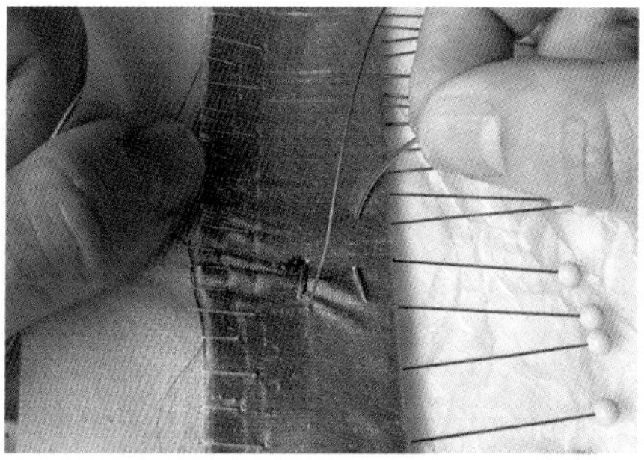

19. Now we work a herringbone stitch along the edge of your board. *Pull your fabric very tightly* every time before you put your needle in. You must make sure that the needle goes through all the layers of fabric to ensure it is secure. The first part of the stitch is a straight stitch as shown. Notice again how the other hand is pulling the fabric tightly. The point of the needle is coming out directly below where the thread was started.

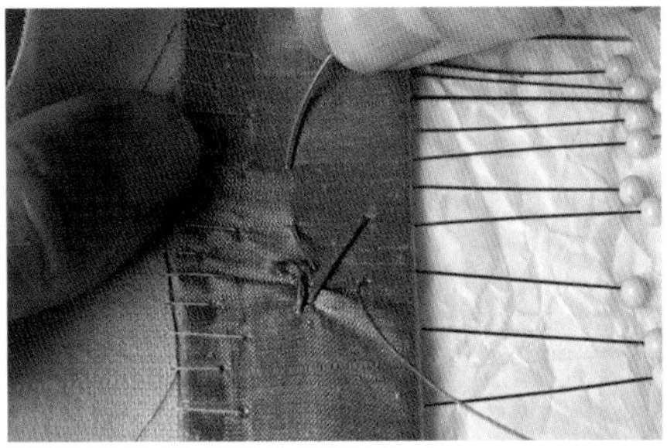

20. Now take your needle and work another straight stitch as shown; notice the point of the needle comes out opposite the end of the previous stitch. Do not try and space your stitches too far apart, your embroidery will not be held tightly enough. Again, pull the fabric tightly.

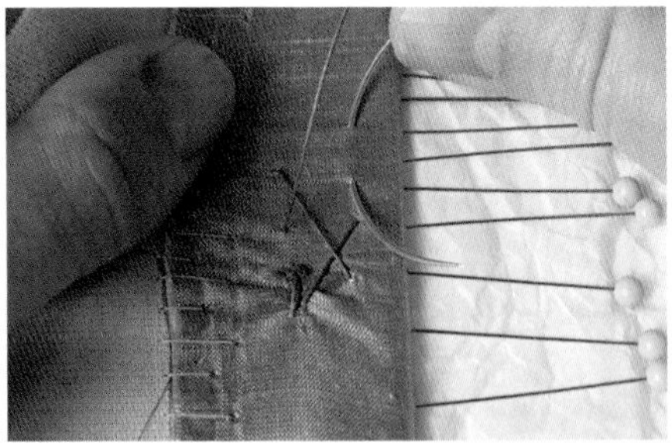

21. Continue the herringbone stitch as shown lining up where the point of the needle comes out with the previous stitch.

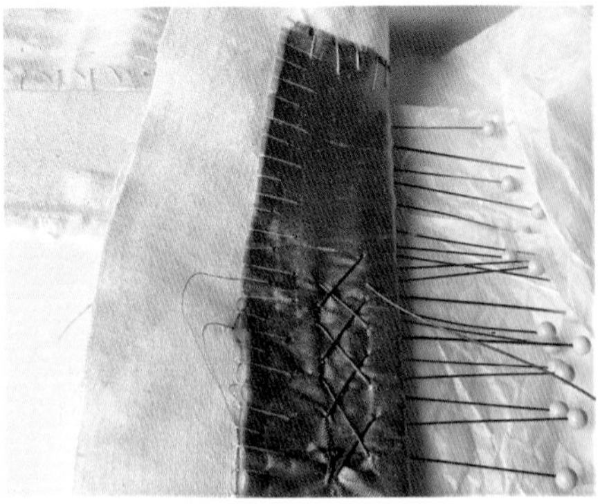

22. Continue along the side of the board, stopping well before the corner so that it can be folded easily.

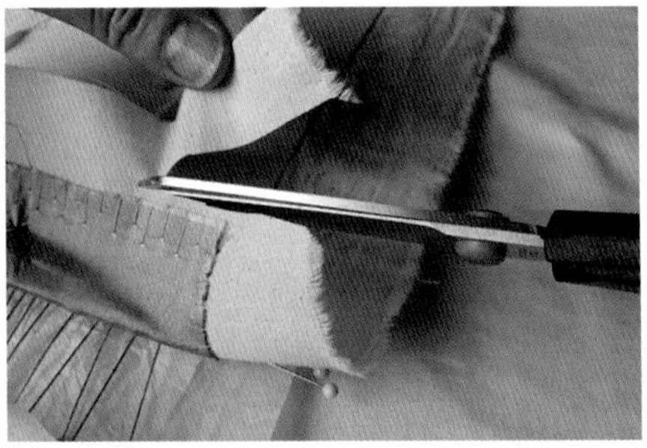

23. To fold the corner easily you will need to cut any excess fabric away. Be careful when cutting as you do not want to accidentally cut in the wrong place, the fabric cannot be glued back!

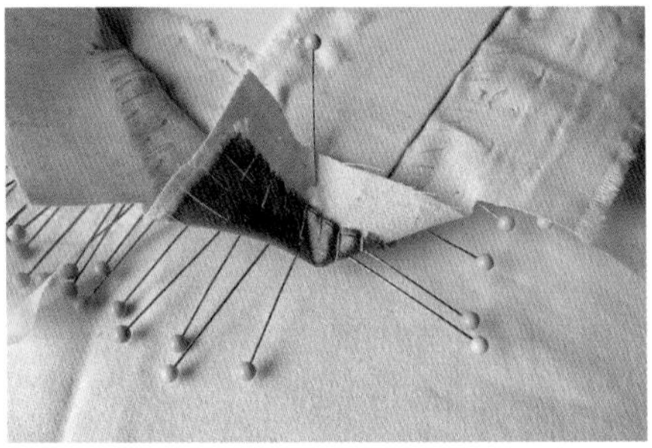

24. Fold the fabric at the corner of the board as shown; it may not be the point of the fabric though!

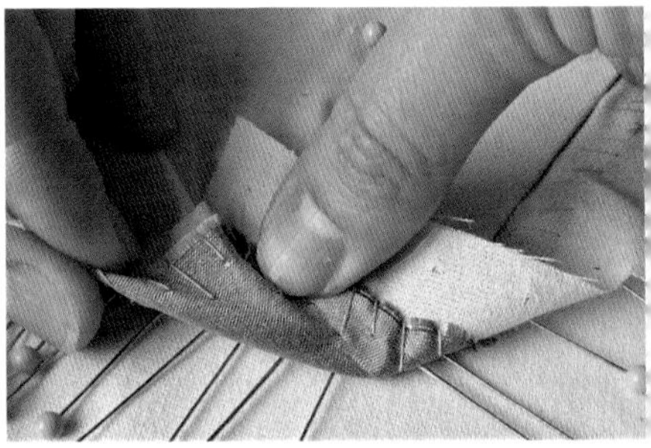

25. Now fold the corners of the fabric in as shown, the fold may rest up against the edge of the board.

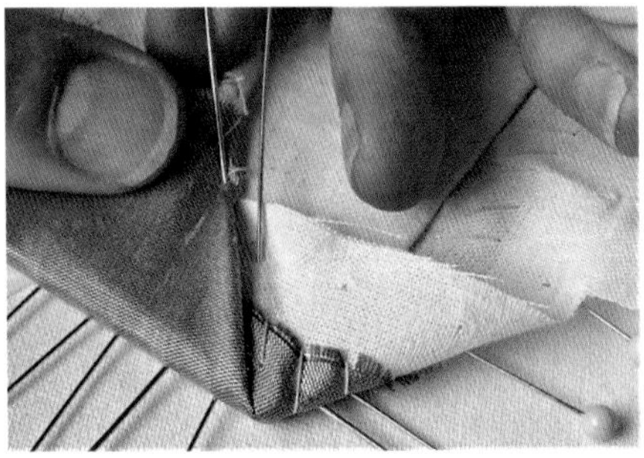

26. Secure with a pin as shown. Notice how the fabric is still being pulled tightly.

27. Fold the other corner in as shown and secure with a pin. Make sure there is a gap running between the two folds. This is so they can be pulled together and not overlap when sewn, therefore creating a flatter and tighter finish.

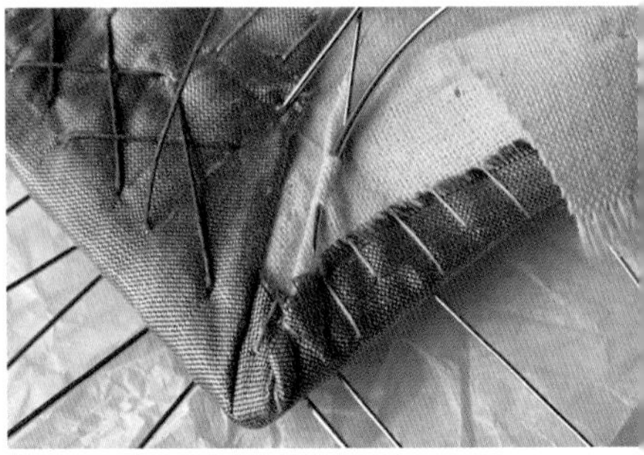

28. Continue to herringbone up to the corner and take your thread across to the opposite side, making a small stitch along the folded edge with the needle pointing towards the corner.

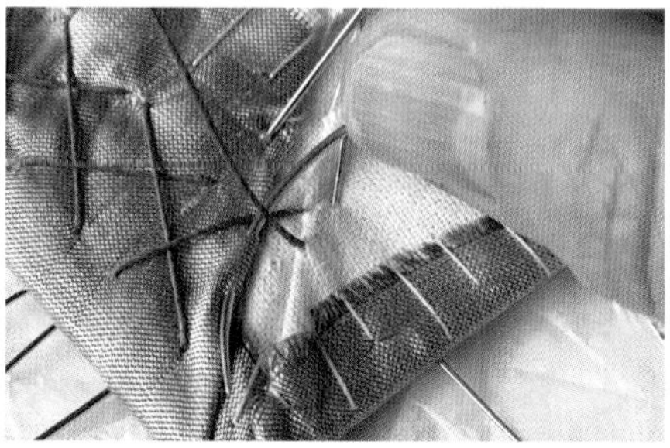

29. Take your needle directly across to the opposite side and take another stitch along the fold, pulling the folds together as you stitch.

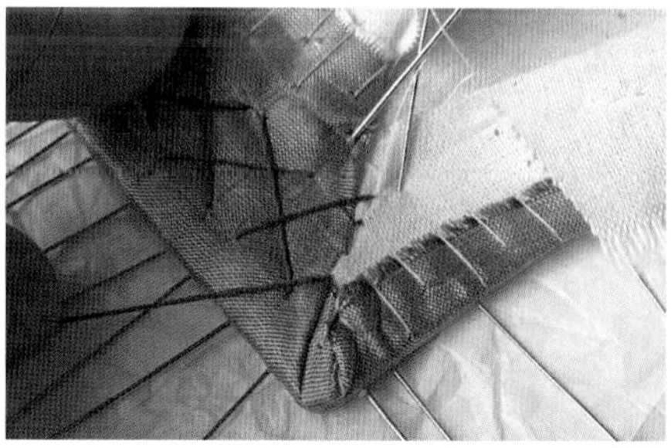

30. Work down to the corner pulling tightly so the fabric is flat and drawn together.

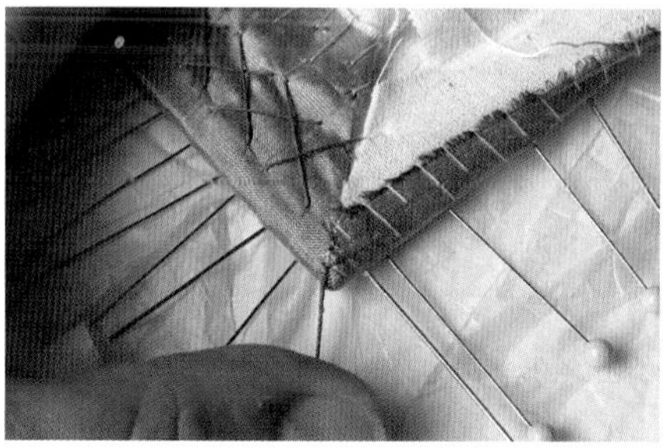

31. When you reach the end push your needle through to the point of the corner, so the thread comes out as shown.

32. Push your needle from the point to the next side of the board.

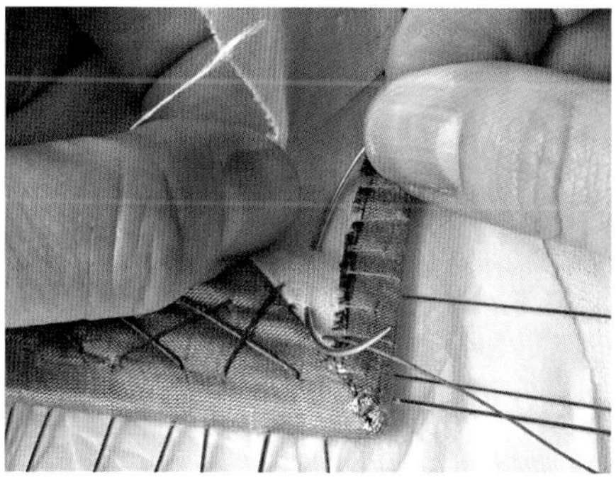

33. Then start your herringbone as before. Repeat all the way round your board.

34. When you have finished turn your embroidery the right way up and remove all the pins. Leave the embroidery for a few days to make sure no wrinkles appear. If they do, you will have to lace parts of your fabric as described below. Cut away any excess fabric from the edges to make a neat line. The embroidery can now be put in a frame.

Lacing your Embroidery on to Board

Mounting your embroidery with herringbone stitch as described before is only one way of securing your embroidery to a board. The other option is to lace it. If your embroidery is very smooth and unlikely to wrinkle or very small in size, then lacing it to a board is suitable. Lacing is sometimes used as well as herringbone stitch for mounting to remove stubborn wrinkles.

The method and materials for mounting this way are the same as for the herringbone method, up to the point of starting to stitch the herringbone.

1. Cut away any excess fabric now as when it is laced it will be trapped under the threads. Try and make a straight line.

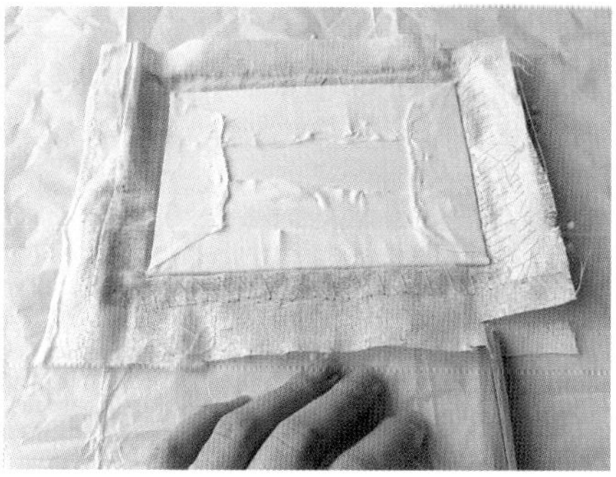

2. Now cut away some of the excess from the corners as shown. We fold the corners flat when we lace so remove the excess now.

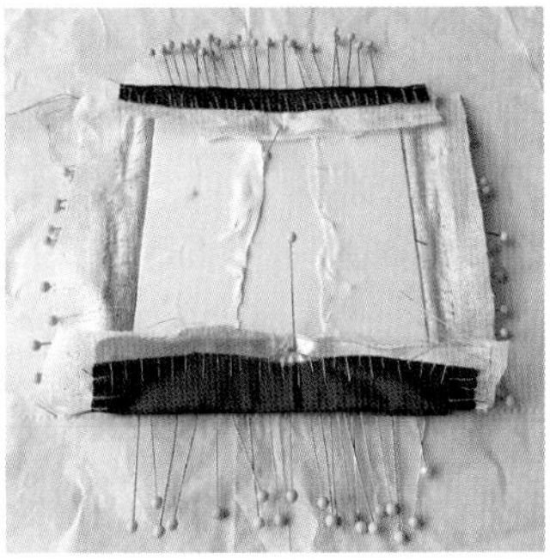

3. Place a pin in the centre of two sides as shown; this is to keep it out of the way and make it easier to lace.

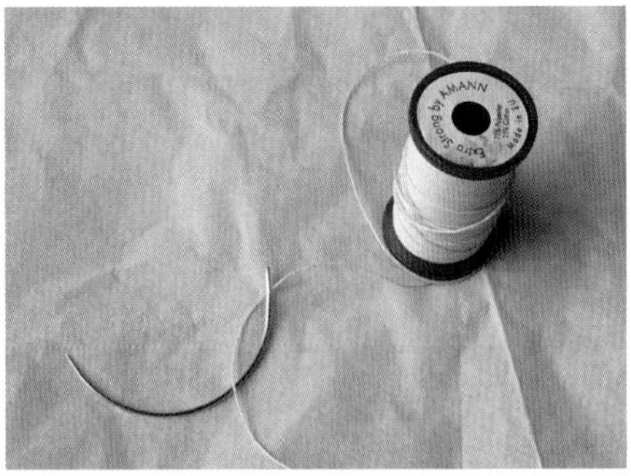

4. Thread up your curved needle with a linen or buttonhole thread but do not cut. Keep it attached to the spool. Make sure you have enough on your spool to enable you to lace one side of your work; you cannot join your thread halfway, it must be one piece.

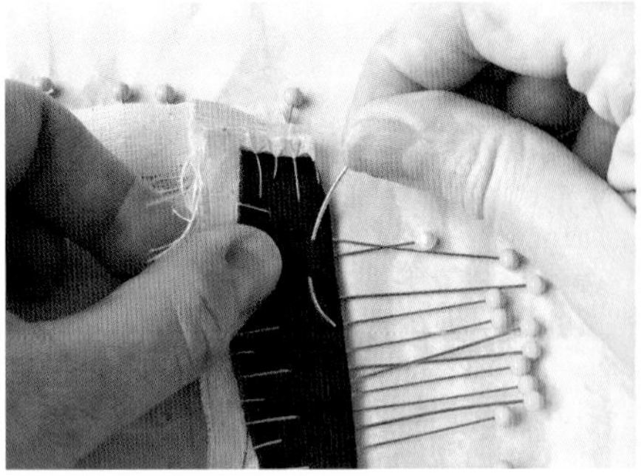

5. Starting at one corner of your board make a horizontal stitch and pull a long length of thread through.

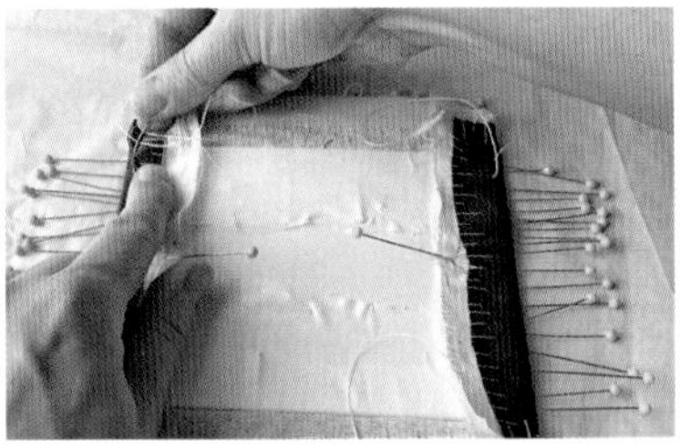

6. Now go to the opposite corner and make another stitch.

7. Go back and forth across your board, making a stitch each time. The more stitches there are then the more secure your work will be and the less chance of wrinkles. You do not need to try and stitch down to the bottom layer of calico with this method. When you get to the end of one side, unthread the needle and leave the thread hanging.

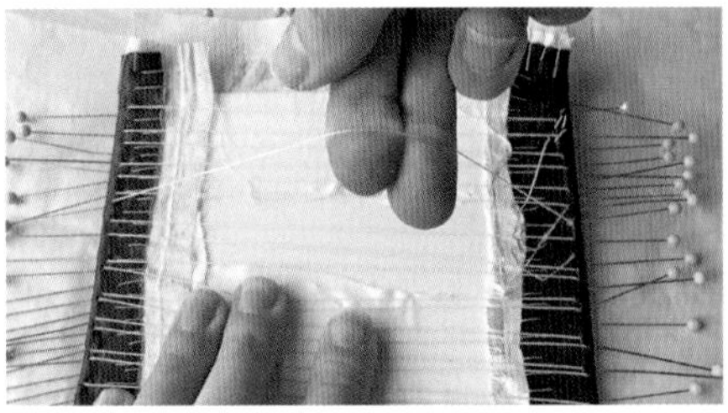

8. Now go back to where you started and cut the thread off the spool. Thread this end onto the curved needle and make three or four little stitches. Make sure it is very secure as you will be pulling tightly against it. Take the needle off and thread it through the other end of your thread; it is best to do this now, so it is ready when you have laced across. Now pull the lacing threads very tightly one by one as shown, from where you have secured the thread all the way across to the other side. When you get to the end, start again to make sure it is tight.

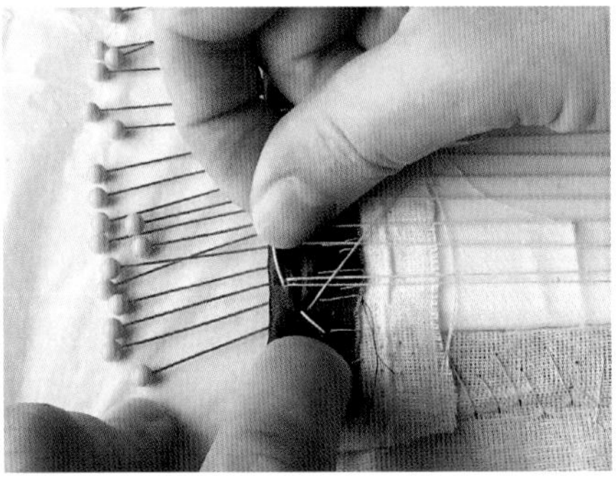

9. When you can pull the thread no more, secure it with your curved needle by doing lots of little stitches. The trick with this method is not to lose tension as you pull across the board.

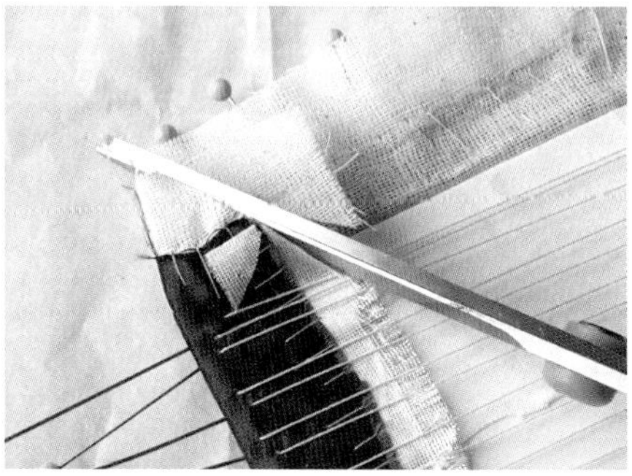

10. Cut the excess off the corners as shown, before you start lacing the other two sides.

11. More excess cut away from the corners.

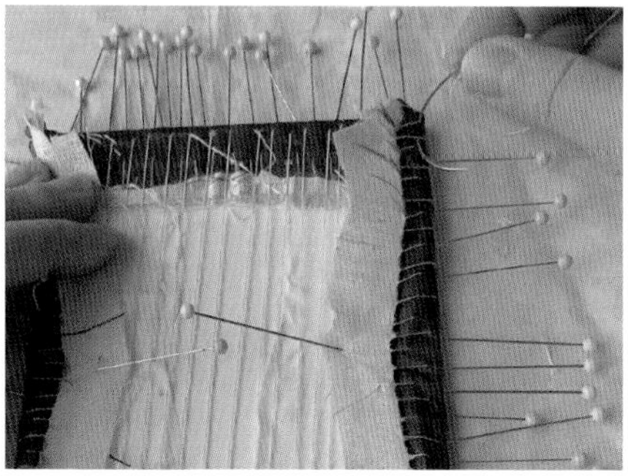

12. Pin the sides to hold as before and then lace in the same way as on the other two sides. Remove the pins and leave for a few days. If wrinkles appear do not take out any lacing, just add additional lacing stitches to the areas that have become loose.

PINCUSHIONS

Pincushions are a useful way to mount your embroidery. If your backing fabric or embroidery is very delicate or a pale colour, then perhaps this is not the best use for them but a patterned fabric or thread painting that is not too delicate would work successfully. Avoid putting pins in the embroidery if you can so as not to ruin all your hard work.

An insert of dried lavender buds to make a scented sachet or emery filings to keep your pins and needles sharp are also useful. You may also want to weight your pincushion, so you can also add a small cushion of dry sand to keep it grounded. Make sure anything you add is in its own separate sachet and is fully dry so as not to come into direct contact with the back of the embroidery, as it may cause staining.

MACHINE-MADE PINCUSHION

This pincushion is made from the Leek embroidery project and stitched on a sewing machine. If you do not have access to a machine then you can hand stitch the pincushion following the same principle.

Materials:

- Embroidered project.
- Set square.
- Tailor's chalk or air-disappearing pen.
- Dressmaking and embroidery scissors.
- Pins.
- Backing fabric for the cushion; this can be the same fabric as you worked your embroidery on or a contrasting one.
- Sewing machine threaded with a matching thread to your fabric.
- Wadding for stuffing your cushion.
- Blunt tool, such as the end of a paintbrush.
- Straight needle such as a number 8.
- Option: A small separate insert of lavender, emery and or dry sand.

1. Work out the size you would like your pincushion and mark on the fabric with pen, tailor's chalk or pins. Use a set square to make sure all the lines are straight, and the corners are 90 degrees. You will be stitching the cushion on the reverse side so make sure you can see the markings on the back. The fabric in the photo is thin enough to see the marking on the back; if yours is not or you have a backing fabric, put your markings on the reverse side.

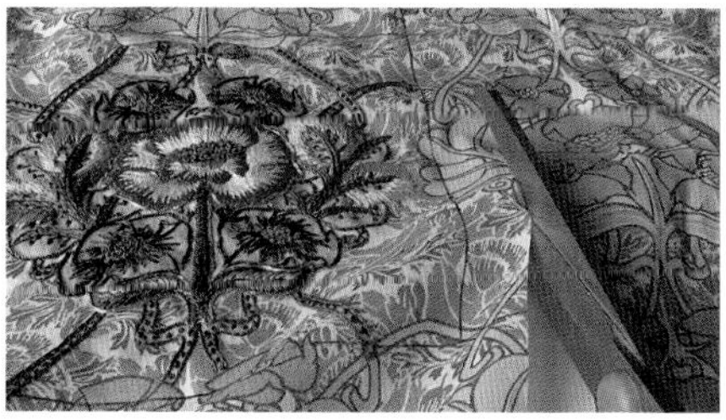

2. Cut an allowance around the embroidery if you have a lot of excess fabric. At least 2cms all round but on the bottom edge leave more excess, at least 4cms.

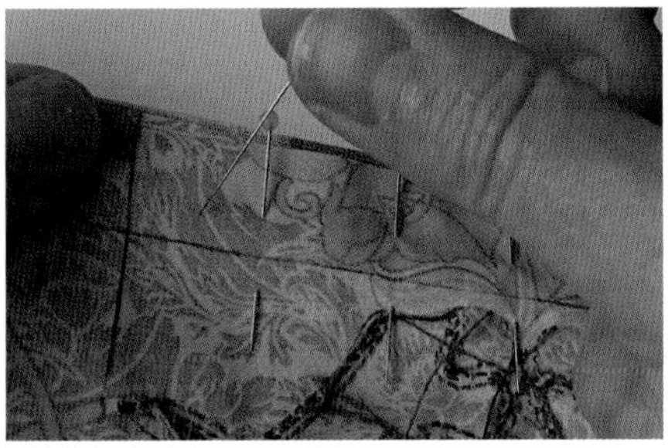

3. Now pin your embroidery and backing fabric together with the right side of the embroidery and right side of the backing fabric together; you should be seeing the reverse side of your embroidery as you pin. In the photograph you can see this is the back of the embroidery. Insert the pins so that they are at 90 degrees to the line you have marked on the fabric. At the bottom edge of your cushion, do not pin all the way across as you will need to leave a hole to turn the cushion through and insert the stuffing. Perhaps use a larger pin to remind yourself to stop stitching, as it is easy to sew the cushion all the way up!

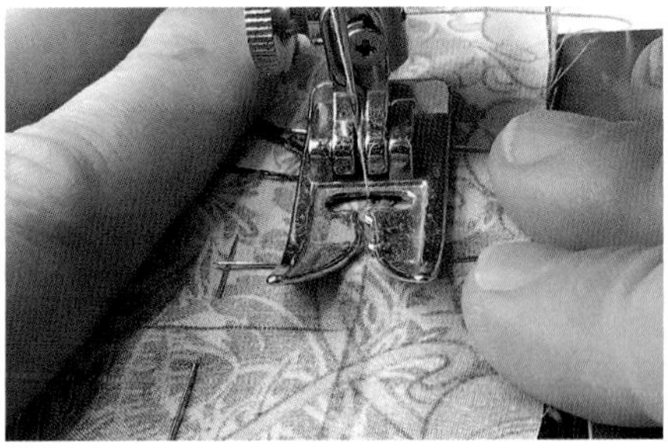

4. Start machining on the bottom edge; as you are not going to stitch all the way across, it is a good place to start. Reinforce the corners a few times so that they are strong. Machine all the way around until you reach the bottom edge again, remembering to leave a space for turning through.

5. Trim the corners of the cushion as shown in the photo to help them get a nice shape when turned through. Do not cut your stitching. Turn the cushion through to the right side carefully.

6. Using a blunt tool such as the wrong end of a paintbrush, carefully push the corners out so they have a nice point.

7. Now stuff the cushion using your wadding. Pull the wadding into small pieces first so that it gives a better shape to the cushion. Use the blunt tool again the get the stuffing into the corners. Add your inserts now, such as lavender.

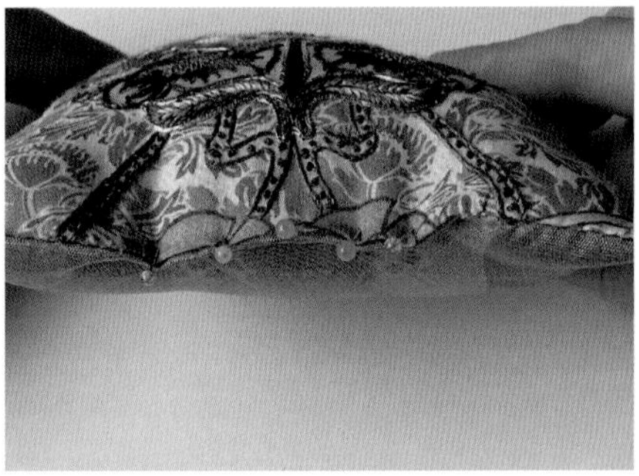

8. When the cushion is as plump as you would like, pin the bottom edges together as shown. We leave an excess of fabric on the bottom edge to prevent fraying when inserting the stuffing and turning the fabric in.

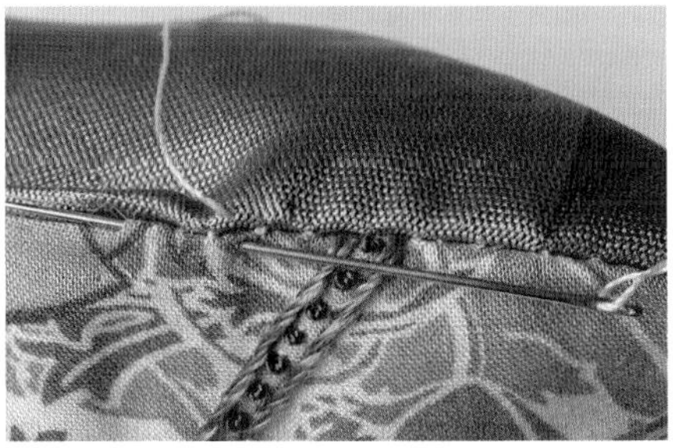

9. Thread your needle with some of the thread you used to stitch up your cushion. Put a knot in the end and insert the needle through the gap in the two fabrics, just at the end of the machine line so the knot is hidden inside the cushion. The needle then comes out on the folded edge of the backing fabric. Now insert the needle on the edge of the top fabric as shown. Pull tight.

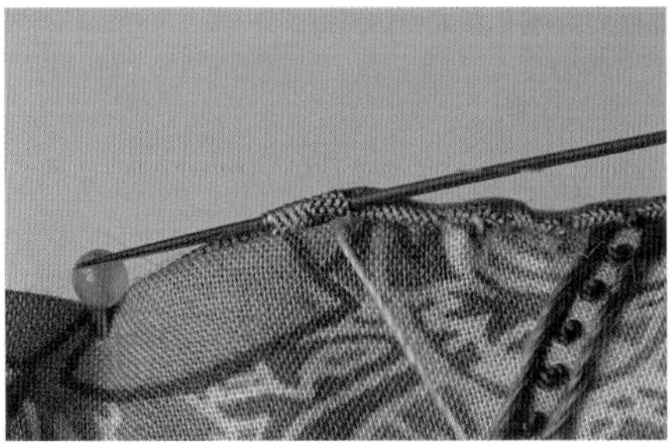

10. Insert the needle through the edge of the backing fabric in the same way, pull tight. This stitch is called slip or ladder stitch and is a great way to join fabrics invisibly.

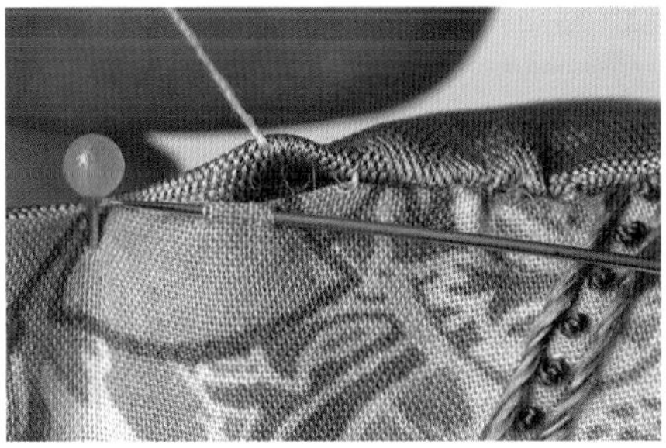

11. Now insert the needle on the front edge and continue until you get to the machined section.

12. When the two fabrics are joined do a few tiny oversew stitches and cut your thread.

Storing your Embroidery

If you are not doing anything immediate with your finished embroidery, then there are things you can do to protect it from future damage.

1. Always wrap your finished work in white acid-free tissue paper. The smoothness of the paper protects the thread fibres from getting rubbed and hairy. It will also protect your work from possible damage from wooden drawers for example, which can leach toxins into fabric and cause staining.
2. Do not fold your work. Strong folds can be impossible to remove over time and silk can break along a fold line. If your work is too big to be stored flat, then roll it around a tube; cover the tube first with acid-free tissue paper then roll your fabric around the tube with the front of the embroidery facing out. A common mistake is to roll embroidery in on itself; you are just crushing your work. Embroidery on the outside makes it much smoother. Make sure you have tissue paper between each roll of the fabric.
3. If you have a few pieces to store, then buying a small acid-free box especially for textiles is worthwhile. You can also store other clean precious textiles in here too, to prevent moth attack as well as damage from outside elements.

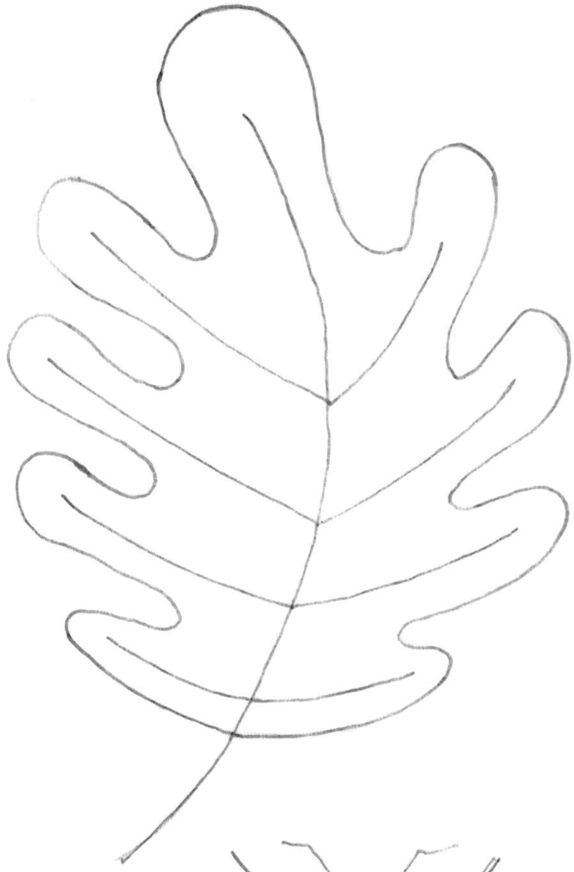

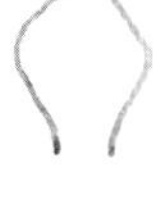

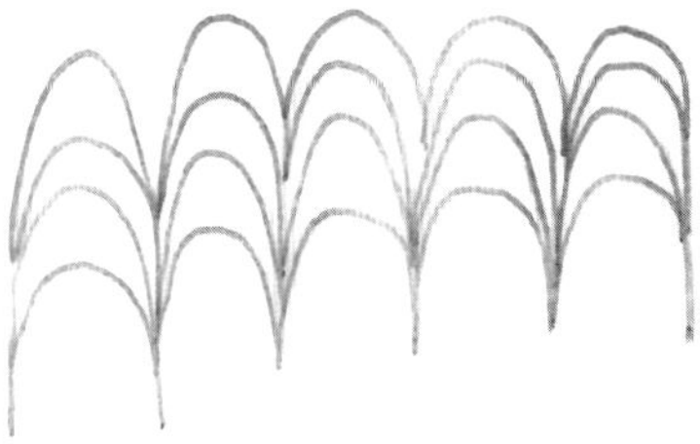

Q: How do I know which needle to use?
A: If you are using fine thread, use a fine needle. One strand of stranded cotton would be a 10–12 embroidery needle, two strands would be an 8–10 needle and so on. Wool can use either an embroidery needle or a chenille needle. Silk can also use either an embroidery needle or chenille needle. The chenille needle makes a larger hole as it goes through the fabric so can help the thread glide through easier. If your needle keeps falling off the thread, try using a smaller size. If you are tugging your needle through the fabric then you do not have a big enough needle, try a bigger size.

Q: How many strands of thread should I use?
A: This is purely a personal choice. One strand of thread will always give a slightly smoother embroidered effect as you only have one thread to control. Two or more strands will obviously make the embroidery grow faster but the threads may twist around each other and if they are not at the same tension, you could get loose stitches or lumps.

Q: How long should my thread be?
A: A shorter thread will keep its sheen and is less likely to get tangled. However, if you particularly like working with a longer thread make sure to finish before you get to the very end. A useful length guide is elbow to thumb.

Q: How many rows of long and short should there be in one section?
A: There is no set answer to this. If your area to stitch is very small, you will not have many rows. Do not try to fit lots of rows in, it may look lumpy. Also, if you have a larger section do not make your stitches too long just to fill it in, you may get a loose tension. A larger area gives you more space to turn the angle of your stitch if you are working natural shading.

Q: Do I have to use split stitch every time I work long and short?
A: No, the split stitch is there to help you. If you think it will get in the way or you want an uneven edge, then do not use one. You do not need one on any true vertical lines in tapestry shading.

Q: How many colours do I need?
A: The answer is as many colours as you want. If you have lots of colours that are almost the same and are confusing you, then drop a couple. If you feel that your colours are not blending smoothly or your work is stripy, then adding a couple could help. If you put your colours in a line from light to dark and there is a big jump between shades, then that is where you need the extra colours.

Q: How long are the stitches?
A: If your stitches are loose and your stitch tension is correct (meaning you have pulled the thread firmly) then they are probably too long. If you come up in a stitch and it moves around when you pull the thread through, then they are too long. If there is not much space to have variation of where to come up in a stitch, then your stitches are too short. There is no set size of stitch, as it will depend on your thread and the number of strands.

Q: My embroidery looks very blocky and I can see all the rows of stitching. What am I doing wrong?
A: Make sure that when you start a new row, you vary where you bring the needle up. You do not want all the stitches in a row to come up in a line. There should be a zig-zag effect to the top and bottom of the stitch.

Q: My embroidery looks very stripy. What am I doing wrong?
A: You are not changing your colour enough or there is a big jump in the shades of your thread. If you have a big jump in colour and there is no other shade available, then you will need to change colour every stitch.

Q: My embroidery looks very lumpy. What am I doing wrong?
A: Your stitches may be too short so that you have more rows than needed; this will just cause the embroidery to build up into lumps and an uneven surface. Make your stitches longer. You may also be coming up too far into your stitches on each row, therefore again giving you more rows than you need. Make sure that you are not crossing lots of threads over on the reverse of your embroidery. If there is a lot of build-up on the back, then when you mount your work it will have unwanted lumps in certain places. You may have a slub in your fabric. You could try and stitch some tiny stab stitches on top of it to flatten it if it is really causing a problem. If you try and cut it out, you may end up with a hole, so this is a very last resort.

Q: Why does my thread keep breaking?
A: Your thread is too long and is getting weak. Start a new thread. You may have a snag on the needle; sometimes the eye of the needle will not have been punched out cleanly, so it effectively cuts the thread as you stitch, or your needle is too small for your thread – try a larger needle or a chenille needle.

Q: Why does the embroidery look 'fluffy' when I am using cotton or silk?
A: Your needle may be too small; change to a bigger one or use a chenille needle. You are using your thread for too long; start a new one more frequently. You are handling your embroidery too much; try not to stroke your work!!

Q: Does it matter if the back of my work is messy?
A: If you have too much mess on the back of your work, it can cause lumps on the front and you may be bringing your thread up through trailing threads on the back which will cause your threads to wear out quicker. It is better to try and have order in the way you work, such as keeping a set of threads for each side and bringing them up close to where you are stitching when you 'park' them.

Q: Where do I start or finish my thread if there is no obvious place or I have finished my work?
A: Take your thread through to the back of your work and weave it under your stitches a few times until it is secure.

Q: Why is my background fabric wrinkling?
A: If you are using two layers of fabric then it is possible the top fabric has not been put on tight enough; it can also be that you need to tighten your frame up. As you work, your frame will slacken off, so it is important to tighten it up regularly. Wrinkles in the fabric can also be caused by a very tight stitching tension or a lot of small, tight stitching in one area. If you think that you are pulling your thread extra tightly then see if you can make your tension a little looser without the stitches looping up from the surface of the fabric.

Q: How do I unpick an area if I make a mistake?
A: It is better to try and correct an area if you think it is going wrong by unpicking a couple of stitches when you first notice. However, you may only realize you have

made a mistake after you have done a large section, or you may have improved your embroidery and want to remove your first part of stitching. It is easier to turn your frame over and cut your threads from the back. Make sure you are removing the right area though. Push a pin through from the right side as a guide of where you need to remove stitches. Cutting them on the back and pulling them out from there will hopefully prevent damage to the top fabric if used and fluff from ruining the front of your work. You can use sticky tape on the back to remove excess fluff; this is important as otherwise it will work its way to the front as you continue stitching. Do not use sticky tape on the front of your work. All you will be doing is lifting the fibres up. Use tweezers on the front to take away excess threads. Try and secure any loose threads that occur by couching them down on the front if possible with some securing stitches, then cut away the excess.

Q: I have unpicked an area and now have a hole; can I stitch over it?
A: If your hole is tiny then yes, you can stitch over it. If, however you have made a hole that is impossible to stitch over then there are two options. If you are just using one layer of fabric, then you could try and darn it as if you were darning socks or gloves; you will need to loosen your frame to do this. However, try and match the weight of thread you are darning with to the weight of the fabric.

If you are using a top fabric and a backing fabric or you are not confident in your darning skills, then cut a small piece of fabric to match your top fabric and secure in place with tiny stitches. You want it to be as flat as possible so that your embroidery does not look lumpy when it is stitched over.

Q: I have pricked my finger and got blood on my work, what shall I do?
A: With a clean (!) mouth, suck a piece of white cotton material or thread and dab carefully on the blood mark. The saliva will dissolve your blood. Use a clean piece of cotton as needed. It will only work if the blood mark is your own and is relatively fresh. It may leave a water mark, but this is preferable to a blood stain.

Q: I have a stain on my fabric; shall I wash the embroidery at the end?
A: Although we try to cover our work, mistakes do happen. Washing is a last resort as it will take away the sheen from your threads and if your colours are not fast, the dyes could run.

One alternative is to add to your embroidery design and therefore stitch over the mark. Perhaps a bee or insect if you are working a flower, an extra tree or bird if it is a landscape. If this is not feasible you could try a clean fabric eraser or a small amount of clear alcohol on a cotton bud. Try them on the edge of your fabric first before rubbing on the stain. You may remove the mark, but you do not want to cause damage to the fabric. Be very gentle and do not rub too hard.

Q: I have mounted my work and there are lots of wrinkles, how do I get rid of them?
A: You may have not pulled your fabric tight enough when pinning or stitching your herringbone stitch. You can add additional lacing to the areas that have wrinkles. If you laced your piece you may have lost the tight tension on the lacing. Add additional lacing to the problem areas.

Acknowledgements

This book has been a huge learning curve and I have loved every minute of planning, writing and stitching it, but there are some 'thank yous' as I have not managed it all by myself.

I would like to thank my parents for supporting me while I was studying on my apprenticeship, I would not have been able to have had this long career in embroidery and learnt everything that is in this book without them, and of course they are my biggest fans.

To Sophie, for the idea and convincing me I could do it. You were right as always, I could!

To Susan K. Williams and The Royal School of Needlework for allowing me 'access all areas' of their historical collection. The treasures were vast, so it was a hard job to not photograph everything they had.

To my teachers that taught me all I know at the Royal School, and yes, I am still learning.

To all my students, who inspire me every day I teach and who over the years have said to me, 'You should write a book and put all those little tips in it, I'd buy it.' Here it is, so please do!

To Anne and David Williams, for all those threads from Doreen that illustrate the colour section. Thank you, I know she would have loved this book. In fact, she may have been my biggest fan.

To Owen Davies and Megumi Sorita for kindly allowing me to photograph and feature items from their own collections.

To All Saints Church in Leek for allowing permission to feature some of their wonderful embroideries. Especially to Angela and Victoria Jervis for all their help.

To Sonia at Dandelyne for all those wonderful little ring frames.

And finally, to Rob, for everything. There is too much to list, just know that I couldn't have done any of it without you. Thank you.

Margaret Dier.

Suppliers

This little bird egg is stitched in tapestry shading and even though all the stitches are vertical, it has a rounded feel to it due to placement of the colour shades.

Many of these suppliers post worldwide.

Fabrics

John Lewis. Fabrics, threads and general haberdashery.
www.johnlewis.com
Liberty London. Liberty print fabric, haberdashery items.
Regent Street, London, W1B 5AH.
www.libertylondon.com
The Silk Route. Silk fabrics and thread.
www.thesilkroute.co.uk
Ulster weavers. Linen fabrics.
www.ulsterweavers.com
Macculloch & Wallis Ltd. Silk and cotton fabrics, threads and haberdashery.
25–26 Poland Street
London
W1F 8QN.
www.macculloch-wallis.co.uk

Threads

DeVere Yarns. Silk threads and wools for embroidery, plus other specialist threads.
www.devereyarns.co.uk
Midori. Japanese silk threads, Japanese silk fabric and transfer paper.
www.midori-embroidery.com
Handweavers Studio. Supplier of threads for weaving but many of these are suitable for embroidery, including very fine wools.
The Handweavers Studio & Gallery
140 Seven Sisters Road,
London,
N7 7NS.
www.handweavers.co.uk
Piper Silks. Specialist silk threads.
www.pipers-silks.com
Lakeside Needlecraft. Stranded cottons, specialist threads, needles.
www.lakesideneedlecraft.co.uk
DMC Threads. Stranded cottons, perlé, ring frames.
www.dmc.com
Cleopatra's Needle. Appletons tapestry and crewel wool.
www.cleopatrasneedle.co.uk
Linladan. Antique threads for embroidery, specializing in linen.
linladan.com

Equipment

Dandelyne. Mini hoop kits for jewellery.
www.dandelyne.com
eWood Story. Miniature wooden frames made with exotic woods.
www.etsy.com/shop/eWoodStory
John James. Suppliers of all types of needles for embroidery.
www.jjneedles.com
Preservation Equipment Limited. Acid-free tissue and board, archive storage boxes, magnifiers, lamps.
www.preservationequipment.com
Daylight Company. Suppliers of specialist lamps, magnifiers, light boxes and daylight bulbs suitable for artists.
www.daylightcompany.co.uk

INDEX

OTHER EMBROIDERY TITLES FROM CROWOOD

Embroideries from an English Garden
978 0 90358 534 7

Ribbonwork Embroidery
978 1 78500 252 6

The Needlework of Mary Queen of Scots
978 0 90358 522 4

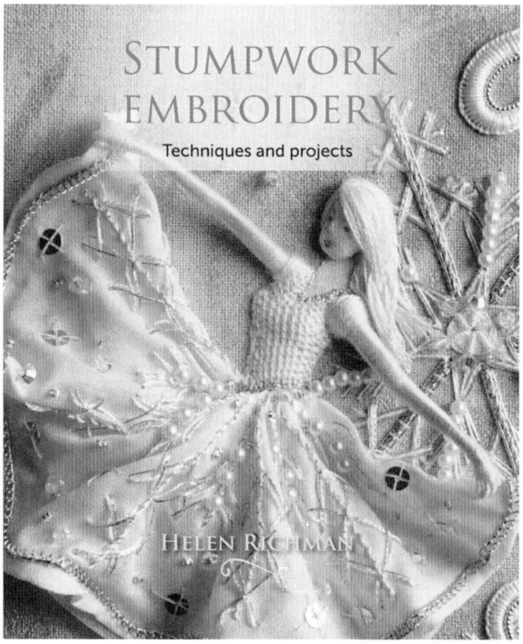

Stumpwork Embroidery
978 1 78500 294 6